D1107714

CONCORDIA
UNIVERSITY

A gift to
Concordia University Library
by Rev. Dr. Theodore Engelbrecht
in memory of

Rev. Dr. Luther
Engelbrecht

ISLAMIC REFORM

Published under the auspices of the Near Eastern Center
University of California, Los Angeles

ISLAMIC REFORM

The Political and Legal Theories of Muḥammad ʿAbduh and Rashīd Riḍā

by MALCOLM H. KERR

UNIVERSITY OF CALIFORNIA PRESS
CAMBRIDGE UNIVERSITY PRESS
1966

University of California Press
Berkeley and Los Angeles, California

Cambridge University Press
London, England

© *1966 by The Regents of the University of California*

Library of Congress Catalog Card Number: 65-24177

Printed in the United States of America

PREFACE

This book is a study of certain Islamic theories of the religious basis of law and government. The first three chapters present an interpretation of the classic juristic tradition of thought, with particular emphasis on those elements of the tradition which modern thinkers have seized upon as the starting point for the reformation they wished to promote. In the succeeding chapters I have critically analyzed the efforts of two leading modernists, Muḥammad 'Abduh and Rashīd Riḍā, to develop concepts of natural law, popular sovereignty, and utilitarian jurisprudence by selectively reinterpreting the classical tradition.

An earlier draft of the book, now substantially revised, was prepared as a Ph.D. dissertation in 1958 under the guidance of Professors Majid Khadduri and Sir Hamilton Gibb. For whatever merit the book may have I am heavily indebted to their inspiration. Others who have read one draft or another of the manuscript and offered valuable comments and criticisms include Albert Hourani, Muhsin Mahdi, Nadav Safran, and G. E. Von Grunebaum. As I have not invariably followed their advice, it is more than perfunctory to say that they are not responsible for the book's faults.

The substance of parts of chapters v and vi appeared in a two-part article, "Rashīd Riḍā and Islamic Legal Reform," *The Muslim World*, L (1960), nos. 2 and 3, and is reproduced here by permission of the journal's editors.

I must record my thanks to Abdallah Abou-Aish and Mrs. Nadia Farag for their kind assistance in bibliographical matters and to my wife Ann for her help in proofreading and preparing the index.

M. H. K.

March, 1965

CONCORDIA UNIVERSITY LIBRARY
PORTLAND, OR 97211

CONTENTS

I

TRADITIONAL AND MODERN AMBIGUITIES

Underlying the Islamic tradition of social thought is a pessimistic consciousness of the tension between ideal and actuality, the spiritual and the temporal, virtue and power, God's command and man's behavior. In past centuries Muslim scholars did not customarily think it their business to reconcile these two sets of contrasting elements. Instead they elaborated their conceptions of the ideal and left Islamic society to cope with actualities by evolving its own practical, but largely unacknowledged, psychological and social mechanisms. But the spread of secular culture in the modern Muslim world has changed this. Instead of rendering the sense of tension obsolete, it has sharpened the tension, and made its resolution a vital problem.

One reason for this is that with the passing of the age of the unquestioned finality of religious dogmas, a new effort must begin to provide social and political life with a basis of moral purpose. Another is that the idea of progress has made the disparity between ideals and actualities seem unnecessary and sometimes insupportable. Whether ideals are conceived within a religious or humanist framework, somehow they must be transformed from slogans into historical realization.

Because Islamic religious doctrine has traditionally claimed full jurisdiction over questions of social morality without always providing practical answers, modern Muslim thinkers have been faced with two broad alternatives. Either they can try to breathe new life into inherited doctrines and adapt them to current needs, or they can seek their inspiration elsewhere. Increasingly it is the latter course that has been followed. Although today the advocates of nationalism do not always explicitly reject the political relevance of Islamic teachings, the intellectual foundations of nationalism are essentially nonreligious. And as

Full bibliographical details of works cited briefly in these notes are given in the Bibliography at the end of the volume.

time has passed, a growing body of educated opinion, wholly and consciously secular in its political outlook, has refused even to pay lip service to religion, thereby signifying a break with thirteen centuries of tradition.

We might suppose, and with some justification, that this is only natural and indeed inevitable in an age in which the march of material progress and the accompanying social revolution have required the abandonment of certain inherited institutions and values in all traditional societies. A revived universal Caliphate, or the deduction of a modern legal system from the Qur'ān and the teachings of Muḥammad, might accordingly be dismissed at a glance as pure fantasy. Retrospectively it does not seem surprising that the congress of religious scholars and dignitaries that met in Cairo in 1926 to discuss a restoration of the Caliphate should only have reiterated ancient formulas, and should have found nothing more constructive to recommend than the convening of another congress sometime in the future. The text of the debates at the congress, marked by an undertone of impotent pessimism, is suggestive less of a call for regeneration than of the last gasp of a defunct idea.[1]

Since the suppression of the Muslim Brethren in Egypt and the demise of the Islamic constitution of Pakistan, there has ceased to be any visible likelihood that Islamic legal and constitutional principles would be made to serve as the operative basis of a modern state in any Muslim country. In Turkey secularism has been celebrated for a generation as the symbol of modern enlightenment. In many other countries vestiges of the Sharī'a, or sacred law, remain in force, but largely on a piecemeal basis, as elements of tradition rather than as manifestations of a governing principle. The appeal to Islamic loyalties is an important psychological instrument for popularizing the domestic and foreign policies of certain governments, but not always the most important one, and it has little to do with the initial shaping of those policies. Islamic publicists continue to turn out a large body of literature expounding the virtues and suitability of the Islamic state, but without practical expectations.

The fact is, however, that earlier in this century serious efforts were made, notably by the Salafiyya movement in Egypt, to reform and restate these medieval doctrines in order to make them applicable to

[1] The text of the proceedings is published in French translation with commentary by Achille Sékaly in *Revue du Monde Musulman*, LXIV (1926), 3–122.

the modern world. The efforts of the Pakistan Constituent Assembly after 1949 to draw up an Islamic constitution, with which we are not directly concerned here,[2] were still more determined and led to a temporary success. The reformers acknowledged that the doctrines in their traditional form were obsolete, but insisted that because they were based on religious principles they must contain a core of validity and should therefore be adapted rather than discarded.

Leaving aside the material historical reasons for the failure of the Salafiyya, we propose to examine their revisions of classical theory on their own ground, that is, as theory, as represented in the work of their leading member, Muḥammad Rashīd Riḍā, and to suggest that the inability of the Salafiyya to come to grips with the inadequacies of the doctrines they set about to revive constituted an intellectual failure that contributed to the political failure.

In what way, then, is classical constitutional and legal theory deficient as a model for modern reform?

In professing to provide man with a political and legal system as well as a spiritual faith, Islam denies at the outset the conception familiar in Christendom of a separation between temporal and spiritual matters. This fact is well known and has been noted by orientalists and Muslims alike with unfailing regularity. But if the temporal and the spiritual are not separate, they are nonetheless distinct, representing two aspects of a single essence. Every human action includes its religiously relevant purpose or motivation as well as its mundane causes and effects. Islamic law and government are in one sense undeniably temporal—they control human behavior of all kinds—regardless of the religious nature of the considerations by which they are evaluated. But if the subject matter and mode of operation of sovereign authority are temporal, the source and objective are spiritual. The Islamic concept of sovereignty cannot therefore be characterized as either religious or temporal without a careful definition of the sense in which "sovereignty" is meant.

This is the meaning of Iqbal's observation:

> In Islam it is the same reality which appears as Church looked at from one point of view and State from another. It is not true

[2] The fullest account of these efforts is Leonard Binder, *Religion and Politics in Pakistan* (Berkeley and Los Angeles, 1961). For a representative example of Pakistani Muslim reformist thinking, see Muhammad Asad, *The Principles of State and Government in Islam* (Berkeley and Los Angeles, 1961).

> to say that Church and State are two sides or facets of the same thing. Islam is a single unanalyzable reality which is one or the other, as your point of view varies.[3]

In the first sense sovereignty signifies ultimate authority above the legal and political system itself, an authority that carries its own justification beyond which there is no moral appeal. In this definition sovereignty is the independent authority to establish values, rights, and obligations. In the second sense it is recognized authority to interpret and apply the values, rights, and obligations that have been created on the higher plane. A constitutional office may be the locus of sovereignty in the second sense, by virtue of being assigned the authority to interpret and apply the constitution. Sovereignty in the first sense belongs to whomever is recognized to have authority over the constitution itself, to create, change, or abolish it.

But this is an insufficient distinction. Does not full power to interpret amount in practice to power to change? Or might not the power to create, if it rests with a definitive person or group, be exercised in the process of interpretation as well? In the British constitution would not Parliament meet both definitions of sovereignty?

In the classical Islamic theories of the Caliphate and jurisprudence the starting point is the assumption that rights and obligations are determined and revealed by God, and that therefore He—or the divine law He reveals—is the ultimate sovereign. The revealed law must in turn be interpreted and applied by qualified individuals, and in the secondary sense these are sovereign. The attribution of ultimate sovereignty to God, of course, in itself is of no practical significance until some agency is identified that can authoritatively decide what God's decrees are. The locus of sovereignty on the secondary plane thus becomes crucial, for it is here that the character of the constitutional and legal systems as functional instruments will be determined. The assertion that Islam provides for a "theocracy" is true in the ultimate sense, but meaningless in the practical sense, for in the latter "theocracy" signifies the rule of a priestly or other supposedly divinely inspired individual or class, which is absent in Islam. An effort to apply the initial premise of divine sovereignty to temporal affairs must inevitably come to grips with the question of interpretation and deal

[3] Sir Mohammad Iqbal, *The Reconstruction of Religious Thought in Islam* (London, 1934), p. 146.

with what have been called "the procedural tests of Islamicity."[4] The need for this came to light in the course of the debate in the Constituent Assembly of Pakistan charged with drawing up a constitution for that "Islamic republic," where it became apparent that Islamic political principles meant many things to different people. This was recognized, for example, in March, 1949, by Prime Minister Liaquat Ali Khan in a statement to the Assembly:

> Sir: I have just now said that the people are the real recipients of power. This naturally eliminates any danger of the establishment of a theocracy. It is true that in its literal sense theocracy means the government of God. In this sense, however, it is patent that the entire universe is a theocracy; for is there any corner in the entire creation where His authority does not exist? But in the technical sense, theocracy has come to mean a government by ordained priests, who wield authority as being specially appointed by those who claim to derive their rights from their sacerdotal position. I cannot overemphasize the fact that such an idea is absolutely foreign to Islam. Islam does not recognize either priesthood or any sacerdotal authority; and therefore the question of a theocracy simply does not arise in Islam. . . .[5]

The classical constitutional theory and, to a lesser extent, legal theory refrained from giving precise definitions of the locus of sovereignty in this procedural sense, and confined themselves instead to setting forth the divine nature of ultimate sovereignty. This limitation, which existed for particular reasons in classical expositions, becomes a serious deficiency in modern times when attempts are made to apply the theory to current practical questions of political and legal organization.

The problem of defining sovereignty in both the ultimate and the procedural senses can perhaps best be described as one of idealism versus positivism. Defining ultimate sovereignty raises the primary question of whether right and wrong are to be viewed as products of the divine will known through revelation, or as products of human judgment and will, known through communication by some recog-

---

[4] Kenneth Cragg, "The Tests of 'Islamicity'," *Middle East Forum*, Nov., 1957, p. 17. Cf. the same author's "The Modernist Movement in Egypt," *in* Richard N. Frye, ed., *Islam and the West* (The Hague, 1956), pp. 163–164, for discussion of this problem.

[5] Quoted by W. Wendell Cleland, "Islam's Attitude Toward Minority Groups," *in* Dorothea Seelye Franck, ed., *Islam in the Modern World* (Washington, 1951), p. 54.

nized agency. Is the promulgation of legal rules essentially a judicial process of discovery and interpretation of preexisting moral principles, or a legislative process? Are the constitutional obligations and rights of the ruler and subjects to be discovered or created by society? Is the legal and constitutional system a static or dynamic one?

The classical theory of the Caliphate affirmed that the institution of the Caliphate and the relationships of right and obligation that it entailed were ordained by God and therefore only to be interpreted and applied by man. It was the preordained duty of the Community to select a qualified candidate for the office of caliph, install him in office, and obey him as long as he performed his duty, which was to apply the Sharī'a and defend the interests of Islam. This is an idealist rather than positivist answer, in that it assumes values to stem from a non-cognitive source rather than from human judgment; their existence and validity are independent of the determinations of some human agency.

Likewise the classical theory of jurisprudence declared that law, to be valid, must be derived by deduction and analogy from the revealed sources: the Qur'ān and the practice (Sunna) of the Prophet. Law that does not conform to this standard is not valid law.

The second question—the locus of sovereignty on the applied or "procedural" plane—demands, as we have seen, a positive answer if the obligations prescribed by the ultimate sovereign are to be practically interpreted, communicated, and enforced. Ascribing these tasks to a body that is not or cannot be precisely defined, or failure to ascribe them to anyone, simply begs the question.

Positivism in relation to this question has nothing to do with what should properly be the sources of law; it is rather a method of classifying and understanding subject matter. Law as a set of rules must be given a form that can be authoritatively validated by some recognized agency. The positivist is concerned with law as a human institution, with the rules it sets for human behavior and the mechanism by which these rules are determined and applied.

Is the Islamic Sharī'a, as traditionally conceived, a system of positive law? Religious morality and positive law can, of course, coincide. In positivist terms, however, they cannot be one and the same thing, and law that is not humanly enacted and recognized, and whose observance is not ascertainable by human faculties, is not law.

All this seems familiar enough in the context of Western social and legal thought. In Islamic thought the distinction has not traditionally been so clearly drawn, and religious obligations, conceived as ideals whose validity is logically prior to their incorporation into the recognized legal structure, attract such preoccupation as to overshadow the separate existence of the legal structure as an independent phenomenon. Such importance has been attached to the divine nature of ultimate sovereignty, in other words, that the distinct nature of procedural sovereignty is often ignored.

But since the underlying premise of the definition of procedural sovereignty is that law exists as a positive order of rules, humanly contrived, interpreted, and applied, even the creation of its values—regardless of their psychological origin or religious worth—must be considered man-made. It is men who choose to derive their legal norms from religious revelation. In the positive sense, it makes no more sense to say that religiously based law is created by God than it does to say that purely secular law is created by inert and impersonal physical circumstances. Law as law is made by men, whatever their motivation. When, as in the case of Islam, the declared source of law is religious morality, this can only mean the positive aspect of religious morality, that is, morality in the form in which men interpret it.

The positive aspect of law, while it might be considered only a poor reflection of the real worth of the moral idealism behind it, assumes a great deal of importance when the material rather than spiritual welfare of the community is at stake. Islam teaches that the Sharīʿa serves to provide both spiritual and material welfare, and that in fact when the latter is seen in its proper light it will prove to be essentially identified with the former. This being the case, it should be asked whether it is legitimate to attempt to distinguish between the two at all; and this leads into the larger question of whether, in the light of the pervadingly religious importance of law in Islam and of the special, almost apocalyptic mission ascribed to the Muslim community in its historical development, there is any place for positivist methods of classification or the positivist definitions and the distinctions they require. Since the Sharīʿa supposedly does not merely combine the purposes of religious morality with those of law, but actually integrates them into a single substance, the whole of which finds its justification in inscrutable divine wisdom, it might be said, as Schacht does, that "the Sharīʿa is not 'law' in the modern sense of the word."[6]

This objection proceeds from assumptions that can be accepted

[6] Joseph Schacht, article "Sharīʿa," in *Shorter Encyclopedia of Islam* (Leiden, 1953) [henceforth abbreviated *SEI*], p. 525.

without weakening the essential point to be made. It must be remembered that the positive approach has been introduced into the discussion of procedural sovereignty only as an objective method of classifying rules and not as an evaluation of their origin. Whether or in what respects it is possible to distinguish between affairs of this world and those of the next is a religious question to which, no doubt, it was only natural for Muslim jurists to assume a Muslim answer. For the non-Muslim there is no reason to make such an assumption. It is legitimate for him to leave religious matters aside and examine the significance of the Sharīʿa, as interpreted by men of this world, for the affairs of this world. If he concludes that in certain areas the Sharīʿa provisions are inconsistent or unverifiable or not binding except as an expression of religious truth, then he cannot but believe there is something important lacking which prevents the Sharīʿa from truly serving to promote the material welfare of the community. In some respects he will certainly find that the Sharīʿa is " 'law' in the modern sense of the word"; this would be true for all those parts of it which have been defined and applied by recognized agencies in society such as the body of the jurists or the judges, police, and other officials. The key requirement in this is the existence of what amounts to a judicial determination of how the law applies to a particular case in question. When in other respects one finds that the Sharīʿa is not what we would call law, it is not merely a question of terms; the question is whether the Sharīʿa, not being law, can fulfill the functions of law. This is the importance of the positive method.

It should not be supposed that the Muslim jurists gave no recognition whatsoever to the importance of positive classifications; rather, it was simply that the method was incompletely applied, especially to the structure of constitutional obligations. Normally the jurists did distinguish between the religious desirability of an act and its legal validity. According to the religious classification, actions are obligatory, recommended, indifferent, frowned upon, or forbidden; according to the legal scale, actions are valid or invalid, not in the sense of being morally right or wrong, but in the sense of having or not having full legal effect. The legal scale, of course, refers only to those actions which are juridically relevant, and within the broad category of legally effective actions (*ṣaḥīḥ*) are recognized the more specific terms of "objectively effective" (*nāfidh*), "subjectively binding" (*lāzim*), and "irrevocable" (*wājib*). There is also the term of "ratification" (*ijāza*).[7]

These legal classifications seem to indicate a desire to examine reli-

[7] Schacht, "Sharīʿa," *SEI*, p. 526.

gious prescriptions from the standpoint of their temporal applicability and of the effects that should be temporally ascribed to them. Although on the whole any action that is religiously permissible (whether obligatory, recommended, indifferent, or frowned upon) is legally valid (assuming that the action is jurdically relevant), and forbidden actions are invalid, there are exceptions: some actions that are not forbidden religiously may be invalid legally, while forbidden actions may be valid; this would usually be the case for reasons of circumstance and perhaps only temporarily so.[8] In such cases as commercial transactions, the positive significance of the legal determination as opposed to the religious appreciation is obvious; in a ritual question such as the announcement of the intention (*niyya*) before performance of devotional exercises, the positive significance is less clear, although it is true that the *niyya* is an outward act rather than an inward spirit of devotion, and that it is certainly considered to be juridically relevant, and valid according to the scale of legal effects. So it is doubtful that in defining the scale of juridically relevant legal effects the jurists intended to develop a system of what we would recognize as positive law, whose temporal significance could be viewed logically apart from its religious significance. Instead what emerges is what might be called a system of positive religious obligations and rights, which have been given an outward form objectively recognizable by human intelligence. They are "juridically relevant" in that, in their outward form, they can be recognized by the judge (*qāḍī*) or the legal consultant (*muftī*) to be with or without outward effect. But this effect is not uniformly temporal in nature, especially in the case of the *'ibādāt* (devotional rituals), whose importance and sanction remain entirely spiritual. While commercial transactions, family affairs, and the like appear to have become matters of positive law, this is not only by virtue of their inclusion in the juridical scale, but also because—unlike the *'ibādāt*—they are considered appropriate matters for litigation and judicial determination.

Thus the identity of religious and temporal values conceived by Islam remains unscathed by the ideas of juridical relevance and juridical validity. What the legal scale does suggest is the existence of what was referred to above as positive religious obligations and rights as distinguished from "true" religious standards. The latter are ascertained not by the normal human faculties of perception but by inward spiritual devotion. As such they go beyond the Sharī'a, which is concerned entirely with externals and has therefore been regarded by

[8] See Schacht, "Bāṭil," *SEI*, p. 60; "Sharī'a", *SEI*, pp. 526–527.

pious Muslims, and particularly the Ṣūfī mystics, as a mere formal structure whose moral value is limited.

The fact that the Sharī'a deals with externals, then, does not mean that it constitutes positive law, while the fact that it remains religious in significance does not mean that it constitutes the real core of the religious spirit. It is ascertained by man as a verbalized scale of religious values, and becomes in this sense positive; its relevance is then evaluated by man according to the "legal" scale, and becomes positive in still another sense; but its actual application to concrete cases by judicial determination or the equivalent is not systematically provided for in juridical theory and is not considered an essential part of the Sharī'a as such. What would be the final step toward the category of positive law is not taken. Insofar as the Sharī'a is in fact incorporated into the judicial process, so that it can be authoritatively determined and applied by human agencies, it is positive law, and it is worthwhile to find out in what fields this has taken place and in what fields it has not, bearing in mind that it is oneself and not the Muslim jurist who thinks the distinction important.

The fact that the Sharī'a does not uniformly constitute a positive system of law can be traced to the lack of procedural positivism in the theory governing its overall determination and application. Since the primary function of the Caliphate is to apply the law, it is essential that the organization of the Caliphate itself be defined in practical terms. Since the substantive rules of the law are to be determined by the consensus (*ijmā'*) of the body of jurists, it is also important that this process be defined. But these definitions were seriously lacking in the case of the Caliphate and were limited in the case of the consensus of the jurists.

The doctrine of the Caliphate did not offer any adequate means of identifying the persons empowered to choose and install the caliph, or, if necessary, depose him, nor did it indicate the processes by which they should come to decisions. A wrongdoing ruler should be deposed if this will not invite anarchy, but the doctrine is silent on who is to decide this, or how.

The doctrine of jurisprudence, for its part, declared that the conclusions of individuals' legal reasoning were to be confirmed as authoritative by consensus. This could be called a positive answer to the procedural question but for the fact that no means was ever prescribed for officially ascertaining what the consensus on a given point of law was. Still, because of the progressive coagulation of judicial opinion into four great schools, in time the consensus was often a matter of common knowledge, while in other questions it was not maintained that the lack of consensus barred the individual *qāḍī* or *muftī* from giving an *ad hoc* judgment.

This lack of positivism in allocating procedural sovereignty both in constitutional and in legal theory appears to follow from the jurists' awareness of the need to protect the idealism of their concept of ultimate sovereignty from the corruptions to which it would inevitably be exposed from a positive process of interpretation and application. A noncognitive, ideal moral value would lose something of its purity in the course of being interpreted by less-than-ideal faculties. If, however, the interpretive process is not clearly spelled out in positive terms, then the ideal is safe from corruption by virtue of the simple fact that no interpretation that does take place is necessarily authoritative. Thus, whenever constitutional practice appears after the event to have deviated from the ideal—if, for example an unqualified caliph is installed—there is no reason to presume that he has been chosen in the correct manner. On the other hand, various allowances in the theory for irregularities ensure at the same time that no presumption can be made that the procedure has been incorrect.[9] There is no agency competent either to validate or invalidate the results. In legal theory, by the same token, *ijmā'* is considered infallible on grounds of the Prophet's statement, "My Community will never agree upon an error." Since there is no way of knowing who is or is not righteous enough to be included in the Prophet's Community, an escape clause is implicit. But even barring this consideration, the fact remains that *ijmā'* was never verifiable except insofar as it had become a matter of common knowledge, and this was only on points that had long since passed from contention, so that an assertion of infallibility was not a very audacious claim. The noninstitutionalization of *ijmā'* was the guarantee of its infallibility, as well as of the ideal nature of the source of law as a whole.

This fear of corrupting ideal values by systematically interpreting their practical applicability appears to have influenced the entire range of classical juristic theory. Formal doctrine could deal with ideals but not actualities, with ultimate authority but not immediate authority. There was simply no room in this attitude for a theoretical explanation of the relation of power to normative values. What pur-

[9] The traditional suspension of judgment by later jurists on the correctness of Mu'āwiya's succession to 'Alī is a typical example.

ports to be political and legal doctrine is really a branch of theology. "Islamic theology," we are told, "is always forced into extreme positions" in its attempt to give a thoroughly logical defense of God's exclusive power; it exhibits a predilection for words and forms, not recognizing them as mere symbols open to the hazards of distortion. But this extremism is characteristic of the "outer formulation" of doctrine rather than the "inner function or reality" of unspoken attitudes, and therefore theological doctrine must not be taken too literally.[10]

This admonition may seem to discourage such efforts as this one to examine and take seriously Islamic doctrines on their formal level, without an accompanying social or historical analysis of what lies hidden underneath. In addition one might reflect on the plea of Louis Massignon for orientalists

> to stop taking apart *a priori* the Islamic system of life into isolated and inert elements, in order to criticise them from "outside": to examine them from the beginning, on the contrary, from the inside, transposing into ourselves the categories of thought imagined by the Muslims, in order to appreciate their original interdependence, their intimate structure, their real historical growth.[11]

This book neither achieves nor attempts this highly desirable, though necessarily somewhat mystical, mental transposition. Classical doctrines are discussed in their outward form with a negative purpose, to show that they were not suitable as a basis for determining, with any precision at least, the processes or substance of medieval Muslim politics. This is important because many modern reformists such as Rashīd Riḍā, under the influence of Muḥammad ʿAbduh, proclaimed it their objective to make these doctrines serve as such a basis in the modern age. For this purpose they thought it worth while to recast them in a more modern image (emphasizing, for example, their flexibility, utilitarianism, and compatibility with certain institutional landmarks of European liberalism), proclaiming at the same time that they were returning to the original purity of what Islamic teaching had been before it was corrupted by tyranny and ignorance. That this

[10] H. A. R. Gibb, "The Structure of Religious Thought in Islam," third of four installments in *The Muslim World*, XXXVIII (1948), pp. 194–195; reprinted in *Studies on the Civilization of Islam* (Boston, 1962), pp. 205–206.

[11] *Revue du Monde Musulman*, XXXIX (1920), 152.

claim was an essentially mythical one may not seem to matter very much, as the world is full of useful myths. What does matter is that the classical doctrines were of a nature inappropriate to modern institutionalization unless stood upside down and turned inside out; and their modern reformist proponents were not willing to go that far. Neither in their own traditional period nor today have the principles in question indicated those unspoken principles by which Islamic life was, or can be, governed.

The failure of the constitutional theory of the Caliphate to provide a sufficiently positive allocation of procedural sovereignty disqualified it from serving as a practical constitutional instrument. It can perhaps be better understood as an apologia for the cumulative historical record of the institution and a defense of Sunnite practice against Shī'ite criticism, than as a reliable expression of what its exponents actually believed was the structure of rights, duties, procedures, and functions that they could normally expect to be observed.[12] Just as the Sharī'a becomes a positive system of law when subjected to human interpretation and application, so the theory of the Caliphate acquires the potentiality of becoming a positive constitutional system in the hands of those modernists who seek to resurrect it, even though for its classical authors it has been something else. But until it is actually applied, as parts of the Sharī'a have been at times, its significance remains in doubt, and must depend on the underlying purposes and expectations of its proponents. Does it really represent to them a program of revolutionary action by which they intend to put it into effect, or does it simply signify an intellectual outlook divorced from prospects of action?

Modern Islamic reformism has lost what Mannheim would have called its utopian character and become merely ideological. Whereas at the turn of the century Muslim reformists appealed, with an earnest sense of concrete purpose and with considerable practical optimism, for the adaptation of legal, political, and social institutions to fit an identifiable Islamic mold, these expectations have now receded, and the appeals convey no more than a state of mind which is well disposed to some regimes and critical of others, none of which has really implemented the Islamic principles in question. In the earlier age the object

[12] This is the view advanced by H. A. R. Gibb, "Al-Māwardī's Theory of the Khilāfa," *Islamic Culture*, XI (1937), pp. 291–302; reprinted in *Studies on the Civilization of Islam*, pp. 151–165.

was to adapt modern society and government to the requirements of Islam; for this purpose the requirements had, admittedly, to be restated. In the present period, by contrast, Islamic principles are often restated as if to imply that Islam has proved adaptable to modern society and government.

Often in history men have sought to justify particular existing systems or policies by reference to irrelevant principles. There was more than a touch of this in the period of the Abbasid Empire, when the orthodox doctrines of jurisprudence and constitutional authority were evolved along lines that bore little relation to the actual state of affairs. However, the ideological purposes were different from those of today. In the face of lawlessness and despotism it was desirable to assert the independence of Islamic legal and constitutional principles from the abuses of temporal power. This was done primarily by emphasizing their divine source and immutable character and, in the field of jurisprudence, the technical complexities (almost deliberately invented) that would render only the professional experts competent to supervise the law's implementation. Both constitutional and legal theory were elaborated as storm shelters: if ignored or abused in practice, they would be at least preserved in doctrinal purity for the day when, by God's grace, the millennium might dawn. Our concern, however, is not with conservatives, but with radicals, that is, the modernists, whose initial intention, two and three generations ago, was to emerge from the storm shelter and build in its place a comprehensive structure into which the whole practical life of Muslim society could be channeled. Such a structure has certainly not been built; another, quite different one is in the process of construction on other foundations, by other people; and many radicals, instead of protesting and resisting or moving back into the old storm shelter, have, so to speak, contentedly taken up residence in the new building as tenants, satisfied that the architecture is at least similar to, if not identical with, their own design.

Other modernists, more clearly aware of the discrepancy between their principles and those of contemporary nationalism, have ceased to be radicals and have become conservatives. They have settled for remodeling the storm shelter. For many Muslim intellectuals modernism is the new conservative orthodoxy. Modernist teachings have found wide acceptance also among the heirs of the premodern conservative tradition. They have adjusted their ideas to make room for reformist notions, but only after reformism lost its prospect of worldly success. Now that it is clear that Islamic law, even in a reinterpreted form, is not to be implemented as the comprehensive basis of the entire legal structure, reformist interpretations are no longer dangerous. Like traditional interpretations, they can retain their integrity only as a catechism, preserved and elaborated by scholars who sense the importance of preserving an intellectual and spiritual heritage. The conservative mythology has thus undergone some changes—indeed, some important ones—which traditionalists have tended to accept as necessary concessions to the modern age, but it remains mythology. Their response to scientific progress in the twentieth century, despite the revisions of dogma, is generically similar to their response to tyranny in the fourteenth century.

Between these alternative gravitations into nationalism and conservatism, the great moral purpose of practical reform that characterized Islamic modernism at the turn of the century has been quietly dissipated. Since modernism's adherents have found other homes, at either end of the spectrum, the dissipation has scarcely been noticed. No one in Egypt, for example, is heard today mourning the legacy of Muḥammad 'Abduh: on the contrary, everyone claims it as his own. The difficulty is that the teachings of 'Abduh and his circle rested on intellectual foundations that were, on the whole, vague and unsystematic. Their social and psychological impact was immense, but it was ambiguous. 'Abduh's heirs were propelled by his impetus in a variety of directions, each divergent movement gathering its own strength and developing its own distinct character in the absence of any basis for consensus on the precise nature of his message. Such diverse individuals as the liberal constitutionalist Aḥmad Luṭfī as-Sayyid, the militant fundamentalist Ḥasan al-Bannā' of the Muslim Brethren, and Gamāl 'Abd an-Nāṣir can all be identified, each in a different way, as heirs of 'Abduh. 'Abduh's historical role was simply to fling open the doors and expose a musty tradition to fresh currents. His intention may have been more specific, but the effect was not. His heirs were, of course, the product of various other influences as well, which sometimes combined with the ambiguity of 'Abduh's legacy to promote additional tensions and equivocations of their own. Such was the case with Muḥammad Rashīd Riḍā, 'Abduh's immediate disciple and principal biographer. Riḍā's intellectual career symbolizes in some ways the political failure of the whole Islamic modernist movement. Without any particular shifts in doctrine his position evolved, under pressure of circumstances, from that of liberal reformer to radical fundamentalist to orthodox conservative. Among those influenced by him, as a transmitter of 'Abduh's ideas, were both the Muslim Brotherhood, who prepared to restore Egypt to the rule of Islamic law by revolution, and Dr. 'Abdarrazzāq as-Sanhūrī, who relegated Islamic law to a minor place in drafting the Egyptian Civil Code of 1949 while praising its adaptability and relevance to modern needs in his published writings. These writings carried the inspiration of Riḍā's preachings, and enabled Sanhūrī to make the 1949 Code seem more or less their fulfillment, which in truth it was not. Under the circumstances the justification was logically absurd but politically effective—a verdict that might, in fact, not unjustly be rendered of many elements of Islamic reformist teaching as they are applied today to law and politics.

The evolution of Islamic modernism from a program of radical reform to simply a set of vague ideological attitudes has been due in large measure to the apologetic mentality among Muslims vis-à-vis Western civilization. Europe in the Reformation and the Enlightenment could dispute theological and philosophical questions within itself, without reference to ulterior standards; Muslims in the nineteenth and twentieth centuries have been in no position to do so, for the ulterior standard has been there for all to see. Hence doctrinal issues could not be disputed solely on their own intellectual or social merits. One must show that one's principles are no less advanced than those of Europe, but no less Islamic than those of the established indigenous conservative tradition. This dual standard has scarcely been conducive to rigorous systematic thought; instead it has opened the market to superficial slogans and angry polemics. Among more capable intellects it put a premium on ingenuity and nimble equivocation rather than on sustained thought. Original thinkers in medieval times, such as Ibn Taymiyya or Ibn Rushd—like Erasmus or Galileo in Europe—had only to assert their intellectual consciences in the face of the established tradition. Modern Muslim thinkers have had the more difficult task of finding their consciences in the midst of two contrasting traditions—or perhaps, since the Russian revolution, even three. Furthermore, there is the pressure of time. 'Abduh and some of his contemporaries recognized that if Islamic beliefs and attitudes were not reformed in time, they would soon be eroded on an increasing scale, leaving in their place a moral vacuum. Perhaps this is what has actually happened. The foundations laid by 'Abduh were only a haphazard beginning; the generation that followed, trapped in the atmosphere of apologetics, could not afford the luxury of clarifying them, but raced ahead to build their own shaky superstructures. The present age of totalitarian nationalism, charged with ideological slogans but devoid of philosophy, is not a surprising sequel.

The theme of this book follows from the assumption, implied in the foregoing, that the practical significance of a set of abstract social ideas may be at least partly dependent on their intellectual worth: on their coherence, profundity of insight and learning, and sincerity of purpose. This may seem at first glance an unexceptionable proposition, but in actuality many people today are embarrassed by it. In this age of foreign aid and cultural exchange programs, where all cultures are equal and none are more equal than others, critical evaluation of other people's beliefs seems arrogant and tactless. Worse yet, modern sociological theory makes critical evaluation seem unsophisticated. With the aid of psychology, it directs our attention to the life situation of those who propound or accept certain ideas, and away from the content and quality of the ideas themselves, reducing them to a forlorn status among the host of dependent variables by which the social process is scientifically explained. The sociologists may, of course, be right, in which case we are only moving bones from one graveyard to another.

But if the intellectual worth of ideas does matter historically, then it is relevant to go on and examine Islamic reformist doctrines on their own ground, that is, as an attempt to adapt traditional Islamic principles to the modern world. Rashīd Riḍā's constitutional and legal theories, on which two chapters of this book focus attention, constitute a leading example of this effort and of the character of the problems it has raised. He sought to revive doctrines that had remained part of the orthodox tradition for many centuries, but which for almost as long had remained bereft of both practical implementation and fresh discussion.

The effort was full of contradiction and equivocation. In the name of a return to the purity of the classic Islamic age, he restated doctrines in modern terms that gave them a radically different meaning, and suited them to markedly different purposes, from those that had traditionally characterized them. On the other hand, his essentially conservative mentality prevented him from following his reinterpretations to their logical and practical implications. He was radical in his theory, while seeing himself as a purveyor of the authentic tradition; he was reactionary in some of his conclusions, while seeing himself as a liberal reformer.

These equivocations, paralleling those of other modern Muslim apologists and generally endemic in the modernist position, stem fundamentally from theological problems which Muḥammad 'Abduh had raised but which neither he nor anyone since him ever resolved. In this sense it is unjust to regard them as the special failing of Rashīd Riḍā; they were the problem of a generation. Later generations have come to fasten their primary concern on other questions, such as the nature of the distinct social and cultural values of the Arab national heritage upon which a system of Arab socialism may be built. The terms of the problem are thus changed, but the search for Arab values presents some of the same difficulties as the search for Islamic ones, and it is appropriate to inquire whether the contemporary problem is essentially different in its origins from that of 'Abduh's immediate disciples.

II

IDEALISM IN THE JURISTIC THEORY OF THE CALIPHATE

The revived interest of modern Muslims in the classical theory of the Caliphate and the effort to find in it the basis for "progressive" institutions of democracy, popular sovereignty, and the like, have not only been stimulated by the political encounter between East and West over the past century but also encouraged by the publications of Orientalists. The eleventh-century jurist Al-Māwardī's treatise on government, *Al-Aḥkām as-Sulṭāniyya* ("The Ordinances of Government"), now generally regarded as the classic statement of the orthodox doctrine of the Caliphate, was resurrected from obscurity in 1853 and edited and published by Maximilian Enger in Bonn; further notice of it was taken by Baron von Kremer in his *Culturgeschichte des Orients unter den Chalifen.*[1] The French translation by the Polish diplomat, adviser to the Porte, and Orientalist Count Léon Ostrorog, published 1901–1906,[2] offered the first attempt by an Orientalist to read into Māwardī a theory of the contractual limitation of the authority of the state along lines familiar in Western thought. This view has since been, and still is, widely accepted by Muslim apologists, but received little serious criticism even among Orientalists until 1954.

That year saw the publication of two important studies: *Institutions du droit public musulman*, Volume I: *Le Califat* (followed in 1957 by Volume II, *Sultanat et califat*), by the Lebanese Christian professor of law Emile Tyan, and *La Cité musulmane: vie sociale et politique* by the French neo-Thomist scholar Louis Gardet. In these outstanding works Tyan and Gardet have made serious criticisms of the contractual theory. Tyan does so on detailed but rather narrow historical and legal

[1] Vienna, 1875–1877.

[2] Léon Ostrorog, transl., *El-Ahkam es-Soulthaniya.* Paris, 1901–1906. 2 vols.

grounds, part of which are cited here below. Gardet, more significantly, addresses himself to the Islamic theological background of constitutional theory, and rejects the notion of contract not as juridically inaccurate but as misleading and irrelevant. Carrying forward Gardet's approach, we are concerned here with points of legal analysis, not to arrive at a precise juridical definition of constitutional relationships in Tyan's manner, but on the contrary to show the absence of certain positive legal elements in the theory of the Caliphate and therefore the inadequacy of a purely legal investigation. This lack of positive content—despite the abundance of writings by medieval jurists on the subject—was due in large part to the theological terms of the theory, and hastened its obsolescence.

The starting point of traditional Muslim political doctrine is the concept of the *walāya*, or vested authority. In the original state of liberty conceived by Islam man has freedom of control over himself (*al-walāya 'alā'n-nafs*); this control can become transitive (*muta-'addiya*), that is, extend over others, only when there is a difference in capacity for liberty (thus, guardianship over a minor) or when control is freely delegated contractually. The *walāya* thus may or may not be inherent in the relationship. In either case it constitutes a trust to be executed in the subject's interest, with the purpose of bringing his capacity for liberty to fruition.[3]

God as man's creator has absolute power over him, and in this sense cannot be said to exercise a *walāya* over him, since the relationship is not subject to qualification. God's will being the only efficient cause, man has no independent existence of his own, and therefore no capacity for interests or liberty, except insofar as granted by God. Generally, however, the relationship is not conceived in these stark terms. Man's actions, as "apparent occasions" of their consequences, are raised fictitiously to the level of free will,[4] so that man may be considered an entity separate from his Creator and thus have a capacity for a responsible relationship with Him. The result is what is called the *mīthāq*, an allegorical covenant by which man voluntarily submits to God's will.[5] In this sense God may be said to exercise a *walāya*, by which it is understood that He will exercise His will for man's benefit.

---

[3] *Ibid.*, Vol. I, pp. 71–78.

[4] *Ibid.*, pp. 68–71. By "fictitiously" is meant not complete absence of validity but the fact that free will has no ultimate reality of its own—only a limited psychological reality valid for the human conscience by virtue of "acquisition" (*kasb*).

[5] Louis Gardet, *La Cité musulmane: vie sociale et politique* (Paris, 1954), p. 183.

Armed with this authority, God then proceeds to furnish man with the rules of conduct necessary for his welfare: the revealed Sharīʻa, governing relations with God (*ʻibādāt*) and with other men (*muʻāmalāt*). In a broad sense the former take precedence over the latter—human relationships being but a function of the spiritual relationship. Leaving this aside for the moment, however, human relations should be placed in a class of their own, since, given the capacity, men are capable of regulating their own relationships and recognizing their material interests through the use of their own reason. But even when reason is supplemented by revelation, social relations are necessarily subject to man's immediate control. The Sharīʻa in respect to relations among men deals only with apparent occasions, that is, human actions, and man is the agent of its interpretation and application. While he is restricted in this by the rules of jurisprudence and, for example, deduces analogies only on the basis of a clearly discernible efficient cause (*ʻilla*), to do so he must rely on his own intellect, which is within the realm of the apparent occasion. The Sharīʻa, then, although a product of the divine will and knowledge, regulates and is regulated in its application by human will and understanding, which have only a limited reality.

A. *The Levels of Meaning*

This brief discussion suggests the existence, implicit in the doctrine described, of four levels of moral significance:

(1) Divine will, the sole metaphysical reality upon which all creation and material or moral relationships depend for their existence. It is the original categorical imperative from which all value derives.

(2) The spiritual relationship between man and God, according to which man is presumed in a derivative sense—even a fictitious sense, if the above use of this term is accepted—to have a will and a conscience of his own, and consequently a capacity for rights and duties and power to enter into contracts. Since God's capacity and knowledge are absolute and man's are conditional and relative, the rights and duties are by no means balanced. Acknowledgment of this fact by man represents piety. This level is of course a function of the preceding one.

(3) The normative relationship between man and man, conceived in terms of law provided by God as a by-product of Level 2 through His perfect knowledge, but applied by man through imperfect knowledge. Because the relationship in this plane is between equals of only limited

capacity, it has a still more contingent character than Level 2; however, there is a constant interaction between the two levels—Level 3 being a function of Level 2—so that the distinction is often unclear.

(4) Non-normative relationships: the world of matter, appearances, and circumstances. This category stands somewhat apart from the others, lacking the qualities of value and will common to them. In any religious system it is bound to be the least meaningful level of the four. It is a direct product of Level 1, but this gives it no special significance. It has no relation to Level 2, and its relation to Level 3 is ambiguous. Human relationships to the extent that they are based on human reason are dependent on material and circumstantial considerations; to the extent that they are conceived as divinely ordained ideal relationships, they are pure spirit. Material circumstances are the basis of material advantage, but cannot be the ultimate basis of moral value; and law is essentially value, although for lack of inspiration men inevitably apply it in terms of material convenience. Ideally, the prescribed relationships of man exist prior to the circumstances to which they are intended to apply.

An example of this anomaly is the notion of the overriding importance of public interests (*al-maṣāliḥ al-mursala*). Ideally the doctrine states that the overall welfare of the Community overshadows any particular legal consideration, especially of the individual. The general right or duty is more important than the particular one, not on a quantitative numerical basis, as if two rights were more important than one, but because of the universal character of the general right. In practice, however, it is difficult to escape basing the doctrine of *maṣāliḥ* on human estimations of relative material convenience, in which absolute principles can seldom if ever be applied absolutely, and the most that one can usually do is to make a more or less educated guess as to which course of action is more likely to produce the most desirable results. It is not surprising, therefore, that the jurists restricted the use of this utilitarian methodology to the nondevotional aspects of law; the devotions (*'ibādāt*) belong to the second level, a spiritual category in which revelation is a more explicit and adequate guide.

The problem of the *maṣāliḥ* is characteristic of the general problem of the positive formulation and application of the law. Law as a normative system of human relationships (Level 3) is ideally only a transposed verbalization of the spiritual content of Level 2; that is, it is a product of religion, created by God and therefore finding its true justification in His will alone. This is the law's ideal nature. But in practical or positive terms it is definable only as a set of rules for the regulation of the empirical world of the fourth level. The problem, therefore, is how law is to be applied without being transformed from an eternal and inscrutable ideal into a mere product of human thought and experience. It is to be expected that there will always be a tension between these two opposite orientations. The tension can be found in various expressions of thesis and antithesis: ideal and positive; spiritual and material; independent and circumstantial; piety and utility; rights of God and rights of man; and so forth. Philosophical and historical analyses of law tend to reflect these opposing orientations respectively.

Much of the difficulty in resolving apparent contradictions in Muslim constitutional theory stems from these ambiguities, that is, from the tendency of the third level alternately to be subjected to the influence of the second and the fourth. The ambiguity enabled Muslim writers to shift with facility from one level of discussion to the other, so that contradictory propositions could be advanced, each of which was true in its own way. Thus for example a judge receives his *walāya* of investiture from his superior, but his authority does not end with the latter's death as usually occurs in delegated offices, because in a larger sense his responsibility is thought to be to the Sacred Law itself, or to the Community.[6]

For this reason much of the juristic theory defies a thoroughly logical analysis. Discussion by modern Western and Muslim writers of such questions as whether the caliph can be said to derive his authority by delegation from the Community (as the contract of the *bay'a* suggests to some) or only directly from God tend to be inconclusive and fruitless.[7]

While the Western jurist is accustomed to dealing with law as an entirely existential phenomenon and relegating the question of its relation to theology to a separate field of study, classical Muslim writers tended to combine their attention to all fields of theology and public and private law in single works. They do not, for the most part, appear to have been troubled by some of the problems most perplexing to modern students of Islam. Shifts among the second, third, and

---

[6] Émile Tyan, *Historire de l'organisation judiciaire en pays d'Islam*, I (Paris, 1938), p. 147.

[7] The clearest recognition of the consequences of this dualism is to be found in Gardet's *La Cité musulmane*.

fourth levels appear to them quite natural and indeed entirely justified, since the distinctions between the ideal and existential are less clear in the Islamic than in the Western tradition.

This state of affairs made possible a wide range of flexibility in the Muslim theoretical system, according to the changing requirements of history: first, within the juristic system itself, and then, when the contradictions between theory and history became too glaring even for the Muslims, from the juristic theory to others quite different. Efforts to escape the implications of Level 4, in the form of the fact of power, had lifted the juristic theory of the Caliphate altogether out of the realm of practical law and into that of pure ideal, where it could be regarded as an expression of God's will and man's duty, but no longer an effective rule of life. With recognition of this fact, the way became clear for drastic revision of the traditional theory (e.g., by Ghazālī, Ibn Taimiyya, and Ibn Jamā'a), formulation of a practical and more opportunistic system of social ethics (e.g., by Ibn Qutaiba, Niẓām al-Mulk, and others of the administrative school of writers), and philosophical expression of both by the Neoplatonists. Since we are only concerned with constitutional theory as a problem of jurisprudence, however, the last two groups will not be included in the following discussion.

B. *Ambiguities in the Classical Constitutional Theory*

Muslim theories of the sources of political authority, being framed within the idea of Islam as a religiously oriented, all-embracing rule of life, are bound to reflect the disparities and ambiguities suggested by the "levels of meaning." Any given problem in political theory is likely to be subject to ambiguity: it can be understood in terms of the second level (the religious significance) or the third (the positive legal or human significance). Furthermore, various institutions in Islamic history as viewed by theorists symbolize one level or the other. The Imamate and the Sultanate, the Sharī'a courts and the *maẓālim* courts, and governorship by voluntary appointment and governorship by usurpation reflect this dualism. On the conceptual level, we can contrast the idea of piety in the ruler to justice in the ruler; virtue as the basis of capacity to power or effectiveness as the basis of capacity; the caliph as *khalīfat Allāh* to the caliph as *khalīfat ar-rasūl;* justice in the ruler as a hope to justice in his subordinates as a matter of enforcement; and the general approach of the juristic school to that of the administrative school of writers. In each of these examples, we find either that one proposition is on the theological level and the other on the juridical level, or that both are juridical, but one is under the influence of theology and the other under the influence of considerations of circumstantial fact and expediency.

Within the confines of the theory of the Caliphate itself, as set forth by the orthodox Sunnī jurists, the various parts of the theory can be looked at in two ways.

The jurists advancing the so-called "classical" theory (Māwardī, Baghdādī, Bāqillānī, and others) thought primarily in terms drawn from the methods and principles familiar to themselves, appropriate to legal transactions. Thus the necessity of the institution of the Caliphate was said to be based on *ijmā'* (consensus); the installation of a caliph and the *bay'a*[8] or oath to him represented a determination of capacity and an affirmation of ensuing mutual obligation between ruler and subjects in a manner suggesting contract, with the implied right of deposition for cause; the qualifications enumerated for the caliph and his electors were clearly designed to ensure performance of their functions; the doctrine of necessity, when invoked, was used to justify exceptional suspensions of legal requirements in the same spirit as in private law. And lastly, the office of the Caliphate, while sanctioned ultimately on religious grounds, was described in terms that excluded what could properly be called religious powers. The caliph's function was to enforce the Sharī'a as a civil executive, not to formulate doctrine.

On the other hand, with the progressive loss by the Caliphate in later Abbasid times of its effective power over the affairs of the Com-

---

[8] The word has many uses in consititutional discussion. Tyan cites the various *bay'as* made to Muḥammad which signified acceptance of Islam and with it the Prophet's authority, and hence may be considered engagements by the Muslims toward God (*Institutions du droit public musulman, I: Le Califat* [Paris, 1954], pp. 144–145 [hereafter cited as *Califat*]). Besides this there is the special *bay'a* (*bay'a khāṣṣa*) given by the electors to Abū Bakr, 'Alī, and certain of the Umayyads; the general *bay'a* (*bay'a 'āmma*) given by the general populace immediately following a special *bay'a* and signifying public acknowledgment of the obligation of loyalty (*ibid.*, pp. 158–159); the general *bay'a* following a testamentary designation (*ibid.*, p. 265); and the repetition of a previously made *bay'a*, called *tajdīd al-bay'a* (*ibid.*, pp. 351–352). An heir apparent would receive a *bay'a* both at the time of his designation and upon his succession (*ibid.*, pp. 329–332).

The term *bay'a* was occasionally used to signify testamentary designation (*ibid.*, p. 264), but other terms were more current: *'ahd, istikhlāf, taqlīd, 'aqd, walāya,* and *waṣiyya* (*ibid.*, pp. 270–272). One would search in vain for the word *bay'a*, for example, in such a lengthy document as Mutawakkil's decree naming his three sons as successors (Ṭabarī, *Tārīkh al-Umam wa 'l-Mulūk* [Cairo, n.d.], II, 39–40).

munity, the aspects of the theoretical structure enumerated in the preceding paragraph had to be viewed differently if they were to retain any meaning. Since the caliph's importance was now primarily as a religious symbol, the procedures and institutions defining his office could only be justified on the religious plane. Thus the necessity of the office could be explained on the grounds that God must have an agent on earth; accordingly the caliph is styled *khalīfat Allāh* ("successor [of the Prophet] approved by God") as well as *khalīfat ar-rasūl* ("successor of the Prophet" in his judicial and executive functions).[9] It follows from this that the *bay'a* is an expression of devotion and submission rather than a contract or a voluntary designation, and that there can be no right of deposition. As for the required qualifications, they lose their importance with the loss of the caliph's practical functions. The one qualification that continued to be stressed was not one of practical ability, but was dynastic: the caliph must be of Quraishite lineage. As the doctrine of necessity came to be invoked on a massive scale, suspension of legal requirements and bowing to the inevitable was not a matter of prudence in exceptional circumstances, but a resigned admission of powerlessness, with no comfort save the thought that times of evil and misfortune were the will of God. And in place of the essentially civil function of the caliph as a law-enforcing executive, emphasis was put on the fanciful spiritual aura of his office and the assumption that while the sultan had been delegated effective civil authority, the caliph retained his symbolic religious prestige.

On historical grounds it would be difficult to argue that the later Abbasids possessed real spiritual powers. Since the failure of the attempt by the caliph Ma'mūn (813–833) and his two successors Mu-'taṣim (833–842) and Wāthiq (842–847) to exercise control over the teachings of the 'ulamā',[10] conservation of religious doctrine had rested unchallenged outside the governmental institution. Nor was it ever incorporated into any other formal institution. It was exercised by the scholars, Ṣūfī preachers, and other individuals to whatever extent their personal prestige would allow.[11]

[9] See I. Goldziher, "Du sens propre des expressions Ombre de Dieu, Khalife de Dieu, pour désigner le chef dans l'Islam," *Revue de l'Histoire des Religions*, XXXV (1897), 335–338.

[10] See Walter Patton, *Ahmed Ibn Hanbal and the Mihna* (Leiden, 1897).

[11] H. A. R. Gibb, "An Interpretation of Islamic History," *Muslim World*, XLV (1955), 11: The issue posed by Ma'mūn's inquisition "proved once and for all that the religious institution of Islam was independent of the Caliphate or any other institution." (Reprinted in *Studies on the Civilization of Islam* [Boston, 1962], p. 12.)

Furthermore, since in theory the caliph stood at the apex of the political system, but passed on authority to the sultan or amir by delegation, whatever power he lost was lost without distinction between the religious and the political, unless he expressly reserved particular powers for himself in the text of the diploma of delegation, which often was not the case.[12]

What the later Abbasid caliphs actually retained was not power but political and religious prestige. In the political sphere the caliph was always the sole titulary of supreme temporal authority. His signature continued to be required for decisions, and during the interregna between sultanates (for example, between the Buwaihid and Seljuk periods) he resumed the exercise of numerous functions without the need for formal authorization.[13]

As for the religious sphere, to judge by the outward forms, procedures, and functions of the caliph it might seem questionable whether he has any genuine religious role at all.[14] Juridically he is simply the legitimate ruler of the Muslim community, subject to a system of law. The Community is therefore governed by a nomocracy, which, regardless of its religious origin, is still the rule of law and not of a priestly class. In interpreting the law the caliph is no more than the chief *qāḍī*.

The only religious element in the caliph's specific powers and duties is the provision for protection of the generally recognized tenets of the faith from attack and perversion; but the caliph has no special religious inspiration or powers of interpretation. This makes Islam an established religion, but does not make the Caliphate an ecclesiastical office, any more than the British Crown, with its duty to protect the established Church of England, is thereby an ecclesiastical office.

It is in its inward rather than outward nature that a religious quality can be ascribed to the Caliphate, that is, on the theological and psy-

---

[12] Emile Tyan, "Notes sur la distinction du spirituel et du temporel dans le califat," *Annales de la Faculté de Droit* (Université Saint-Joseph de Beyrouth), 1951, no. 1, p. 12: "The Caliphate, having always been considered as the sole depository institution of all authority, under its two aspects, civil and religious, was reduced, when the effective exercise of this authority passed to the sultans, to a purely theoretical role of sovereignty, from both the civil and religious points of view, which was legally necessary only for validating the *de facto* position of the sultans."

[13] Tyan, *Institutions du droit public musulman, II: Sultanat et califat* (Paris, 1957), p. 247. (Hereafter cited as *Sultanat.*)

[14] Thus C. Snouck Hurgronje writes that the Caliphate never enjoyed anything that could be called spiritual authority "unless by 'spiritual authority' we are to understand the empty appearance of worldly authority" (*Mohammedanism* [New York, 1916], pp. 112–113).

chological rather than juridical level. The law from which it is derived is of religious inspiration, and its performance or nonperformance has a religious as well as temporal sanction. The religious source and sanction are always at the forefront of consciousness; in a given situation the legal formula is often conceded a special religious significance. Thus for the sultans to seek diplomas of investiture from the caliphs was in large part a demonstration of piety: it was "less to obtain a confirmation properly speaking of their authority, than to assure their integration into Islam and to make a proclamation of faith."[15] The fact that the maintenance of the institution of the Caliphate was often considered an article of religious faith[16] explains why the destruction of the Caliphate by the Mongols in 1258 was viewed with such consternation.[17]

Those writers such as Ibn Khaldūn, Nasafī, and Ibn Taimiyya who subscribed to the doctrine that the true Caliphate had lasted only for a short time, were in effect defining the office in terms of the motivation of its incumbent: the ruler was legitimately styled "caliph" only as long as the guiding spirit of his rule was to apply the Sharī'a and promote the best spiritual as well as material interests of the Community. Nasafī and Ibn Taimiyya were only following the ḥadīth, common especially in the Ḥanafī school, according to which the Prophet said: "After me there will be a Caliphate for thirty years, then it will become a tyrannical kingdom."[18] For Ibn Taimiyya the Caliphate was not even necessary.[19] Ibn Khaldūn, for his part, did not consider the Caliphate incompatible with "kingdom" (*mulk*) or temporal sover-

---

[15] Tyan, *Sultanat*, p. 240.

[16] *Ibid.*, p. 239.

[17] Tyan, in the course of an admirable clarification of the question of temporal and religious powers (*Sultanat*, pp. 238–251), sums up: "The Caliphate conserved its character as a religious institution, not in the sense of an organism of spiritual power or function, but, quite precisely, in the sense that in the Islamic conception of the Caliphate, as the titulary repository of supreme sovereignty in both the religious and civil aspects closely bound up with each other, is an institution that constitutes an element of the faith. It is a fundamental element of Islam, the pillar on which rests the whole edifice and which conditions the organization and life of the Community. The Islamic faith includes belief in the necessity of the Caliphate as the titular organism of the civil and religious attributes of sovereignty" (p. 250).

[18] E. E. Elder, *A Commentary on the Creed of Islam:* translation of Sa'd ad-Dīn at-Taftazānī's commentary on the catechism of Abū Ḥafs 'Umar an-Nasafī (New York, 1950), p. 144.

[19] H. Laoust, *Essai sur les doctrines sociales et politiques de Taḳī-d-Dīn Aḥmad b. Taimiya* (Cairo, 1939), pp. 279–283.

eignty. He allowed that power and compulsion were entirely admissible instruments of rule, the important question always being to what end power was used. The early caliphs had found compulsion unnecessary, owing to the special circumstances of voluntary social cohesion in the early Community; the Umayyads through the reign of 'Abd al-Malik and the Abbasids through Hārūn ar-Rashīd combined the good intentions essential to the Caliphate with the necessary compulsion and thus were both caliphs and "kings" at the same time. The latter Umayyads and the later Abbasids were caliphs in name only.[20]

Among classical Muslim writers Ibn Khaldūn appears to have been most prominent in recognizing the importance of the distinctions between the spiritual and positive levels of observation and judgment. He first of all uses the term *mulk* to denote political control in human society as a generic term. This is divided into *mulk ṭabī'ī* and *mulk siyāsī*. *Mulk ṭabī'ī* or "natural sovereignty" denotes the unregulated exercise of power by a ruler based on sheer force, only one step removed from the law of the jungle. *Mulk siyāsī* or "political sovereignty" is rule by law, or nomocracy. It is subdivided into two types: *siyāsa 'aqliyya* or rationally derived nomocracy, and *siyāsa dīniyya* or religiously derived nomocracy. The Caliphate is of the latter type.[21]

Sovereignty of some type, whether political or natural, is recognized by Ibn Khaldūn as necessary and inevitable: necessary for the protection of persons and property, and inevitable because of the workings in history of human nature,[22] principally through the force he identifies as *'aṣabiyya* or group solidarity. It is characteristic of Ibn Khaldūn's distinction as a historian that he subjects Islamic institutions to the same considerations of human nature as non-Islamic ones, recognizing that irrespective of their religious significance, they are all, on the existential level, human institutions.

But it subsequently becomes clear that by "religiously derived nomocracy" he means only Islamic nomocracy, and that he has by no means separated religious evaluations from the discussion. For after

---

[20] Ibn Khaldūn, *Al-Muqaddima*, chap. iii, sec. 26: "The Transformation of the Caliphate into Royal Authority;" English translation by Franz Rosenthal, *Al-Muqaddimah: An Introduction to History* (New York, 1958), I, 414–428.

[21] Ibn Khaldūn, *Muqaddima*, chap. iii, sec. 23: "The Meaning of Caliphate and Imamate," Rosenthal translation, I, 385–388.

[22] Ibn Khaldūn, *Muqaddima*, chap. i, First Prefatory Discussion: "Sovereignty is a natural quality peculiar to man which is absolutely necessary to him." Cf. Rosenthal translation, I, 92.

setting forth his classification, he proceeds to an argument congenial to Muslim pietist minds:

> Mankind is intended for its religion, which leads it to bliss in the hereafter in the path of God. . . . The systems of divine law were thus issued to guide mankind in this direction in all circumstances of devotions and transactions. . . . Sovereignty resting on force . . . is reprehensible in the eyes of God. . . . But sovereignty resting on a rational system of law is also reprehensible, since it is conceived other than by the light of God; and whomsoever God has not enlightened, what light has he?
>
> . . . From this the meaning of the Caliphate will be clear. Natural sovereignty means ruling men in accordance with the aims and desires of the ruler. Political sovereignty [i.e., rational nomocracy] means ruling men in accordance with the dictates of reason, in order to secure worldly interests and avert harm. The Caliphate [i.e., religious nomocracy] means ruling men in accordance with the dictates of the Divine Law, securing thereby both the interests of the hereafter and those of this world which are contributory to them. For the affairs of this world, in the eyes of the Lawgiver, are viewed in the light of the interests of the hereafter. Thus in truth the Caliphate represents the Lawgiver in protecting the Faith and guiding men's earthly affairs.[23]

With these words Ibn Khaldūn has turned from an objective classification to an evaluation that has meaning only on the religious level. The religion on which one type of law is based in his classification is now assumed to be true religion. There is evidently no room for, say, a pagan religious nomocracy in his categories. Neither the religious inspiration nor the spiritual benefits of divine law can be recognized by a purely legal or sociological analysis; the latter can only recognize the existence of religious belief as a positive phenomenon.

Thus even so detached a thinker as Ibn Khaldūn did not confine his analysis entirely to the objective characteristics of the objects of his inquiry. In terms of our levels of significance, we should say that he treats the materials of the third and fourth levels with an awareness of their value in the second.

If this was true for Ibn Khaldūn, it should not be surprising to discover the same practice in the constitutional expositions of the jurists, since the religious implications of jurisprudence are still more direct than those of sociology.

---

[23] Ibn Khaldūn, *Muqaddima*, chap. iii, sec. 23: cf. Rosenthal translation, I, 386–388.

One way to demonstrate this tendency in the juristic theory of the Caliphate is to call attention to the practice of relying on what we may call self-sufficient facts. By this is meant that in a particular situation a particular fact is considered juridically relevant even though no means are provided for its authoritative verification, or even though it is not susceptible of verification.

The most obvious example of this is the failure of the jurists to describe the procedures by which certain constitutional functions were to be performed. In the election of the caliph by the *ahl al-ḥall wa 'l-'aqd* (leaders of the Community), not only do we never have a precise account of who these electors are or how they are to be chosen and on what basis, but there is no means described of authoritatively determining whether or not the election has been correctly carried out. The legally relevant facts in this case are (1) the competence or incompetence of the electors, (2) their fulfillment or nonfulfillment of their functions in a proper way,[24] and (3) the completion or perfection of the resultant legal relationship between caliph and Community by the new caliph's adherence to the electors' designation and their swearing of allegiance to him. It is only assumed that the process will be followed in a valid manner; there is no means prescribed of determining authoritatively whether this has been done.

It can be argued, of course, that the election of the caliph by the electors is itself a verification of his capacity, and that the oath of loyalty is a verification of the completion of the legal transaction. But this is only self-verification; there is no provision whereby the competence of the electors themselves is to be verified by an outside body before their acts can be pronounced valid. The jurists customarily were content to assume that only those qualified as electors would play the role, and that they would choose the caliph in the correct manner; the assumption was sufficient, and the correct behavior was presumed to take its legal effect without the need of being pronounced valid. In the absence of these procedures of verification the whole notion of the *bay'a*-election becomes a matter not of legal machinery but of moral justification of courses of action that may or may not be followed. If, in other words, qualified electors choose a qualified candidate, their action is valid; but since there is no recognized means of ascertaining whether this has been the case, the validity itself is not verified, and so cannot have any positive legal significance, but only a moral significance not dependent on recognition by a competent authority.

[24] That is, by competently judging the candidates' qualifications.

Similarly, it was argued by some jurists that a sole qualified candidate for the Caliphate was to be considered installed by virtue of the simple fact of his unique qualifications.[25] According to this view, the sole qualified candidate for a judicial post still needed an express *walāya* of investiture, because the judge is only the delegate of the caliph, who could exercise the functions himself, while the caliph, by contrast, is not the delegate of a higher official, but exercises an original authority. He is not, therefore, dependent upon a *walāya*, and his investiture is no more than a confirmation of his authority which already exists by virtue of his capacity.[26]

But this argument overlooks the fact that without such confirmation the candidate's capacity, from the juridical point of view, is nonexistent. The legally relevant fact—the candidate's unique capacity—is deemed effective without needing even to be recognized.

Other self-sufficient facts are assumed in the doctrine that only the pious and just caliph is truly a caliph, and in the doctrine that forceful usurpation of authority, when effective, automatically is to be considered legally confirmed on grounds of necessity.[27] Whether in the one case the caliph is pious and just, and in the other the usurpation is effective, are questions that apparently do not have to be answered by any authoritative procedure; the mere facts, recognized or not, are sufficient in themselves.

Two points should be noted in these examples. In the first place, the doctrines in question were designed to provide a justification for events that had already taken place, rather than an adequate mechanism or procedure for the regulation of constitutional questions in the future. In the second place, the doctrines were more moral than legal, since they did not depend on any human recognition and were therefore nonpositive. Or, in another sense, they were legal doctrines, inasmuch as they were framed in legal terminology and purported to have legal significance, but only if the word "legal" is understood in a purely ideal sense. But this ideal meaning can only be understood on the higher level, where law is not simply a recognized body of rules, but something more, namely, the ultimate justification of those rules. In the case of the Sharī'a, this justification is religious truth.

---

[25] This view is cited noncommittally by Al-Māwardī, *Al-Aḥkām al-Sulṭāniyya* (ed. Enger; Bonn, 1853), p. 9.

[26] *Ibid.*, p. 10.

[27] See Badr ad-Dīn Ibn Jamā'a, *Taḥrīr al-Aḥkām fī Tadbīr Ahl al-Islām*, ed. H. Kofler, in *Islamica*, VI (1934), 357, for the most extreme position in this regard.

C. *Social Contract and the Caliphate*

As a rule, theories of the Caliphate as a contractual delegation are derived from the process of election (by acclamation) by the *ahl al-ḥall wa 'l-'aqd* ("people of loosing and binding"), followed by the *bay'a* (oath of loyalty) by the populace at large. The procedure that is historically more relevant—that of designation by the incumbent caliph of his successor with the oath following—is customarily treated as a variant of the "classic" formula of election. There is little justification for this assumption, however. As Tyan remarks, it is more logical both historically and juridically to consider the election as the subsidiary process, resorted to only when the preceding caliph fails to exercise his prerogative.[28] Thus, for example, although Māwardī mentions election before testamentary designation, he says: "The testamentary designation is an explicit and binding declaration, and only in its absence is election resorted to."[29] Similarly the Egyptian fifteenth-century scholar Qalqashandī says: "There are two means of empowering the caliph: either by testamentary designation from the preceding caliph, or if there is no previous designation from the caliph, then by a *bay'a* from the *ahl al-ḥall wa 'l-'aqd.*"[30]

Nevertheless, even in the case of election, the modern supposition that this signified a contractual delegation of the authority of the Islamic Community to the caliph is a questionable one, and in the case of nomination, all the more so.

A prime example of the delegation theory is found is Ostrorog's commentary accompanying his translation of Māwardī. All political relationships, says Ostrorog, must be understood in terms of the *walāya* or title to authority under which the caliph and his delegates exercise their functions. "Every legitimate authority in Islam is a *walāya*, acquired by delegation *from the general walāya with which the Nation has invested the Caliph* in entering with him into the contract of the Caliphate."[31] That the transaction is a contract, says Ostrorog, is attested by the fact that every contract must include a "condition" (*sharṭ*) and a "pillar" (*rukn*) which consists of offer and acceptance; these elements are found in the investiture of the caliph, and hence the

[28] Tyan, *Califat*, p. 188; *Sultanat*, p. 336.

[29] Māwardī, *Aḥkām*, p. 11.

[30] Abū 'l-'Abbās Aḥmad al-Qalqashandī, *Ṣubḥ al-A'shā* (Cairo, 1916), IX, 252; cited in Tyan, *Sultanat*, p. 336.

[31] Ostrorog, *El-Ahkam*, pp. 194–195 (my italics).

investiture is a contract.[32] The *ahl al-ḥall wa 'l-'aqd* are the representatives of the Community, as attested by their authority to act on its bchalf not only in selecting the caliph but also in deposing him and in deciding questions of *ijmā* (consensus).[33]

Ostrorog admits the difficulty of reconciling all this with Māwardī's opening statement: "God has instituted a chief over the Nation in place of the Prophecy, including under him the entire Community, and has delegated to him control of their affairs so that they may be regulated in accordance with the Faith He has ordained."[34] This pronouncement appears to rule out any capacity of the *ahl al-ḥall wa 'l-'aqd*, on behalf of the Community, to delegate authority. In answer to Shī'ite objections in this vein, Ostrorog cites the "orthodox" reply: it is indeed not the Community that grants authority; the caliph's *walāya* finds its real efficient cause in God; the election by the Community is only the "apparent occasion" bringing the *walāya* into effect.[35]

What Ostrorog is quite rightly saying is that Māwardī's statement refers to the higher religious level: it is God, from a religious point of view, who sanctions human political authority, and the Caliphate is justified ultimately on religious grounds. But on the positive level, an agency is necessary to pronounce the dictates of the Law, regardless of the Law's source.

The "orthodox" argument to which he refers is well represented in a passage by the eighth-century (i.e., pre-Māwardī) theologian 'Aḍud ad-Dīn al-Ījī in which he enumerates and refutes the Shī'ite arguments.[36] The first objection is as follows:

> The Imamate is God's and the Prophet's lieutenancy, and so the validity of the office cannot be established by the decision of others, i.e., the electors (*ahl al-bay'a*); if it were so, then the Imam would be their caliph, not God's and the Prophet's.

'Aḍud ad-Dīn replies:

> The electors' choice of the Imam is itself an indication of the lieutenancy of God and the Prophet, who set him up as a sign of

[32] *Ibid.*, pp. 155–156. Note the inductive reasoning.

[33] *Ibid.*, p. 107.

[34] Māwardī, *Aḥkām*, p. 2.

[35] Ostrorog, *El-Ahkam*, p. 107. No sources are cited.

[36] *Kitāb al-Mawāqif:* Parts 5 and 6 and Appendix edited by T. Sorensen under the title *al-Ilāhiyyāt wa 's-Sum'iyyāt wa 't-Tadhyīl min Kitāb al-Mawāqif* (Leipzig, 1848), p. 304.

> their judgment in favor of that lieutenancy, as is the case with the signs of other ordinances. The explanation according to our view is that the *bay'a* is not what validates the Imamate, in the sense you referred to, but rather it is a sign bringing the Imamate to light, as is the case with analogy and consensus which indicate (but do not create) the ordinances of the Sharī'a.

The second objection is:

> The electors have no authority (lit., disposal) over other persons, and therefore their action and their choice cannot have any binding force over others. They do not themselves enjoy authority over the Muslims, so how can they invest someone else with such authority?

And the answer:

> If their action and choice is a procedure established by God and His Prophet as an indication of their judgment in favor of the Imamate of whomever the electors decide to recognize, then the objection falls. For their *bay'a* becomes a decisive proof for the Muslims and must be followed. Your position is also refuted by the example of the witness and the judge. They must be followed because the Lawgiver made their words an indication of divine judgment which must be followed, even though they have no authority over the object of the testimony and of the judicial verdict.

This is a decisive rejection of the contract theory; the *ahl al-bay'a* are considered mere functionaries, not interested parties.

The Shī'ite objection, then, distorts the issue by lifting it entirely out of the realm of law and into that of theology, rendering meaningless any notion of human rights and duties conceived on their own level. But while 'Aḍud ad-Dīn's words establish this, they serve not to support a theory of delegation from the Community but to refute it by distinguishing between designation and delegation. For him as for the Shī'ite critics, the source of authority is theologically conceived.

The next difficulty arises in regard to the *bay'a* given after nomination of the caliph and his acceptance. Māwardī implies that the oath is obligatory.[37] Since offer and acceptance form a complete contract, argues Ostrorog, the oath merely "perfects" it.[38] The same view is

---

[37] Māwardī, *Aḥkām*, pp. 7, 12.
[38] Ostrorog, *El-Ahkam*, p. 107.

advanced by others,[39] and is in accord with Māwardī's text: "They (the *ahl al-ḥall wa 'l-'aqd*) offer him the Imamate, and if he accepts it they swear allegiance to him on it; and by their oath the Imamate becomes fully contracted to him."[40]

While it is indeed true that a contract is generally not fully binding until perfected in the manner appropriate to the case—a marriage contract, for example, becomes binding only after consummation—it is questionable whether much juridical importance can be attached to the *bay'a* as a perfection of the alleged contract of the Imamate. If the *bay'a* is considered obligatory after nomination and acceptance, it appears to be no more than an acknowledgment of already existing obligations. This is true of both the public and the private *bay'as*. Ostrorog recognizes the dilemma: when Māwardī doubts that any *bay'a* need follow a testamentary designation,[41] Ostrorog objects that no homage can be considered due until freely professed by the Community's representatives.[42] It is, of course, rather pointless for Ostrorog to dispute points of this kind with a jurist of the eleventh century. In any event, he fails to follow Māwardī here because he clings to his own preconception of a *walāya* delegated from the Community, if not by election, then at least by an act of ratification, while Māwardī was thinking along other lines according to which not the oath of allegiance but only the nomination had any constitutive significance.

In his amply documented study of the process of investiture of the caliph, Tyan finds that despite the pretensions of latter-day Abbasid writers, from a time early in the Umayyad period the rendering of homage by the notables had in practice been considered obligatory and not subject to individual discretion,[43] and that the general *bay'a* by the populace at large had been considered so from the beginning.[44] Both *bay'as* were considered necessary for a full consummation of the caliph's authority, although the validity of his investiture was not affected and although they were not given voluntarily. They represented only an affirmation of recognition and hence were accorded to the designee both after his designation and upon his actual accession to

[39] Cf. for example Santillana in T. Arnold and A. Guillaume, eds., *The Legacy of Islam* (Oxford, 1931), p. 297; Gardet, *La Cité musulmane*, p. 167.

[40] Māwardī, *Aḥkām*, p. 7.

[41] *Ibid.*, p. 12.

[42] Ostrorog, *El-Ahkam*, p. 129.

[43] Tyan, *Califat*, pp. 321–326.

[44] *Ibid.*, pp. 168–172.

office.[45] The finality of nomination as a constitutive act may be gauged from the case of 'Umar b. 'Abdal'azīz, the eighth Umayyad caliph, nominated without his knowledge by his cousin and predecessor, Sulaimān, in a sealed document. On Sulaimān's death, according to the chroniclers, an assembly of notables was convened and their obedience to the anonymous beneficiary of the sealed testament secured; only then was the document opened and 'Umar proclaimed Caliph.[46]

A similar issue arises in the question posed by Māwardī as to whether the sole qualified candidate for the Imamate may be considered installed without the usual procedure of formal nomination, acceptance, and homage. The general view, says Māwardī, is that the formalities are necessary even though the electors have no choice.[47] Presumably he considers this merely a matter of declaratory recognition, for he quotes the following argument of those who would dispense with the formalities, without troubling to refute it: A judge must receive an express *walāya* of investiture even if he is the only qualified candidate for the post, but the caliph need not, because of the fundamental difference in their positions. The judge is the caliph's deputy, and the latter could in his absence perform the function himself; the caliph's functions, by contrast, can be performed by no one else, since they involve the rights of both God and man. The qualified candidate is therefore indispensable and, as Māwardī declares, "in consideration of his special qualifications, his investiture needs no confirmation."[48]

This again reflects Māwardī's unconcern for even the appearance of free selection, and hence Ostrorog is disturbed. If the contract becomes superfluous, he says, this contravenes *ijmā'*, according to which the caliph must be chosen and installed by a full contract that not merely confirms but actually *confers* authority.[49] He does not enter the more limited but more plausible objection that the procedures of declaratory acknowledgment cannot be dispensed with without inviting chaos.

Some explanation for the inconsistencies sensed by Ostrorog may

---

[45] *Ibid.*, pp. 315–319.

[46] *Ibid.*, p. 268, citing Ṭabarī, Mas'ūdī, and Suyūṭī. As Tyan notes elsewhere, in the case of 'Umar b. al-Khaṭṭāb's succession of Abū Bakr on the latter's nomination, it is doubted whether he ever received a formal public *bay'a* at all (*ibid.*, p. 182).

[47] Māwardī, *Aḥkām*, p. 9.

[48] *Ibid.*, p. 10: "Lam yaftaqir taqlīdu mustaḥiqqihā ma'a tamayyuzihi ilā mustathbitin lahu."

[49] Ostrorog, *El-Ahkam*, pp. 120–121.

seem to emerge from the dual status of the Imamate which, in Māwardī's words, "combines the rights of God and of men."[50] In this context Ostrorog cites a dual limitation on the caliph's authority: there is no obligation of obedience unless the caliph conforms to God's Law on the one hand and to man's best interests on the other.[51] The latter part of the stipulation, of course, is far from being universally accepted, being subject to varied interpretation, but it is essential to the view that Ostrorog holds, and he quotes Ibn Nujaim to this effect:

> If the action of the Imam is based on the principle of public benefit in what concerns the affairs of the populace, his decree is effective, but only insofar as it does conform to it [the principle]; if opposed to it, it [his decree] is not effective.[52]

In reality Ibn Nujaim was only applying these words to a specific case —that of division of public funds—so that Ostrorog's citation is out of context. Be that as it may, he evidently seeks to equate disregard of public welfare with what Māwardī terms *jarḥ al-ʿadāla*, or disqualification on grounds of lack of moral probity.[53] He notes that the majority of jurists, unlike Māwardī, hold that deposition of the caliph is only optional in case of such disqualification, and thus again he betrays his insistence on Community discretion in contrast to Māwardī; but it is doubtful whether he interprets the grounds of this majority opinion correctly, for the issue is not properly one of Community sovereignty.

The notion of the caliph as dual trustee is generally accepted and cannot be dismissed, but it does not really lend itself to the theory of contractual delegation. The rights of God and those of man cannot be conceived to be on an equal footing. The latter are valid from the religious point of view only by virtue of the fact that they are included in the former: safeguarding public welfare is a religious duty, and in that sense a "right of God." By the same token, religious duties, when incorporated in a system of positive law, acquire a civil aspect, and in that sense can with equal logic be called "rights of man."[54] Therefore it

---

[50] Māwardī, *Aḥkām*, p. 10: "Al-imāmatu min al-ḥuqūqi 'l-mushtarikati baina ḥaqqi 'llāhi taʿālā wa ḥuqūqi 'l-ādamiyyīn."

[51] Ostrorog, *El-Ahkam*, p. 170.

[52] Ibn Nujaim, *Kitāb al-Ashbāh*, I (Istanbul, 1290 H.), p. 158.

[53] Māwardī, *Aḥkām*, p. 26.

[54] In positive law the distinction becomes one of Community or state rights as opposed to private rights. It is the Community that views the operation of the whole Sharīʿa, including both religious duties and private transactions as well as public policy, as its concern. This is true whether the Community chooses to enforce certain aspects of the Sharīʿa (such as religious duties) or not.

becomes essential to define the level of discourse and maintain a careful distinction between the levels from which seemingly contradictory concepts derive.

If constitutional relationships are to be examined on the legal level as a purely existential phenomenon, whose only identified source is its habitual recognition in men's minds (irrespective of the grounds on which they recognize it), then it might logically be said that the community stands above the law, for the law is nothing but what the community chooses to recognize as law. In this sense any ruler subject to the law is *ipso facto* subject to the community, and all his obligations are owed to them through the medium of the law. Since his authority is defined by the law, it can be said that by this means the community has delegated authority to him. A notion of contract in this context would necessarily be extremely limited, since its maintenance would be purely at the discretion of the community.

But the analysis soon proves to be unsatisfactory if it continues to ignore the grounds on which law is recognized as binding, that is, its acknowledged sources. In saying that maintenance of the legal system defining the ruler's position is at the community's discretion, it is necessary to know by what assumption this discretion will be exercised. For one set of assumptions would encourage wide exercise of discretion with few or no limitations, while another set would render the element of discretion meaningless by circumscribing it with inhibitions on all sides. Any system of rule by law is a nomocracy, as distinguished from absolutism on the one hand and anarchy on the other, but according to the process of its determination and recognition, nomocracy can approach either extreme in practice. The legal system is but the outward form; the assumptions behind it may be theocratic, voluntaristic, naturalistic, and so forth.

Furthermore, it is of great importance to what extent the community maintains an awareness of the law's assumed ultimate sources in its interpretations of it. This awareness, to the extent that it exists, serves as a guarantee that the assumptions will continue to be influential in limiting or encouraging change in the law itself. This means that in a divine law system, the more the law is viewed in the light of its religious sources, the less important its immediate existential source—that is, human recognition—is thought to be, and the less tendency there is to emphasize man's existential sovereignty over the exercise of legal functions, as distinguished from God's sovereignty over the initial authorization of those functions.

In the case of classical Islamic theory, it is essential to keep in mind not only that the nomocracy is a religious one deriving from the contents of scriptural revelation, but that the consciousness of the religious origin and significance of the law is constant and vivid. To use scholastic terminology, the "apparent occasion" (*as-sabab aẓ-ẓāhir*) of a given object of inquiry is seldom viewed without awareness of its "efficient cause" (*'illa*). Relations between men are thus habitually conceived in conjunction with the ulterior relation between man and God, and it is not surprising to find the two levels entangled in discussions of particular questions where they ought logically to be kept separate. The important fact is that they are not separated, and that therefore an analysis of constitutional relationships entirely on the positive and immediate plane of law, while it might prove a rewarding technique to the historian,[55] tends only to mislead the political theorist, since it assumes a consistency of thought that its Muslim expositors did not observe.[56] The theory, after all, is significant not for the conclusions that we might logically draw but only for the conclusions that its architects themselves drew. The inconsistent shifts from one level to another can best be studied for the negative purpose of showing that the theory is important not as a practical instrument but as an idealized, specifically Muslim rationalization of the structure of political authority. The materials are necessarily legal in nature, but the the rationalization has unmistakable religious overtones. If, then, positive considerations of law—for example, authoritative determination or recognition of legally relevant facts—are sometimes ignored, even if this should seem to constitute a breach in consistency, the theorist has served his purpose if he has shown where the relevant rights or duties in the particular case lie, regardless of the mechanics of application. It is more important to the Māwardian theorist, for example, to decide whether a sole qualified candidate for the caliphate needs a formal designation to *constitute* his authority than whether he needs it for declaratory purposes; once it is decided that his unique qualifications are sufficiently constitutive in themselves, the declaratory question is of comparatively little importance, and disagreement among the jurists is easily tolerated and hence left unresolved.

---

[55] It might have done so, but in fact it has not, since the theory did not serve the positive function of an organic law so much as a euphemistic, therefore distorted, justification of the historical record.

[56] Tyan sees in this "one of the most striking manifestations of the essential character of Islam: the congenital and irreducible confusion between the political and religious elements . . ." (*Sultanat*, p. 267).

The level of religious relationships, then, as the source of legal relationships, remains ever-present in the discussion of the latter. Psychologically and morally, the *bay'a* binds the subject more to God than to the caliph; the latter exercises God's authority, not his own. God's will is conceived as being too immediate to make possible a genuine delegation of power and authority to men, and the absolute gratuity of God's grace (according to the more orthodox view, though not to the mu'tazilite) rules out any concept of natural law or natural social function.[57]

Not only the general lines but even the details of the functional relationship between the caliph and the Islamic Community are spelled out in learned interpretations of the Sharī'a. An agreement by the caliph and the *ahl al-ḥall wa 'l-'aqd* to abide by these rules adds nothing new. The reaffirmation may have a psychological importance, and in fact this seems to have been the significance of at least the second, or public, *bay'a*—as the following pages will suggest—while the process of election or nomination signifies the determination of capacity. But these facts do not imply contract in the sense of voluntarily constituted obligation.[58]

D. *The Investiture as a Determination of Capacity*

We have maintained that the concept of authority in the traditional theory of the Caliphate, because of its theological overtones, left the

[57] See Gardet, *La Cité musulmane*, pp. 36–40, for an elaboration of this point, and throughout for a general critique of the contract theory, largely based on a comparison of traditional Islamic notions with the natural law of the Thomist tradition to which he adheres. A theory of social contract, in Gardet's view, is incompatible not only with the idea of divine voluntarism on which the Sharī'a is based, but with the idea of a more autonomous natural law as well, because of the functionalist implications in the latter (pp. 181–182). Only the denial of religious or natural obligation altogether, in favor of unfettered human voluntarism, raises the possibility of a social contract; and even in this case the emphasis upon the General Will, as in Rousseau's thought, tends to reduce the ruler to the position of mere agent, rather than delegate, of society (p. 338).

[58] The point is admirably put by N. J. Coulson: "For Islamic religious law sees as its essential function the portrayal of an ideal relationship of man to his Creator: the regulation of all human relationships, those of man with his neighbour or with the State, is subsidiary to, and designed to serve, this one ultimate purpose. A distinction is indeed drawn between the rights of God and the rights of men, but most authorities would regard only property rights as belonging essentially to the latter class; and in any case, on the higher plane, the whole Sharī'a is *ḥaqq Allāh* [i.e., the right of God], for all rights and obligations are derived from His command" ("The State and the Individual in Islamic Law," *International and Comparative Law Quarterly*, IV [1957], 50).

Islamic Community with no powers of its own to delegate, and consequently no place for a notion of social contract properly speaking.

Nonetheless, the purely legal, nontheological aspects of the jurists' writings should be studied to determine what contractual elements are present, explicitly or implicitly, at this level. Furthermore, Islamic law recognizes other types of contracts than those defining new mutual obligations, so that the above arguments do not exclude the use of the term altogether. In what follows we shall suggest that while the idea of contract may certainly be found on the positive or nontheological level of the theory of the Caliphate, the chief concern of its exponents was not with contractual obligation, but with the determination of the capacity of the parties.

The installation of the caliph was frequently likened to a contract of marriage. Thus it is stipulated that the elector or electors cannot revoke the contract, once completed, without cause, just as the bride's guardian cannot do so;[59] they cannot select themselves;[60] if more than one caliph is chosen, each by a different elector or group of electors, the first one chosen takes precedence, as in the case of marriage;[61] and if the elector lacks moral probity, his designation is void.[62]

The marriage analogy should not be pressed too far, for it is generally used only as just cited: to prescribe the limits of the electors' authority and, to a lesser extent, to determine the requisite qualities of capacity for that authority. The fact that it was this analogy that most habitually came to mind among the writers, however, does suggest that they considered the resemblance significant. The implications of this are very different from those of the contract of *walāya* envisaged by Ostrorog. The marriage contract serves to specify the parties who choose to enter into an already defined relationship, which can be affected in detail but not in substance by any special arrangements made. The contract of the Imamate, if it is to be so called, is similar to this except for the fact that one party—the Community—is obliged to "marry" and to do so at once, and furthermore is bound to try to select the most ideally suitable "partner." The essential questions are thus (1) who may fill the role of guardian in marrying off the

---

[59] Abū Bakr al-Bāqillānī, *al-Tamhīd fī 'r-radd 'alā 'l-mulḥida wa 'l-Mu'aṭṭila wa 'r-Rāfiḍa wa 'l-Khawārij wa 'l-Mu'tazila* (Cairo, 1947), p. 179.

[60] *Ibid.*, p. 180.

[61] *Ibid.*; Māwardī, *Aḥkām*, p. 10; Abū Ya'lā al-Farrā', *al-Aḥkām as-Sulṭāniyya* (Cairo, 1357 H.), p. 9.

[62] 'Abdalqāhir al-Baghdādī, *Uṣūl ad-Dīn* (Istanbul, 1928), I, 281.

"bride," and (2) who is eligible to be chosen as "groom"? These are questions of capacity.

1. Capacity of the electors

A *walāya* may exist by virtue of contractual delegation from a superior to a subordinate or by virtue of inherent capacity. As in the case of the prospective bride, it is assumed that the Community is not in a position to act for itself and therefore needs a "guardian" or "guardians," who exercise their function not by delegation but because their influential position enables them to "loosen and bind" public affairs with effectiveness, and because they may be depended upon to act in the Community's interest—and here enters the other implicit ingredient of capacity, namely, fulfillment of some moral or normative standard.

Whether this role is filled by a group of notables or by the preceding Caliph their effective and benevolent influence remains the determining factor. When in later times the role was filled by irresponsible military commanders, the element of benevolence was lost, but this fact was conveniently obscured by the doctrine of *maṣlaḥa* (public welfare), by which it was considered in the public interest to accept their choice even if the choice itself was not made in the public interest. Thus although the term *ahl al-ḥall wa 'l-'aqd* was theoretically applied to some unspecified group of wise, benevolent, and influential men, in fact the most important element was influence.

We can now turn to specific doctrines of the jurists. Al-Bāqillānī makes it clear that to him the number of electors is of no importance and that his only concern is with their qualifications and those of the designee. No particular number was specified in the Sharī'a sources, and therefore it must be assumed that one or more is sufficient.[63] The qualifications of Abū Bakr, the first caliph after the Prophet's death, and those of the Community leaders who elected him by acclamation, are sufficient justification for his Imamate;[64] Abū Bakr's unilateral nomination of 'Umar as his successor was accepted, despite a certain lack of enthusiasm for the latter's heavy-handed ways, because Abū Bakr was recognized as a qualified elector.[65] As for 'Umar's appointment of a conclave to select his successor, it was not because he appointed them, but because they were individually qualified that their

[63] Bāqillānī, *Tamhīd*, p. 178.
[64] *Ibid.*, p. 187.
[65] *Ibid.*, p. 201.

election of 'Uthmān was valid. Even had they not been appointed, their capacity was sufficient to justify their role.[66]

Similarly, Baghdādī states on the authority of Al-Ash'arī that a single elector is sufficient, provided that he is a qualified interpreter of the law (*mujtahid*).[67] The notion that electing an Imam is an exercise of *ijtihād* lends added weight to the evidence that making the choice is primarily a determination of capacity. The requirement of the quality of *mujtahid* for the electors is familiar among juristic theorists, as are those of moral probity and sound judgment.[68]

The requirement of power or influence as an element of capacity, in the case of election, is not so clearly stated; but it must be inferred. Al-Bāqillānī refers to the electors as "the best of the Muslims from among the people of loosing and binding and those entrusted with this matter."[69] The phrase "loosing and binding" so commonly used is never clearly defined by the authors, but the words themselves suggest prestige and capability, as do the words "those entrusted with this matter."

In the case of nomination by the Imam of his successor, the element of power is evidently present and did not need to be identified by the writers. Bāqillānī's reference to Abū Bakr as a qualified elector of 'Umar[70] indicates his disinclination to distinguish between election and testamentary designation, although among other writers such a distinction is the general rule. Among the others one finds the assumption, however, that the Caliph, already being required to have the qualifications of the electors, can be depended upon to choose the most qualified candidate. The Imam is in fact the most qualified of electors *ex officio*, according to Māwardī.[71]

2. Capacity of the caliph

On the side of the prospective caliph, again it is a matter of capacity. The role exists, waiting to be filled. It is the nature of the role that accounts for the near perfection required of the candidate by the traditional theory. It is noteworthy that these ideal qualifications were

---

[66] *Ibid.*, pp. 202–204.

[67] Baghdādī, *Uṣūl ad-Dīn*, I, 280–281.

[68] Māwardī, *Aḥkām*, p. 4; Abū Ya'lā, *Aḥkām*, p. 3.

[69] Bāqillānī, *Tamhīd*, p. 178.

[70] *Ibid.*, p. 201.

[71] Māwardī, *Aḥkām*, p. 12: "The Imam is more entitled to it [the selection] because his choice in it is more incisive and his word is more effective."

discarded by the same rationalizing process that eliminated the quality of benevolence from the electors: the essential ingredient of capacity comes to be influence. Even if the caliph himself has no influence, he may be credited with capacity as long as the regime bearing his name wields effective power. Even if his character itself is not such as to promote the public welfare, the public welfare dictates acceptance of his character.

This overriding importance of effective power is stressed by Ibn Khaldūn and Ghazālī, each in his own way. Ibn Khaldūn maintains that no society, religious or otherwise, can be effectively maintained without social solidarity (*'aṣabiyya*), which is the foundation of power. "Without *'aṣabiyya* the laws would be ineffective, for they are applied rightly only through *'aṣabiyya*."[72] This is the real significance of the requirement of Quraishite lineage: "Whoever is entrusted with the affairs of the Muslims must be of a people possessing a strong *'aṣabiyya* by which they predominate over other peoples of their time, so that they may secure the following of others and authority may be unified in protecting [the Community]. . . . "[73] Ibn Khaldūn cites the opinion held by some, without directly refuting it, that when the Quraish lost their influence, the requirement of Quraishite lineage was no longer valid.[74]

Other qualifications are recognized (knowledge, moral probity, aptitude and experience, and sound physical condition),[75] but these may be overridden in favor of effective influence based on *'aṣabiyya*. Thus Mu'āwiya's installation of his dissolute son Yazīd as his successor was justified, the interests of the Community being served by Umayyad solidarity. Witness by contrast the trouble that ensued from Ma'mūn's nomination of 'Alī ar-Riḍā, whom the Abbassids would not accept.[76]

On the other hand, Ibn Khaldūn does not lose sight of the intended purpose, which is of course the promotion of Islam through application of the Sharī'a. More important than the ruler's personal qualities is his relationship to his subjects: he must not only defend the peace but

---

[72] Ibn Khaldūn, *Muqaddima*, chap. iii, sec. 26; cf. Rosenthal translation, I, 414.

[73] *Ibid.*, chap. iii, sec. 24: "The Differences of Muslim Opinion Concerning the Laws and Conditions Governing the Caliphate"; cf. Rosenthal, I, 401.

[74] *Ibid.;* Rosenthal, I, 398–399.

[75] *Ibid.;* Rosenthal, I, 394–396.

[76] *Ibid.*, chap. iii, sec. 28: "The Succession [by testamentary designation]"; Rosenthal, I, 431–434.

treat his subjects with equity and forbearance. The key to this is moderation and balance in the ruler's character. By an excess of intelligence, for example, "he may impose on the subjects what they are unable to bear, because he perceives what is beyond their grasp."[77]

By the same token *'aṣabiyya* may be pushed to immoderate proportions and employed solely for the purpose of domination. When this happens, the Imam becomes a secular monarch, and this is what in fact progressively occurred in Islam during the Umayyad and early Abbasid period, until the later Abbasids were caliphs in name only.[78] One recalls the similar view of Ibn Taimiyya that the Caliphate, after the first four (*rāshidūn*, "rightly guided") incumbents, existed only as a fictitious and anachronistic institution no longer filling its supposed function.[79] We have already referred to the Ḥanafī tradition according to which the Prophet predicted that the Caliphate would last only thirty years, after which it would become a tyrannical kingdom.[80] Taftazānī explains that this does not necessarily exclude occasional virtuous rulers such as 'Umar b. 'Abdal'azīz from the category of caliph, but means only that as a rule the Umayyads and Abbasids were unworthy of the title. He further suggests the possibility of a distinction between the usually synonymous terms "imam" and "caliph" but admits that evidence for this is lacking.[81]

The implication of these views for the question of capacity appears to be that if the ruler either lacks the required qualifications or fails to fill the office successfully, he simply is not considered to be a caliph. This of course assumes that the Caliphate is not obligatory (though perhaps the Imamate, if distinguished, may be) and therefore simplifies the problem of capacity immensely by virtually denying that the problem exists; it is not therefore very helpful to us.

Al-Ghazālī recognizes the usual list of qualifications for the Caliphate,[82] but subordinates them to broader considerations. He proceeds from the assumption that "the authority of the caliph is primarily circumstantial, i.e., he has authority for what he does rather than what

[77] *Ibid.*, chap iii, sec. 22: "Extreme Harshness is Harmful to Sovereign Authority and in Most Cases Undermines It"; cf. Rosenthal, I, 384.

[78] *Ibid.*, chap. iii, sec. 26; Rosenthal, I, 414–428.

[79] Laoust, *Essai*, p. 283.

[80] Elder, *Commentary*, p. 144; Abū 'l-Ḥasan al-Ash'arī, *Al-Ibāna 'an Uṣul ad-Diyāna* (Hyderabad, 1321 H.), p. 95.

[81] Elder, *Commentary*, pp. 145–146.

[82] Ghazālī, *Al-Iqtiṣād fī 'l-I'tiqād* (Cairo, 1320 H.), p. 106.

he is."[83] This is essentially an application of the principle of public utility (*maṣlaḥa*). The purpose of Islamic government is to promote the Sharī'a, with a view in turn to furthering the religious life of the citizens. "When we speak of the right ordering of religion we mean that state of knowledge and piety which are only attained with a healthy body, preservation of life, and assurance of the necessities of living. . . . [These] cannot be established without an obeyed ruler [*sultān*]."[84] Here enters the power element as a qualification. The important consideration in choosing a ruler is his ability to preserve security:

> Indeed I say that, after the death of the imam, should there be only one Qurayshite who commands obedience and following, then he should assume the Imamate. . . . His Imamate would be lawfully contracted and obedience to him would be obligatory, for he would assume power by virtue of his power and qualifications, and to oppose him would cause civil strife.[85]

Power, of course, may rest not with the caliph himself, but with others nominally subordinate to him, and this is permissible:

> The point in brief is that we are mindful of the characteristics and qualifications of the sultans, with a view to attaining the public welfare. If we were to pronounce the *walāyas* void, the public interests would be completely nullified. How would the capital be used up in quest of the profit? Rather, the *walāya* is now only the consequence of power, and whomever the holder of power swears fealty to, is the caliph, while whoever exercises unrestrained power, while remaining [nominally] obedient to the caliph through the *khuṭba* and coinage, is a sultan, exercising rule and justice throughout the land by an effective *walāya*.[86]

So as not completely to neglect the qualities of knowledge and virtue, Ghazālī permits a ruler to depend for them on others, that is, the 'ulamā'.[87] From this and the foregoing, the view has been advanced that Ghazālī distinguishes between the person of the caliph and the office of the Caliphate, the latter being separable into its institutional, constitutional, and functional aspects, represented respectively by the caliph, the sultan, and the 'ulamā'—the essential object being only to

83 Leonard Binder, "Al-Ghazālī's Theory of Islamic Government," *Muslim World*, XLV (July, 1955), 231.

84 Ghazālī, *Iqtiṣad*, p. 105.

85 *Ibid.*, pp. 106–107.

86 *Ihyā' 'Ulūm ad-Dīn* (Cairo, 1289 H.), II, 130.

87 Ghazālī, *Iqtiṣād*, p. 107.

ensure that these roles are filled effectively by one party or another.[88] One might add that a similar idea was expressed by Naṣīr ad-Dīn Ṭūsī[89] and, less directly, Ibn Taimiyya.[90]

This may be reading too much into Ghazālī's opinions. It must be remembered that Ghazālī is ready to waive all qualifications but power on the part of the ruler and his associates if the only alternative is civil strife. This is particularly clear from a reading of his famous passage in the *Iqtiṣād* in which he asks:

> Which is better—to say that the judges are dismissed, appointments void, marriages not lawfully contracted, all transactions of the governors of every corner of the earth without effect, and all the people living in sin—or to say that the Imamate is validly contracted . . . ?[91]

There is no reason given in this passage for us to suppose that the judges or governors will be properly qualified, any more than the imam. The latter's function of enforcing the Sharī'a has been reduced to the mere maintenance of the formal structure of the legal institutions which are all theoretically delegated and subdelegated from him. Originally the personal requirements for the office of caliph were justified as a guarantee that a righteous influence would be exerted downward from the apex of the governmental pyramid upon the lower offices. Now this influence is gone, and the judges and governors must be depended upon to supply their own moral inspiration. But the pyramid structure of delegations which Ghazālī seeks to maintain was in the first place predicated on the assumption that this could not be expected. In waiving the personal qualifications of the ruler, Ghazālī abandoned the letter of the law for what was supposed to be its spirit, but this appears to have been in vain, since the qualifications were the guarantee of the spirit. The desire to avoid violence has overridden all other considerations, and power has become the dominant element in the determination of the caliph's capacity.

---

[88] Binder, "Al-Ghazālī's Theory . . . ," *op. cit.*, p. 241.

[89] *Akhlāq-i-Nāṣirī* (lith. 1883), pp. 410–411, quoted by Gibb in *Law in the Middle East*, Khadduri and Liebesny, eds. (Washington, 1955), p. 25; see also Gibb, "Some Considerations on the Sunni Theory of the Caliphate," *Archives d'Histoire du Droit Oriental*, III (1948), 405.

[90] Laoust, *Essai*, 315–317. This is but a step toward a recognized separation of religious and ruling institutions, reflected in Persian theory. Cf. Ann K. S. Lambton, "Quis Custodiet Custodes?", *Studia Islamica*, V (1956), 125–148.

[91] Ghazālī, *Iqtiṣād*, p. 107.

This tendency finds considerable support in the familiar pronouncements that the imam need not be the "most excellent" of his time[92] and that different qualities in the candidate are most important in different circumstances.[93] It is nonetheless conceded that the electors normally must choose the best qualified candidate. The first four caliphs are said to have been the most virtuous members of the Community in the order of their succession. "If the Khalifate had not been Abū Bakr's right, the Companions would not have agreed to him."[94] If only one candidate is qualified, says Māwardī, the electors are bound to choose him, and the actual exercise of such a choice, while necessary as a recognition of his capacity, does not signify any discretion on the part of the electors.[95]

The secondary or public *bay'a*, furthermore, is equally a recognition of fact. By it the Community acknowledges that a man of capacity has been duly determined by the elector or electors. The act has only a declaratory significance, and therefore it follows as a matter of course. It is a useful means of avoiding possible confusion, but if it is dispensed with or even refused, the duty to obey still stands. Māwardī cites the example of 'Umar, who became caliph by Abū Bakr's designation without benefit of *bay'a*.[96]

Taftazānī explains that "the one who is equal to the most excellent in virtue (but) less fit as to knowledge and practice may be more experienced . . . and more able to perform the necessary duties, especially whenever the appointment of the less excellent is better for warding off evil and removing the outbreak of sedition."[97] While "less excellent," in other words, he is more effective, and for this reason has a greater claim to capacity.[98] Similarly Māwardī states that an inferior designee, once installed, is not removed by the appearance of a more qualified candidate.[99] The implication is that to retract would only produce confusion; thus the public welfare is protected more effec-

---

92 Elder, *Commentary*, p. 149. The doctrine was primarily used as a defense against the criticisms of the Shī'ites.

93 *Ibid.*; Abū Ya'lā, *Aḥkām*, p. 8; Ibn Jamā'a, *Taḥrīr*, p. 357.

94 Elder, *Commentary*, p. 143; see also Ash'arī, *Ibāna*, pp. 92–95.

95 Māwardī, *Aḥkām*, p. 9.

96 *Ibid.*, p. 12.

97 Elder, *Commentary*, p. 149.

98 This is not entirely consistent with the statement of Nasafī and other Ḥanafīs that the Caliphate lasted only thirty years, unless, as suggested before, the Imamate and Caliphate are distinguished.

99 Māwardī, *Aḥkām*, pp. 8–9; also Bāqillānī, *Tamhīd*, p. 182.

tively by retaining the incumbent, and in that sense his capacity is recognized. None of these writers denies that the person best fulfilling the ideal requirements should be chosen when practicable, but the important point is that even when this is not practicable, the prime consideration of capacity is not theoretically violated. A line of reasoning that assumes that whoever is chosen has, *ipso facto*, the greatest capacity no doubt seems highly sophistical, and yet this is quite in keeping with the Sunnī jurists' tendency to seek theoretical justification for the record of history.

The notion that might makes right, which is the final absurdity in any constitutional system, is well represented by Badr ad-Dīn b. Jamā'a (d. 1333), a leading Shāfi'ite jurist in Cairo during the period of the puppet Abbasid regime in Egypt under the Mamluks. Ibn Jamā'a has been said to have sought, by an extreme extension of the doctrine of necessity, to make the classical formula of the Caliphate applicable to the Sultanate.[100] His free use of the terms *imām*, *khalīfa*, and *sulṭān* virtually interchangeably lends particular credence to this view.

Imamates (or, apparently, rulership in general), says Ibn Jamā'a, may be of two kinds: that of selection (*ikhtiyār*) and that of conquest (*qahr*). His brief exposition of the imamate of selection is along orthodox lines—with the usual necessary qualifications, procedures to be followed in choosing between equally qualified candidates, and so forth —adding only an exceptionally strong injunction against the slightest disobedience.[101] His remarks on the "imamate of conquest," on the other hand, read like Ghazālī's view of the sultan, extended one step further by being applied to the imam himself:

> If the Imamate is vacated and someone ordinarily ineligible seeks it, and conquers the people by force of arms, even without a *bay'a* or designation, his *bay'a* is considered contracted and he must be obeyed, in the interests of the order and unity of all Muslims. It does not matter if he is ignorant or evil-doing on the whole. If the Imamate is contracted by power and force to one person, then another arises and defeats the first by force of arms, the first is deposed and the second becomes imam, for the reasons we have given concerning the interests and unity of the Muslims. This is why Ibn 'Umar said, "We are on the side of the victor."[102]

---

[100] H. A. R. Gibb, "Constitutional Organization," *in* Khadduri and Liebesny, eds. *Law in the Middle East*, p. 23.

[101] Ibn Jamā'a, *Taḥrīr*, pp. 356–358.

[102] *Ibid.*, p. 357.

It should be recalled that although caliphs by Ibn Jamā'a's time had long been made and unmade by force, and accepted accordingly, not since the reign of al-Ma'mūn five centuries earlier had a caliph installed himself by force that he could call his own; subsequently it had always been the amirs, sultans, and other kingmakers who played this role—the caliph being no more than the nominal beneficiary of the imposed *bay'a*.

Ibn Jamā'a surely did not overlook the distinction between caliph (usually synonymous with imam) and sultan, but presumably thought the distinction unimportant. By transferring the might-makes-right reasoning from the sultanate (where Ghazālī applies it) to the caliphate he may indeed have intended to indicate that the latter no longer deserved any measure of formal dignity not accorded to the former, beyond mere existence in office for the purpose of granting such an appearance of legitimacy to operations of the government as popular expectations required.

This reasoning served less to raise the dignity of the sultan than to acknowledge the unimportance of the caliph's special character. The passage quoted above may be taken not as an invocation of necessity in the sense of a repugnant last resort but as a practical recognition that force is essential to all authority, and that it matters little whether such force is styled Caliphate or Sultanate.

This approach, of course, renders the original theory of capacity in the Caliphate meaningless. Once the capacity of the elector and that of the candidate are determined solely by considerations of expediency—let alone by bowing to the inevitable—the very notion of capacity loses all significance. The real foundation of authority will then depend on the unspoken attitudes and expectations of the public mind, and power will become legitimate authority whenever it is generally accepted as such. If the attitude is one of submissive resignation—as it appears to have been in later Abbasid and Mamluk times—power will be easily accepted. Virtually any working system of government could follow from a theory of capacity, in accordance with whatever process actually determines capacity.

But it should not be concluded from this that the idea of capacity as the basis of authority has no significance of its own. The idea that might makes right is not a principle of authority but its very denial. Authority is a normative conception, which in Islam further means a moral conception, and therefore capacity for authority implies a moral definition of capacity (although, as we have seen, the element of power must also be present). Power has no moral quality, although it may affect morality's fortunes. In stipulating that the parties to the contract of the Imamate must have a certain capacity, the juristic theory was logically bound to consider the moral content of that capacity as absolutely essential. It might bc reduced by force of circumstances, but it could not be eliminated. Power is also a necessary ingredient, but it cannot be the exclusive one. When it becomes exclusive, by definition the result is anarchy, tempered only by the public attitude.

Whether and under what circumstances the imam could be removed from office was, to be sure, the subject of widely differing views at different times among the jurists. The historical tendency was to move away from the early presumption that physical or moral incapacity disqualified the imam and necessitated his removal—a view expressed by al-Bāqillānī[103] and to a lesser extent even by Māwardī[104]—toward the presumption of absolute submission made by Ghazālī[105] and Ibn Jamā'a.[106] The arguments back and forth and the implications of the tendency toward quietism have been amply discussed by many Orientalists and need no repetition here. It needs only be noted that while in time the issue of obedience to tyranny as a matter of moral duty was largely resolved by the doctrine that the subjects should submit as long as they were not commanded to commit sin, the more significant aspect of the question—whether the oppressive ruler possessed legal capacity for his office—was more difficult. The theories of Ghazālī and Ibn Khaldūn discussed above should be reviewed in the context of the question of capacity, the issue being whether interpretation of the Sharī'a really had any relevance to the type of rule prevailing in the later Abbasid period. Ghazālī thinks so; Ibn Khaldūn thinks not.

E. *Conclusion*

The juristic theory of the Caliphate was not of course the only vehicle of systematic political thought in medieval Islam, and probably not the most sophisticated. With the decline in the historical fortunes of the Caliphate it was natural that other modes of speculation less bound up with the juristic categories of thought should rise in importance. For the lawyers' role had been principally to find legal justifications for historical *faits accomplis*, reconciling the various

[103] Bāqillānī, *Tamhīd*, pp. 186–187.

[104] Māwardī, *Aḥkām*, pp. 25 ff.

[105] Ghazālī, *Iḥyā'*, II, 130; *Iqtiṣād*, p. 107.

[106] Ibn Jamā'a, *Taḥrīr*, p. 357.

practices that obtained with the Sunna of the Rāshidūn caliphs whenever possible or appealing to the doctrine of necessity when not. Eventually this could only lead to a mass of fictions and sophistry, to overreliance on the spiritual significance of the caliph's office and person, and on the pietistic rectitude of doctrine irrespective of practice, and eventually to acknowledgments such as Ghazālī's that the theory was inadequate.

In these circumstances the secretarial-administrative and the Neoplatonist schools of writers came into greater prominence—the one advancing a concept of functional ethics according to which the individual's conscience was to be conditioned by his social position in the hierarchy of authority,[107] the other seeking to fit the ideal of the philosopher king into an Islamic mold,[108] and both concentrating on the theme of the dependence of all subordinate classes on the benevolence of the ruler, whoever he might be. But these theories were constructed with little direct reference to either the Sharī'a or to the Caliphate. Their ethical and philosophical content was more Persian and Greek than Islamic;[109] the most that can be said is that they were conceived by Muslims and therefore products of an Islamic culture.

---

[107] E.g., Ibn Qutaiba, *'Uyūn al-Akhbār. I: Kitāb as-Sulṭān* (Cairo, 1925); Niẓām al-Mulk, *Siyaset Nameh* (French tr., C. Schefer, *Siasset Nameh*, Paris, 1893); Ghazālī, *Naṣīḥat al-Mulūk* (Teheran, 1928) and pp. 131–141 of *Ihyā' 'Ulūm ad-Dīn*, II. For secondary sources see G. Richter, *Studien zur Geschichte der älteren arabischen Fürstenspiegel* (Leipzig, 1932); Ann K. S. Lambton, "The Theory of Kingship in the Naṣīḥat al-Mulūk of Ghazālī," *The Islamic Quarterly*, I (1954), 47–55; Ishaq Musa al-Huseini, *The Life and Works of Ibn Qutayba* (Beirut, 1950).

[108] E.g., Abū Naṣr al-Fārābī, *Ārā' Ahl al-Madīna 'l-Fāḍila* (Cairo, 1323 H.; German tr., Friedrich Dieterici, *Der Musterstaat von Alfarabi*, Leiden, 1900) and *as-Siyāsāt al-Madaniyya* (Hyderabad, 1346 H.); Naṣīr ad-Dīn Ṭūsī, *Akhlāq-i-Nāṣirī* (lith. 1883); Jalāl ad-Dīn Dawwānī, *Akhlāq-i-Jalālī* (tr. W. F. Thompson, *Practical Philosophy of the Muhammadan People*, London, 1839). For secondary sources see Lambton, "Quis Custodiet Custodes?", *Studia Islamica*, V (1956), 125–148; Leo Strauss, *Persecution and the Art of Writing* (Glencoe, Illinois, 1952); H. K. Sherwani, *Studies in Muslim Political Thought and Administration* (Lahore, 1945); Erwin Rosenthal, "The Place of Politics in the Philosophy of Al-Farabi," *Islamic Culture*, XXIX (1955), no. 3; Carra de Vaux, *Les Penseurs de l'Islam* (Paris, 1926), IV, 7–18; Ibrahim Madkour, *La place d'al-Farabi dans l'école philosophique musulmane* (Paris, 1934), pp. 182–92.

[109] Gardet and Anawati take note of this fact in their *Introduction à la théologie musulmane* (Paris, 1948), pp. 318–324. The philosophy of Farabi, Avicenna, and Averroes, they observe, tended to coincide with Islamic religious dogma only where the latter offered no challenge to reason; in fact, theology and philosophy operated each as a thought system sufficient within itself and taking little note of the other except as an antagonist.

Thus while the secretaries' and philosophers' general contribution to political thought in Islam was an important one, and indeed may better reflect the political attitudes and expectations of medieval Muslim society than do the constitutional theories of the Caliphate, they did not offer a specifically Islamic interpretation of the problems of power and authority. It is therefore not surprising that Muslim modernists of recent generations, in their search for antecedents for a revived religious society, should interest themselves in the Caliphate (more particularly, the Rāshidūn caliphs) rather than in the pious sultan or the philosopher king.

III

IDEALISM IN TRADITIONAL JURISPRUDENCE

For modernist reformers the Caliphate is only a means to an end. That end is the application of the Sharī'a and, today, its rejuvenation. An examination of constitutional theory thus leads directly to a consideration of the spirit in which the law itself has been conceived; and the extent to which law has been regarded as a humanistic enterprise bears on the character of the source of authority of the state.

Modern reformism has sought to identify a principle of dynamism in the Sharī'a by which to loosen the grip of rigid and all-inclusive finality that has characterized orthodox jurisprudence since the third century of Islam. This effort—strikingly represented by Rashīd Riḍā, but also by more cosmopolitan minds such as the Lebanese Muslim lawyer Ṣubḥi Maḥmaṣānī[1] and the former president of the Egyptian Council of State 'Abdarrazzāq as-Sanhūrī[2]—assumes that the great jurists of the early period of development and indeed throughout Islamic history, when properly understood, will be seen to have had a dynamic view of the Sharī'a. The element in their jurisprudence which the modernists have particularly seized upon as the basis for dynamism and humanism is the notion of *maṣlaḥa* (welfare, benefit, utility). Chief among the classical jurists cited in this regard are Al-Ghazālī (d. A.D. 1111), Ibn Taimiyya (d. A.D. 1328), and Najm ad-Dīn Ṭaufī

[1] See particularly his *Falsafat aṭ-Tashrī' fī 'l-Islām* (Beirut, 1946; English translation by Farhat J. Ziadeh, *The Philosophy of Jurisprudence in Islam*, Leiden, 1961), and his article "Muslims: Decadence and Renaissance—Adaptation of Islamic Jurisprudence to Modern Needs," *Muslim World*, XLIV (1954), 186–201.

[2] See his "Le Droit musulman comme élément de réfonte du code civil égyptien" in *Introduction à l'étude du droit comparé: recueil d'études en honneur d'Edouard Lambert* (Paris, 1938), II, 621–642; also "Wujūb Tanqīḥ al-Qānūn al-Madanī al-Miṣrī" ("The Need for Revision of the Egyptian Civil Code"), *Majallat al-Qānūn wa 'l-Iqtiṣād*, VI (1936), 3–144. See below, pp. 218–219.

(d. A.D. 1316). It is notable that all these jurists lived well after the definitive evolution of the four orthodox schools, and that both Ibn Taimiyya and Ṭaufī held eccentric views.

Like the traditional doctrine of the Caliphate, traditional jurisprudence was closely tied to its theological foundations. Here, however, we are concerned not so much with a disregard for the positive importance of institutionalizing and formally recognizing the rules of conduct, as with an insistence on minimizing the influence that human faculties can have on the content of the revealed Law in the process of its interpretation.

An idealism of the kind discussed in the preceding chapter did in fact exist in the minds of certain pious scholars whose conception of the law was wholly bound up with its religious origins to the exclusion of its modes of application. The significance of this view will be considered briefly below. But it did not dominate the theory of jurisprudence as it did constitutional theory. The administration of justice was in the hands of scholars to an extent sufficient to ensure that the science of jurisprudence would treat the Sharī'a as a practical instrument to be applied to actual cases. Whether theory actually kept pace with practice is another question; the point remains that great efforts were made to work out methods of interpretation which were presumably suitable for application. Where the idealist spirit made itself most strongly felt was in the jurists' concern that these methods should not distort the true substance of revealed values.

It is in examining the modernists' treasured concept of *maṣlaḥa*, particularly in the hands of Ghazālī, Ibn Taimiyya, and Ṭaufī, that we can best assess this idealist concern, since the technique of *istiṣlāḥ* (judgment on grounds of welfare or utility) was the most liberal principle of legal interpretation in traditional currency, and the one in which human value judgments were allowed their widest role. If these value judgments were suspect and circumscribed even with regard to *maṣlaḥa*, as we shall suggest they were, then the same can be said *a fortiori* of the system of legal interpretation as a whole.

The first task is to set forth the general theoretical principles according to which law was traditionally conceived: the divine (as opposed to natural) source of law, the law's function, its relation to religious values, and the extent to which its rules are accessible to human intelligence. The role of human judgment in applying the nontextual sources of law (analogy and consensus) will then be examined, followed by a discussion of *maṣlaḥa*.

A. *The Religious Nature of Law: General Principles*

1. The divine source of law

Both natural and divine law doctrines assume that right and wrong are not a matter of relative convenience for the individual, but derive from an eternally valid standard. This stand is ultimately independent of human cognizance of it or adherence to it.

Both also assume, though on different grounds, that men are capable of learning the true nature of right and wrong, and that having done so, they can elaborate their knowledge rationally and apply it to concrete situations.

Beyond this base of agreement, however, theories of natural and divine law diverge. The first distinction is a normative one. Natural law is supposedly inherent in the nature of the created, finite, material world. What men ought to do or not do follows from the reality—what is—of nature; self-fulfillment comes only from performing their "natural" functions. Modern positivists object that this derivation of the "ought" from the "is" lacks a logical connection. It can be made to have logical sense only if we assume one of two things: (a) that strictly on grounds of material self-interest or practicality, the wise man chooses to follow certain broad principles of ethical behavior in order to maximize his personal satisfactions and to escape unwelcome natural consequences of contrary conduct; or (b) that behind the concept of obligation to conform to "nature" is an ulterior imperative of a religious or mystical character: God, or conscience, commands this conformity. In this case the sanction is a spiritual one. The first of these two alternatives is not much removed from the ethics of simple utilitarianism, except for the fact that it purports to look further afield than the more or less immediate situation for its determination of what enlightened self-interest really is.

Divine law, on the other hand, does not depend on an assumption that right and wrong are inherent in nature. They are simply creations of God's will, directly applied to the circumstances of human behavior and having nothing in particular to do with nature as a universal ordered system. God commands men to act in certain ways by directly communicating His will to them, by textual revelation; He does not simply command men to look into the world of creation and find rules of behavior there.

To the religious mind, inasmuch as nature is God's creation, if God commands men to conform to nature, then natural law is a form of divine law, and nature is a form of revelation. But this is so only by derivation. The difference is a vital one, and it is most appropriate to use the term "divine law" to denote directly rcvealed, textual law as opposed to law revealed implicitly through nature. Divine law is formed in a spiritual rather than material mold; it is extranatural, and logically precedes the creation of nature itself.

The second difference is an epistemological one. Since natural law is supposedly implicit in the created world, it can be known through the same human faculties by which natural phenomena are known: sense perception and reason. The basis of obligation may be nonrational, that is, religious, but the rules of conduct themselves have a rational substance.

Since divine law is based on explicit divine commands, and comes not from nature but from beyond it, knowledge of it cannot come from reasoned observation of the created world but from study of the revealed texts. Such study is itself rational, but is much more limited in scope than the study of nature, for it has a large body of substantive rules of conduct which it must accept *a priori*, whereas in natural law all substantive rules must be logically or empirically derived. In divine law reason must resist the urge to penetrate beyond its appointed sphere of deductive elaboration, under the surface of the revealed rules in quest of their ultimate rationale.

The normative difference between divine and natural law is meaningful only in religious terms. The epistemological difference, which follows from the normative one, is significant for the objective study of legal theory quite apart from theology. Regardless of why one accepts human or inanimate nature or religious texts or anything else as a source of recognizable obligations, the fact that he accepts one rather than the other is important. Does the jurist base his rational analysis on the traditional textually revealed sources, keeping within their confines, or does he allow his speculation to wander wherever reason and curiosity may lead it? When the question is put this way it is irrelevant what religious commands and sanctions lie behind each system. What matters is how much of the law is placed beyond discussion and how much is left to discretion.

Ash'arite theology, which came to prevail over that of the Mu'tazilites as the accepted Sunnī orthodoxy after the tenth Christian century, gave support to the divine rather than natural law conception on both normative and epistemological grounds. The Mu'tazilites emphasized God's ominiscience and justice; the Ash'arites emphasized His omnipotence and absolute will. The Mu'tazilites conceived of the universe as a rationally integrated system governed by laws of cause and effect, which God had created and set in motion once and for all. The Ash'arites, refusing to accept any implied limit on the will or power of God, denied the existence of an inherent order of any kind in the universe by which it might be characterized as natural or rational. By a doctrine of continuous divine creation and recreation they held that the processes of the universe are essentially miraculous, and that what passes for continuity and causality is no more than the habitual regularity, or, in the Qur'ānic phrase, "custom," of the Creator (*sunnat Allah*).[3] Likewise, as theistic subjectivists combating the objectivism of the Mu'tazilites and the philosophers,[4] they held that good and evil have no intrinsic quality of their own but are simply products of the Divine Will conveyed in Revelation and systematically elaborated in the Sharī'a. Accordingly there is really nothing for men to learn in the moral sphere except the revealed obligations, which have no foundation in a natural order in the world, nor in a natural order in the human personality, nor in a rational order of justice. Right and duty are conceivable only in terms of God's command, and perceptible only within a submissive spirit. Thus Al-Ash'arī explained the orthodox ("Sunnite") position of his time as follows:

> They believe that there is no good or evil on earth, except what God wishes; and that things are by the wish of God, as He has said, "But wish it ye shall not, unless as God wisheth it," [Q. lxxxi:29] and as the Muslims say, "What God wishes is, and what He does not wish is not."[5]

The problem of free will was accordingly simplified. Free will does not exist, since natural causality itself is denied, even in the secondary

[3] Duncan Black Macdonald, *Development of Muslim Theology, Jurisprudence, and Constitutional Theory* (New York, 1926), pp. 204–205; by the same author, *Aspects of Islam* (New York, 1911), pp. 136–137; also Tor Andrae, *Die Person Muhammeds in Lehr und Glauben seiner Gemeinde* (Uppsala, 1917–18), pp. 92–123.

[4] George F. Hourani, "Averroes on Good and Evil," *Studia Islamica* XVI (1962), 15 and *passim*, 13–40; by the same author, "Two Theories of Value in Medieval Islam," *Muslim World*, L (1960), 269–278.

[5] *Maqālāt al-Islāmiyyīn wa 'khtilāf al-Muṣallīn*, cited by Walter C. Klein in his translation of *Al-Aš'ari's Al-Ibānah 'an Uṣūl ad-Diyānah* (American Oriental Series, Vol. 10, New Haven, 1940), p. 31.

sense that causes may produce effects by virtue of a power with which God endows them.[6] But neither the nominality of ethics nor the divine determination of men's actions need diminish the moral responsibility of the individual, given the sweeping transcendentalism and divine voluntarism of the Ash'arite position. The individual is responsible by virtue of divinely created "acquisition" (*kasb*)—not acquisition of immediate capacity of choice in his actions, which is the sense in which some of the Mu'tazilites used the term, but simply acquisition of responsibility in the life hereafter for his actions. God doeth what he will, and giveth and taketh away.

In terms of practical psychology and behavior, this is a sweeping overstatement. "God's custom" was assumed to be unchanging, as it must be if life is to go on. His commands expressed in the Sacred Law, if not ultimately natural in any philosophic sense, were considered in practice to be responsive to human needs and to common sense. As for the doctrine of predestination, Muslims, like Calvinists and modern scientific determinists, were quite capable of treating it as the theological abstraction it was. But we are concerned with the intellectual spirit and methods of Islamic jurisprudence. These could not entirely escape the influence of the Law's theological underpinnings, which proclaimed that reason is essentially irrelevant to the substance, determination, and obligatory character of moral principles.

2. *Pietist and practical attitudes toward law*

The prime purpose of the Sharī'a is to provide men with a criterion of distinction between good and evil.[7] Its function is therefore inseparable from the function of religious revelation, of which the Sharī'a is a part. The question of the origins and ultimate authority of the Law is a theological one, and the individual's legal obligations are religious obligations as well.

Nonetheless legal and religious obligations are not identical, and scrupulous adherence to the law is not sufficient by itself to assure salvation for the individual. The law limits itself to external behavior, while the truly religious spirit is a matter of inward intention. It might be said that since law is an expression of religiously ordained obligations and a religiously "true" distinction between good and evil, in its original form it is identical with religious morality; but in such a form it is not law. The distinction between piety and justice, or between

[6] Louis Gardet, *La Mesure de notre liberté* (Tunis, 1946), pp. 18–21.

[7] Qur'ān xxv:1: "Blessed is He who hath revealed unto His slave [Muḥammad] the criterion [of right and wrong], that he may be a warner to the peoples."

moral truth and rules of behavior, draws the line between religion and law. Within the definition of law there are other distinctions that can be drawn which, taken together, provide a descending scale from the ideal to the existential: the law may be conceived as an eternal set of rules, as the revelationary verbalization of those rules, as human understanding of the verbalization, as a set of logical derivations from what is understood, and finally—wherever logical derivation is thought to fail to provide for given situations—human value judgments.

But since the law, if distinct from ultimate religious truth, is still considered to be derived from it, it is the concern of jurists to find ways to minimize the possibility that the original revelationary basis will be distorted in the process of interpretation. This is done by regulating this process as carefully as possible. It being the function of law to provide a revealed distinction between good and evil, the object of the jurists' rules must be to ensure that the distinction will not, through the distortions of interpretation, come to be based on human tastes and preferences.[8]

There is for this reason a great deal of difference between the use of deductive logic and the use of human value judgments. The former accepts revelation as axiomatic, the latter provides its own axioms. The difference between these two methods is the prime consideration in discussions on *qiyās* (analogy) and the related concept of *maṣlaḥa*, as we shall see. The rules formulated to govern *qiyās* and *maṣlaḥa*, as legal techniques, reflect the theological principle involved: that man must rely on revelation to know good from evil. In the same spirit, the rules governing interpretation of the Qur'ān and ḥadīths, the elaborate philological studies, and the examination of the chains of authority by which ḥadīths were transmitted are all designed to provide the most authentic possible determination of the content of the revealed commands in such a manner as to eliminate speculation, which would be presumptuous value judgment.[9]

---

[8] See Octave Pesle, *Les Fondements du droit musulman* (Casablanca, n.d.), p. 106, for discussion of this question. But, observes Pesle, "God, in taking an interest in man, is called on to grant him many sacrifices." Again: "Let us not forget that the word of God addresses itself to man and that in fact it is the latter who gives it impulsion. The Law, whatever high idea one may conceive of it, fatally implies a cooperation of man with God" (*ibid.*, p. 114).

[9] Thus for example the ḥadīth: "Every new law is an innovation; every innovation is a deviation [from the sacred path], and every deviation leads to eternal hellfire" (quoted by Ahmad Sakka, *De la souveraineté dans le droit public musulman sunnite* [Paris 1917], p. 55).

It is this derivation of law from a higher source that causes Vesey-Fitzgerald to remark that the whole Sharī'a is a formalized system of equity in the Western sense of the word. The formalism of the system, he observes, served the Community as a barrier against tyranny, since it was more difficult for the ruler to manipulate a rigid system of divine law than a flexible man-made one.[10] But formalism, it must be remembered, protects the law not only against conscious attempts at manipulation but also against any involuntary tendencies to distort the divine sources in the process of interpretation.

Although the concept of law is necessarily on a lower level than the concept of piety because it is limited to rules of external behavior, many jurists were acutely conscious of its theological origins, and of the fact that law was not only an instrument for human use but an imperfectly grasped expression of God's will, and that its ultimate sanction was religious. For this reason, while conveniently distinguishing as jurists between "rights of God" and "rights of man," they could remember that from the theological point of view the latter were also "rights of God." For the same reason some jurists sensed that there was something inevitably, almost tragically, profane about interpreting and applying the Sharī'a. The Law finds its source in a set of religiously ideal relationships independent of the material circumstances in which it is to be applied; the ideal of its observance by man lies not in scrupulous performance of external obligations but in the inner spirit of devotion with which he performs those actions. It is this spirit of piety rather than mere justice that the religious sanction takes into account, and this is what is meant when it is said that outward performance, for example, of ritual duties (*'ibādāt*), gains nothing for the individual unless accompanied by sincerity of intention (*ḥusn an-niyya*); in fact, it would probably not be denied that the same rule applies to social transactions as well as to ritual.

This awareness of the potential gulf between piety and justice, and between the law as a revelationary command and as it is imperfectly understood, appears to have contributed to the well-known reluctance of many jurists to accept positions of judicial administration. These persons felt, according to a recent study of the question, that by accepting office they would only become responsible before God for the

---

10 "Nature and Sources of the Sharī'a," *in* Khadduri and Liebesny, eds., *Law in the Middle East* (Washington, 1955), pp. 105–106. Where the ruler could not alter the law, however, he could often by-pass it, being sanctioned in this by the flexibility of his powers of *siyāsa* (political management).

corruption of the ideal of the Sharī'a that must inevitably accompany its interpretation and application.[11]

The more practical-minded jurists, however, accepted the limitations of their profession, recognized that an external code of behavior was preferable to no responsibly interpreted code at all, and argued that the judge was to be commended in the sight of God and man for an honest effort.[12] The sincere but mistaken *mujtahid*, according to one ḥadīth, would be rewarded in heaven for his pains, while correct *ijtihād* would bring double reward.[13] These jurists and the first group appear to represent two general schools of thought, not only on this particular issue of externals, but also on the overall question of a theological-pietistic versus a professional and systematic approach to law.[14] These alternatives parallel the idealist and positivist possibilities in political theory discussed in the preceding chapter.

Of course, if the view of the former group were to prevail, there would be no effective system of law at all. Who is to judge whether a given obligation is performed with sincerity of intention? The very term *niyya*, used in its legal rather than religious sense, does not truly signify sincerity of intention at all; it is merely a formal declaration by the believer of his intent to perform an act of ritual, so that it can be established that the act is done consciously as ritual, and not frivolously or with some other purpose in mind. Ironically, then, the very

[11] N. J. Coulson, "Doctrine and Practice in Islamic Law: One Aspect of the Problem," *Bulletin of the School of Oriental and African Studies*, XVIII (1956), 211–226. See also H. F. Amedroz, "The Office of Kadi in the Ahkam Sultaniyya of Mawardi," *Journal of the Royal Asiatic Society* [*JRAS*] (July, 1910), 773–776.

[12] The celebrated instructions of 'Umar, the second caliph, to his *qāḍī* admonish the latter to do his best with full confidence: "God concerns himself with your secret character and leaves you to follow appearances. . . . For when a man's conscience towards God is clear, God makes his relations with man satisfactory; whereas if a man simulate before the world what God knows that he has not, God will put him to shame" (D. S. Margoliouth, "Omar's Instructions to the Kadi," *JRAS* [April, 1910], 312).

[13] I. Goldziher, "Über eine Formel in der jüdischen Responsenlitteratur und in den muhammedanischen Fetwas," *Zeitschrifte der Deutschen Morgenländischen Gesellschaft*, LIII (1899), 649.

[14] Coulson, throughout the article just cited (note 11), refers to the religiously oriented group as the "idealist" school and to the practical-minded as "classical." The attitude of the latter is well expressed in a passage by the Shāfi'ite jurist Al-'Izz b. 'Abd as Salām: "All obligations refer to the interests of God's creatures in this world and the next. God is not in need of people's worship, nor is He benefitted by the obedience of those who obey, nor harmed by the disobedience of those who disobey" (*Qawā'id al-Aḥkām fī Maṣāliḥ al-Anām* (Cairo, 1934), II, 70, quoted in Maḥmaṣānī, *Falsafa*, p. 170; Ziadeh translation, p. 106).

term that in one sense refers to something beyond the scope of law is also used in another sense to denote part of the outward formality itself. The *niyya* as a ritual declaration does not, and cannot, indicate the presence of *niyya* as an inward attitude.[15]

It is not clear whether the pietist attitude or the practical attitude contributed more to a systematization of the rules of legal interpretation in such a way as to circumscribe the role of human value judgments. At first blush it might be supposed that the pietist, being more preoccupied with the theological foundation of the Sharī'a, would be the more concerned with preserving its revelationary content, and therefore more ready to devise a methodology that would serve this purpose. On the other hand, since the pietist took a pessimistic attitude toward practical jurisprudence as a profession, he was perhaps less favorably equipped for the systematic reasoning it required, and more susceptible to the tendency to replace rigid formulas with what he flattered himself to be the dictates of his own piety or mystic insights, thereby introducing his own value judgments.

The practical jurist, for his part, might be impelled by his desire to solve particular questions that arise from time to time, to accept a principle of convenience or common sense; on the other hand, irrespective of his religious consciousness or lack of it, he was bound to see the need to systematize the rules of interpretation in defense of his own professional position, and in this case the only question is on what basis the systematization is to take place. Since perhaps by Shāfi'ī's time—certainly by Al-Ash'arī's—the consensus was well established that the Qur'ān and the Prophetic ḥadīths offered the most authoritative distinction between right and wrong, the systematizing legal theorist was more or less compelled to accept these as his fundamentals.

In view of these alternative considerations it would be unreasonable to presume an association of either the pietistic or professional school of thought with a particular view of legal methodology. The historical evidence appears to be only fragmentary, and to the extent that it is available, it seems ambiguous. It is true, for example, that the Ḥanafī school, which enjoyed an official status under the Abbasids and Ottomans, was the most liberal of the four *madhāhib* in admitting the claims of *ra'y* (opinion), in utilizing legal fictions (*ḥiyal*), and in setting aside strict analogies by the process of *istiḥsān* (preference). Yet its

---

[15] Joseph Schacht, article "Niya," *Shorter Encyclopedia of Islam* [*SEI*], p. 449.

founder, Abū Ḥanīfa, is reported to have accepted a judicial post only after being flogged.[16] Again, one writer attributes the more literalist and deductive methodology of the Mālikite and Shāfi'ite schools to a pietistic attitude, in contrast to the liberal methodology of the practical-minded Ḥanafīs;[17] but elsewhere we are told on good authority that Shāfi'ī himself—who was more than anyone else responsible for the systematization of methods of interpretation and securing the authority of formal Prophetic traditions—was seldom influenced "in his conscious legal thought by material considerations of a religious and ethical kind" in contrast to Abū Ḥanīfa and Mālik; he consistently separated legal from moral concepts.[18] Ghazālī (a Shāfi'ite) is cited as typical of those "religious minds" that rebelled against an over-reliance on legal formalities at the expense of piety,[19] and yet his own legal methodology is described as rigidly logical, and in fact his legal work *al-Mustaṣfā* is prefaced with a study of logic.[20] And Ibn Taimiyya, a keen religious revivalist who recognized that legal methodology was inseparable from a theory of prophecy, found formal logic of the Shāfi'ite type responsible for the rigidity and consequent moral stagnation of the Sharī'a.[21]

What the development of the system does apparently reflect is an assumption common to both the pietist and the professional schools. The former was disturbed by the disparity between law itself and religious spirit, while the latter accepted it. But both recognized another disparity on a lower level, within the scope of law: the disparity between the authority of axiomatic rules derived from revelation on the one hand, and the presumptuousness of human preferences, unrooted in revelation, on the other. In other words, the authority of the Qur'ān and Sunna was generally accepted by *ijmā'* and was not in question. Therefore, even when the more liberal schemes for *qiyās* and *istiṣlāḥ* were put forth by some authors, the apologetic effort was always made to show that the proposed method did not really depart from the accepted confines of revealed values. How different this is

---

[16] Gustave E. von Grunebaum, *Medieval Islam. A Study in Cultural Orientation* (Chicago, 1947), p. 167.

[17] Coulson, "Doctrine and Practice. . . ," *op. cit.*, pp. 222 ff.

[18] Schacht, *The Origins of Muhammadan Jurisprudence* (Oxford, 1950), p. 317.

[19] Schacht, article "Sharī'a," *SEI*, p. 525.

[20] Henri Laoust, *Contribution à une étude de la méthodologie canonique de Taḳī-d-Dīn Aḥmad b. Taimiya* (Cairo, 1939), pp. 4–5.

[21] *Ibid.*, pp. 7–9.

from the modern situation, in which apologists seek to show that Sharī'a methodology does not really exclude humanist values!

B. *Qiyās*

Qiyās, or analogy, is the method of interpretation in which logical reasoning on the basis of the Qur'ān and Sunna is generally accepted as fully legitimate. The procedures of analogy are designed to eliminate independent value judgments, although as we shall see this is not always possible in practice. Ideally, the concept of *qiyās* rests on the assumption that in a given rule revealed in the Qur'ān or ḥadīth, a particular attribute of the subject ruled upon is the governing consideration, and that by discovering what this attribute is, the rule can be systematically applied to other comparable situations. For instance, to cite the usual example, the Qur'anic ban on wine is clearly due to the consideration of intoxication, as is evident from the wording of the relevant passages.[22] It is generally agreed that by analogy, any other intoxicating drink is also forbidden. By the same token, a ḥadīth declares that a virgin not yet of age may be given in marriage only by her father or guardian; the Qur'ān, meanwhile, specifies that an orphan's property should be held for him until his coming of age. The Ḥanafī school of jurists resorted to the latter rule to aid in interpretation of the former, and reasoned analogically that the girl's minority was the determining element rather than her virginity; consequently a widow or divorcee not yet of age could remarry only by decision of her father or guardian, while an adult woman marrying for the first time could do so independently.[23]

The Mālikī jurist Shihāb ad-Dīn al-Qarāfī (d. 1285), an authority on methods of jurisprudence frequently cited by modern writers, defined *qiyās* as "establishing the applicability of a ruling in one case to another case on grounds of their similarity with respect to the attribute upon which the ruling is based."[24]

[22] Q. ii:219, iv:43, v:90–91. In iv:43, which was revealed before the definitive ban in v:90–91, Muslims are forbidden to pray while intoxicated "until ye understand what ye say." Various ḥadīths confirm the conclusion that intoxication is the guiding consideration. (See A. J. Wensinck, article "Khamr," *SEI*, pp. 243–245; see also Maḥmaṣānī, *Falsafa*, pp. 133–134.

[23] The Shāfi'īs, on the other hand, drew a different analogy and reached the contrary conclusion that virginity was the determining element.

[24] *Tanqīḥ al-Fuṣūl fī 'Ilm al-Uṣūl*, published as chapter 2 in *Adh-Dhakhīra*, a collection of Qarāfī's writings (Cairo, 1961), I, 119.

This definition leads us directly to what is in principle the starting point of every legal analogy in Islamic law: the *'illa* (sometimes translated as "efficient cause;" more specifically in this instance, the attribute or characteristic of the matter under consideration that gives rise to the judgment).[25]

The *'illa* in the prohibition of wine, for example, is the wine's intoxicating property. The *'illa* does not, properly speaking, signify the value judgment itself, that is, that intoxication is bad, but only the objective fact of intoxication. The interpreter of the law is therefore not primarily concerned to identify the underlying reason for the prohibition of wine, but only to identify the attribute that occasions the prohibition. The underlying reason, which is a value judgment, is known as the *ḥikma* ("act of wisdom"). The *ḥikma* may in some cases be rationally comprehensible and identified explicitly or implicitly in the language of the Qur'ān or ḥadīth, or seem readily apparent to common sense; but this need not be so, and even where it is, it is traditionally controversial whether the jurist may or may not go beyond the *'illa* to base his analogy on the *ḥikma* itself. Modern Muslim scholars anxious to convey the humanism of the Sharī'a tend to emphasize the rational comprehensibility of the *ḥikma* and its relevance to the promotion of man's material interest. In this process the distinction between *ḥikma* and *'illa* is sometimes lost, the latter term being employed to cover the meaning of the former.[26] When the "wisdom" underlying a rule is not rationally comprehensible, however, as is universally agreed to be the case in certain matters of ritual (e.g., selection of the month of Ramaḍān for fasting rather than some other month), some jurists have traditionally substituted the more general term *sabab* (cause, occasion) for *'illa*.[27]

Thus every *'illa* is a *sabab*, but a *sabab* is an *'illa* only if based on an intelligible *ḥikma*. But this distinction of terms was not always used; more commonly scholars would say, as Qarāfī does, what came to much the same thing in practice: that there was disagreement as to whether every legal rule must have an *'illa*, but that in any event no

[25] As variants of the term *'illa* in certain contexts the terms *manāṭ*, *maẓinna*, and *ma'inna* are used. See 'Abdalwahhāb Khallāf, *Maṣādir at-Tashrī' al-Islāmī fīmā lā Naṣṣ fīh* (Cairo, 1955), p. 41.

[26] See for example Maḥmaṣānī, *Falsafa*, p. 133; Ziadeh translation, p. 79: "The jurists derived this new source (i.e., *qiyās*) from the fundamental juridical premise that all rules are based upon objectives and interests (*maqāṣid wa maṣāliḥ*), and that such objectives and interests are the causes (*'ilal*) for the rules."

[27] Khallāf, *Maṣādir*, p. 42.

analogical reasoning was permissible in matters of ritual, nor (in the opinion of the majority) for the purpose of extending the application of established criminal penalties (*ḥudūd*) or penances (*kaffārāt*).[28] To hold that an *'illa* or *sabab* must always exist even where admittedly it may not be used for the purpose of legal reasoning, is to take a position of purely theological relevance.

The rules governing the use of analogy in making legal judgments were the cause of considerable dispute among medieval jurists precisely because of the scope it gave to the use of reason beyond the confines of explicit revelation. Generally the Ḥanafī school, which accepted the authenticity of relatively few Prophetic traditions, compensated for this by a particularly liberal use of analogy, including methods that their critics considered intellectually sloppy. By contrast Aḥmad b. Ḥanbal, who insisted on recognizing a very large number of ḥadīths, many of which were considered suspect by others, and who thus considered divine judgment to be explicit on many matters, was correspondingly chary of *qiyās*. The Ẓāhirites ("Literalists") and some Shī'ites rejected *qiyās* altogether. Between these poles the main body of Mālikīs and Shāfi'īs, and some later Ḥanbalis such as Ibn Taimiyya and Ibn Qayyim al-Jauziyya, developed the use of analogy along carefully defined lines, characterized especially by a regard for precise and systematic logic.

Qarāfī's classification of the methods and rules of *qiyās* offers an example of the detailed attention that the medieval legal scholars, like an army of ants picking clean a bone, devoted to the elaboration of God's Holy Word beyond the immediate context in which it was revealed, and illustrates the care they took to ensure that formal logic should fill every possible space before human preference, with its many fallibilities, could arrogate judgment of right and wrong to itself.

Qarāfī lists eight means used to identify the *'illa* in a given legal ruling.[29] These are as follows:

(1) Explicit textual indication (*naṣṣ*).

(2) Implicit textual indication (*īmā'*). An example is provided by "Flog both the adulteress and the adulterer"[30]—a specific causal con-

[28] Qarāfī, *Dhakhīra*, I, 125–126.

[29] *Ibid.*, I, 120–123.

[30] The logical key here is the Arabic grammatical particle *fa*, signifying consequence: "Az-zāniyatu wa 'z-zānī fa'jlidū kulla wāḥidin minhumā" (Q. xxiv:2).

nection being apparent between the deed and its consequence. Evil intentions of adultery, on the other hand, do not bring an analogous retribution, because the *'illa* is implicitly the deed itself. This method of deduction includes three subcategories. The textual language may imply a causal link, as in the case just mentioned. It may indicate a distinction; for example, "The murderer shall not inherit"—here, a distinction of incompatibility between the act of murder and the capacity of legal heir. Or the textual language may forbid an action that would obstruct the performance of an established obligation, thereby implying that the obstructive consequence is the *'illa* of the prohibition.

(3) Suitability (*munāsaba*): conduciveness of a rule to the promotion of a benefit (*maṣlaḥa*) or the prevention of an evil. Thus wealth is the *'illa* of the obligation to pay the poor tax (*zakāh*), and intoxication is the *'illa* of the prohibition of wine. The underlying premise here is that the law serves a recognizable social purpose. Although Qarāfī lists this as only one method among others for identifying the *'illa*, and does not insist that it is always appropriate, nor that promotion of social benefit is a necessary property of all *'ilal*, he nonetheless attaches particular importance to it; and so must we, since superficially it appears to support the modern doctrine that the Sharī'a is a utilitarian, or at least adaptable, social instrument.

Qarāfī treats "suitability" as a broad category comprising several subdivisions. First, what is "suitable" (*munāsib*) may either be so on grounds of compelling necessity (*ḍarūra*), importance (*ḥāja*), or mere supplementary embellishment (*tatimma*). In case of contradictory considerations, precedence is to be given in that order. Compelling necessity signifies the protection of the "five universals" (*al-kulliyyāt al-khams*) deemed to be recognized in the Sharī'a: life, religion, family, reason, and property; some would add a sixth, namely, honor. "Importance" signifies need, but not of an imperative kind: for instance, the duty of a guardian to arrange a suitable marriage for his ward if at all possible. "Embellishment," finally, signifies the general encouragement of good works and good character; Qarāfī's examples include the support of relatives and discounting the testimony of slaves.

A given quality may vary in significance from compelling necessity to importance to mere embellishment, according to the case. Thus it is a first requirement for a man to provide for his own support; it is important for him to support his wife, and merely desirable for him to support his relatives.

The second subclassification concerns the degree of specificity of the *'illa* and of the case on which a ruling is made. These may each belong to a general category, or genus (*jins*), or a particular one, or species (*nau'*). The strongest form of analogical reasoning is one whose terms are both specific, since greater precision is thereby achieved; correspondingly, the weakest form is one whose terms are both general, and thus subject to loose reasoning. Between these two positions, the *'illa* may be general and the ruling specific, or vice versa. For example, prohibition of wine-drinking because of intoxication is a more specific proposition than prohibition, say, of any action likely to lead to immoral or unseemly behavior. Hence an analogy extending only to consumption of other intoxicants is sounder than one extending to frivolous behavior generally. This appears to be a way of confirming that the *ḥikma* itself is a poor substitute for the more specific *'illa* as a basis of analogy.

Thirdly, Qarāfī distinguished between *munāsaba* analogies in which the social benefit promoted is one that is recognized in some clear fashion by the textual sources, those where the textual sources specifically exclude the benefit from consideration and thereby overrule the analogy, and those where the texts neither endorse nor exclude the benefit but simply ignore it. A recognized benefit is a *maṣlaḥa mu'tabara*, an excluded benefit *maṣlaḥa mulghāh*, and an ignored one *maṣlaḥa mursala* (*mursala* signifying "unrestricted"). The recognized benefit is a more reliable basis for analogy than the ignored, unrestricted one, for the latter has no logically determined *'illa* but simply a presumptive or intuitive one, and hence in the strict sense is not really an analogy. Nevertheless, Qarāfī notes that "we [the Mālikī school] use it, and the truth is that it is general among [all four of] the schools."[31]

(4) General resemblance (*shabah*), in which there is no "suitability" or promotion of benefit inherent in the comparison in question, but a ruling is required and hence for the sake of convenience an analogy is adopted. For example, when one man kills the slave of another, what compensation shall he pay? The dead slave might be considered comparable to a freedman, or alternatively, to some other form of prop-

[31] *Dhakhīra*, I, 122.

erty. Neither analogy has any particular support, and hence is not considered in some quarters to be authoritative.

(5) Concomitance (*daurān*): if in a series of cases a particular authoritative judgment and a particular attribute are consistently present or absent altogether, the attribute is taken to be the *'illa*. Again there is disagreement over this method.

(6) Experimentation and enumeration (*sabr wa taqsīm*): a process of elimination, in which each attribute in an established case is individually examined to determine its qualifications as a determinant of the ruling. If all attributes save one are clearly irrelevant for one reason or another, that one must be the *'illa*. The crucial question, of course, is the criterion of relevance; this we shall return to presently.

(7) Examination from all sides (*ṭard*): a method closely related to the two preceding ones, and defined by Qarāfī as "the conjunction of the ruling with the attribute in all its forms," but without any regard for "suitability." Again the jurists disagree on its use.

(8) Refinement of the basis of the ruling (*tanqīḥ al-manāṭ*), that is, isolating the *'illa* from the accompanying superfluous, but connected, elements of its context in a given case. This, as Khallāf makes clear in his explanation of the term, is a subsidiary method of clarification. It is used when the Qur'ān or Sunna indicates the *'illa* in a general and unspecific way. For example, a ḥadīth tells of the Bedouin who came to Muḥammad and confessed to having deliberately had relations with his wife during the daytime in Ramaḍān, the month of daytime fasting and abstinence. The Prophet told him to do penance. By the process of *tanqīḥ al manāṭ* the jurist eliminates the clearly irrelevant circumstances: that the man was a Bedouin, that the woman was his wife, that his act occurred in that particular year. He concludes that the *'illa*, thus "refined," is a composite one, namely, deliberate daytime sexual relations during Ramaḍān, and that this is an offense punishable by penance. This is the Shāfi'ite ruling; the Ḥanafīs rule from this case that all intentional daytime breaking of the fast in Ramaḍān, including eating and drinking, requires penance.[32] The Ḥanafīs have, in other words, "refined" the case still more than the Shāfi'is, holding that there is nothing in it to distinguish one form of fast-breaking from another, any more than there is anything to distinguish Bedouins from other men.

[32] Khallāf, *Maṣādir*, p. 55.

> From this it is apparent [explains a modern commentator] that *tanqīḥ al-manāṭ* is different from *as-sabr wa 't-taqsīm*. *Tanqīḥ al-manāṭ* exists where a text [of Qur'ān or Sunna] indicates the basis (*manāṭ*) of a ruling, but it is unrefined and not free of irrelevant accompanying attributes. *As-sabr wa 't-taqsīm* occurs where there is originally no textual indication of the basis of the ruling and it is desired, by means of this method, to identify the *'illa*, not simply to refine it from something else. Seeking to extract the *'illa* that is not indicated by texts or by consensus, by means of *as-sabr wa 't-taqsīm* or by any other method, is called *takhrīj al-manāṭ:* that is, deduction of the *'illa* of a textually indicated legal ruling where the *'illa* itself is not indicated by textural sources or by consensus. *Taḥqīq al-manāṭ* is the effort to verify the presence of an *'illa* established by text or consensus or any other means, in a particular situation or occurrence other than the one with which the text was immediately concerned. . . . *Tanqīḥ al-manāṭ* means refining, specifying, and separating the *'illa* from its surrounding conditions.[33]

These eight methods of identifying the *'illa* are of uneven importance. They may be considered under three general headings. The first two (*naṣṣ* and *īmā'*) are obvious and self-explanatory examples of the law's respect for directly revealed principles. The last five (*shabah*, *daurān*, *sabr wa taqsīm*, *ṭard*, *tanqīḥ al-manāṭ*) are cases of exterior, circumstantial reasoning, some more convincing than others, but differing little from one another in the abstractness that surrounds the inductive element in their logic and hedges its possible use as a tool of social convenience. If the logic of these methods is partially inductive, the purpose in any case is to arrive at a principle—the *'illa*—that can be applied deductively and thereby serve as a control over the vagaries of human preference.

The third method, *munāsaba*, may seem to constitute an escape clause, and a particularly significant one in view of the fact that according to Qarāfī it takes precedence over the last five methods (some jurists, he notes, dispute this in the case of *daurān*).[34] It is widely held among the jurists that suitability is a condition required of the *'illa* in all analogies, and not simply one possible means of identifying it.[35]

---

[33] *Ibid.*

[34] *Dhakhīra*, I, 130.

[35] Khallāf, *Maṣādir*, pp. 42–43; Nicholas P. Aghnides, *Muhammadan Theories of Finance* (New York, 1916), p. 81.

According to this conception, the methods of *al-sabr wa 't-taqsīm* and *tanqīḥ al-manāṭ*, while being legitimate tools in identifying the *'illa*, are always subject to the test of *munāsaba*. The purely exterior analogies based on mere coincidence (i.e., *shabah* and *ṭard*), in which no established element of suitability is involved, are rejected as methods "which have no connection with the [original] ruling nor with its *ḥikma*."[36]

The twentieth-century Egyptian commentator 'Abdalwahhāb Khallāf—whose methodology is careful and, by contemporary standards, rather conservative, but who nonetheless reflects the modern urge to emphasize the social utility of the Sharī'a where it may be found—explains that the requirement of suitability means that the *'illa* must be plausibly conducive to the *ḥikma* underlying the ruling. He thus presumes that the *ḥikma* may be known, and equates it with what Qarāfī only referred to as the "promotion of a benefit or the prevention of an evil." The *'illa*, however, must not only be "suitable" (*munāsib*) but also "objectively recognizable" (*ẓāhir*) and "clearly defined" (*munḍabiṭ*). The *ḥikma*, while known, may not itself have these qualifications.

> For the true motive for [God's] enactment of the ruling, and its intended purpose, is its *ḥikma*. If the *ḥikma* in all rulings were objectively recognizable and clearly defined, then it would be the *'illa*, being the motive for their enactment; but for lack of objective recognizability in some rulings and of clear definability in others, its place is taken by objectively recognizable and clearly defined attributes that are appropriate and suitable to it. What allows for the consideration of these attributes as *'ilal* for the rulings and for their replacing their *ḥikmas* is simply that they are presumptive (*maẓinna*) to the latter. If, then, they are not presumptive to them, they are neither suitable nor appropriate, and will not serve as *'ilal* for the ruling.[37]

The principle of suitability, whether in the usage of medieval jurists like Qarāfī or of modern interpreters like Khallāf, must be understood for no more than what it is: a conservative, circumscribed, rather timid acknowledgment of the place of social utility in the implementation of God's sacred commands. In the first place, as all agree, recourse to it in determining the *'illa* is subordinate to the use of indications of

---

[36] Khallāf, *Maṣādir*, pp. 44, 54.

[37] *Ibid.*, p. 43

the revealed texts. In the second place, even where it is used, one must still determine whether the particular utility in question is endorsed, excluded, or ignored by the revealed texts. Only in the last case, known as *maṣlaḥa mursala*, which is the least authoritative of the three, is the interpreter really in the position of exercising an independent value judgment. Thirdly, as we have also seen, the Sharīʿa is held to attach greater moral importance to the promotion of some benefits (*maṣāliḥ*) than others; those which are matters of compelling necessity are, in fact, explicitly spelled out: the preservation of life, religion, family, rationality, property. Fourth, it was commonly recognized that account should be taken of the degree of certainty with which the benefit in question would be furthered by the ruling in question: definitely (*qaṭʿan*), presumably (*ẓannan*), doubtfully (*shakkan*), or illusorily (*wahman*).[38]

Qarāfī, in his commentary on his own treatise, discusses the proposition advanced by some jurists that if the attribute in question is not clear and specific (*munḍabiṭ*), then the *ḥikma* itself may serve as the *ʿilla* as the basis of an analogy. The argument in favor, he says, is that the *ḥikma* is the source of the *ʿilla* and comprehends it, and therefore must logically be an even more authoritative basis of judgment than any given attribute whose significance is only derivative from it. The contrary argument, which Qarāfī appears to accept, is that if it were permissible to reason directly from the *ḥikma*, it should then logically be impossible to reason from a derivative attribute without implying some deficiency in the *ḥikma*; yet the permissibility of reasoning from attributes is confirmed by consensus. Relying on the *ḥikma*, furthermore, would lead to certain legal judgments contradicted by the conclusions of consensus. The prohibition of adultery, for example, might be ascribed to the *ḥikma* of the necessity to protect genealogy; but on this basis, it would be logical also to prohibit intermarriage between persons of unknown parentage, which by consensus is not in fact the case.[39] The *ḥikma*, in other words, is an unacceptable criterion for judgment because of its generality and uncertain character; reliance on it is presumptuous and likely to lead to distortion. The conservatism of this view goes a step beyond the principle, referred to earlier, of excluding *munāsaba* analogies when the benefit in question has been set aside by an explicit textual indication.

[38] *Ibid.*, p. 50.

[39] Qarāfī, *Sharḥ Tanqīḥ al-Fuṣūl*, with additional commentary by Aḥmad b. ʿAbd ar-Raḥmān al-Yazlīteni (Tunis, 1910), p. 359.

Qarāfī also cites the well-known view, although as a Mālikī he does not endorse it, that the *'illa* in a ruling may be an attribute inherently restricted to the original case itself and therefore excluding the possibility of analogy. There are two technical variants of this, the "substrate" or "thing itself" (*al-maḥall*) and the "insufficient cause" (*al-'illa 'l-qāṣira*). The former refers to the nature of the object of judgment as a whole, which is coterminous with all its attributes. Hypothetically, wine might be prohibited because it is wine; no particular characteristic of wine is relevant, but simply "winehood." The second variant refers to a specific attribute, but one which is peculiar to the object: for example, to take the example of wine again, the fact that it is made from pressing grapes.[40] The *maḥall* and *qāṣira* forms of *'illa* seem to be practically indistinguishable, and tantamount to denial of rationality in the legal prescriptions concerned. They negate the requirement generally laid down by the Ḥanafī and Mālikī schools that an *'illa* must be "transitive" (*muta'addiya*), that is, applicable beyond its original context. Otherwise, as Qarāfī cites the Ḥanafī view, the *'illa* is useless, and the result would be to diminish people's acceptance of the original ruling and their sense of the law's intent. Nonetheless, Shāfi'ī and "most theologians" accept the notion.[41] It is interesting that Khallāf, in his presentation of *qiyās*, excludes the *'illa qāṣira* and insists on transitiveness as a general condition, as he insists on "suitability" (*munāsaba*), without referring to the existence of disagreement.[42]

The underlying question concerning us in the methods of analogy is not whether they promote the use of reason as opposed to sole reliance on revelation. Certainly they do this, and analogy is nothing if not rational. Reason and revelation should not be regarded in this context as antithetical but rather as complementary. The question is one of boundaries: where does revelation end, where does reason begin, and what, if anything, lies in between? The analogy itself must be logically tight, but at its starting point it may or may not be contiguous to revelation. The principle of *munāsaba* does not logically represent a lack of contiguity if the element of utility promoted by it is textually indicated, but only if it is ignored, in which case it is *maṣlaḥa mursala*. At this point the reasoning involved crosses the boundary and into territory that is properly speaking not *qiyās* but the child of *qiyās*,

[40] *Ibid.*, p. 358.
[41] *Ibid.*, p. 362, *Dhakhīra*, I, 125.
[42] Khallāf, *Maṣādir*, p. 44.

called *istiṣlāḥ*. The latter, which signifies explicitly utilitarian jurisprudence, was not regarded by the jurists as a source of law in its own right, as *qiyās* is, but only as a subsidiary and occasional technique of disputed validity. *Istiṣlāḥ* was primarily regarded as a Mālikī method; Qarāfī, as a Mālikī, observes that the other schools make use of it, but this may be taken simply to mean that in practice the formal restrictions on legal reasoning were much honored in the breach, or at least applied rather loosely, as surely they had to be if the necessary tasks of jurisprudence were not to await the solution of some extremely abstract and complicated logical problems. The declared methodology was, to this extent, more a statement of moral intent than practical accomplishment, and presumably an ideological device enhancing the prestige of the Law as a legitimate extension of theological principles. From this standpoint it matters as much what the jurists declared as what they did. It is significant, for example, that the Ḥanafite and Shāfi'ite schools generally acknowledged the authority of *qiyās* only on the basis of an *'illa* indicated by the sources.[43] It is noteworthy also that the imposition of the qualification of *munāsaba* as a condition for all analogies, even those whose *'illa* is textually indicated, amounts to a restrictive rather than permissive principle.

Hedged by its restrictions, *qiyās* was evolved in the first instance by Abū Ḥanīfa and his school as an application of Qur'ān and Sunna rather than as a means of disregarding them, and as a systematic alternative to the resort to simple personal preference (*ra'y*) for which the champions of the Sunna in the Ḥijāz had castigated the early jurists of Iraq. The process of systematization of analogical method and of its relation to the other sources remained after Abū Ḥanīfa to be completed by Shāfi'ī. For Shāfi'ī, *qiyās* was the only legitimate form of legal reasoning, precisely because of its systematic dependence on revelation and its contrast to personal preference; and he equated it with the term *ijtihād*, or personal endeavor. *Qiyās* and *ijtihād*, wrote Shāfi'ī, are "two terms with the same meaning. On all matters touching the [life of a] Muslim there is either a binding decision or an indication as to the right answer. If there is a decision, it should be followed; if there is no decision, the indication as to the right answer should be sought by *ijtihād*, and *ijtihād* is *qiyās*."[44] To be authoritative, however, it must be confirmed by consensus.

---

[43] Aghnides, *Muhammadan Theories*, p. 800.

[44] Shāfi'ī, *Ar-Risāla*, translated by Majid Khadduri, *Islamic Jurisprudence: Shāfi'ī's Risāla* (Baltimore, 1961), p. 288. See also Schacht, *Origins*, pp. 124–127.

Qiyās was thus a means of protecting the authority of revelation in jurisprudence. If it can be held that the immediate basis, that is, the *'illa* of legal rulings can be rationally determined, the field is more effectively pre-empted from the exercise of human preference. Even such a conservative as the fourteenth-century Ḥanbalī jurist Ibn Qayyim al-Jauziyya, disciple of the puritan reformer Ibn Taimiyya, insisted that in the majority of cases the *'illa* could be determined with assurance. To the objection that the commands of the Qur'ān and Sunna are full of inconsistencies that make a reasoned analysis impossible, and that the Sharī'a "makes distinctions between similar things and treats dissimilar things as if they were the same," Ibn al-Qayyim replied that this allegation only showed the objector's lack of perception.[45] He goes on to quote with approval Ibn al-Khaṭīb:

> Most of the ordinances of the Sharī'a are based on clearly recognized considerations (*maṣāliḥ ma'lūma*), and disagreement arises only in the very few cases of exception to this. The occurrence of rare exceptions does not give grounds for bringing a reasoned approach altogether into doubt.[46]

As for Ibn al-Qayyim's master Ibn Taimiyya, the monumental studies on his legal and social thought by Henri Laoust[47] lead to the conclusion that he considered *qiyās* the chief means of authoritatively developing the teachings of the Qur'ān and Sunna into a comprehensive body of law. By denying any conflict between revelation and sound reason or between the outward expression and inner meaning of revelation, while asserting that revelation contained a guide for decision on all occasions, Ibn Taimiyya was able to view *qiyās* neither as the legitimate field for mystic speculations, nor as an exercise in morally sterile pedantry, nor as a debasement of the content of revelation.

> We must equally refute the thesis of those who reject *qiyās*—the Mu'tazilites of Baghdad, the Ẓāhirites, and a sizeable number of partisans of ḥadīth and Ṣūfīs—and the no less reprehensible extremism of the People of Opinion (*ahl ar-ra'y*) who have

---

[45] Ibn Taimiyya and Ibn Qayyim al-Jauziyya, *Al-Qiyās fī 'sh-Shar' al-Islāmī* (Cairo, 1346 H.), pp. 92 f.

[46] *Ibid.*, pp. 97–98.

[47] *Essai sur les doctrines sociales et politiques de Taḳī-d-Dīn Aḥmad b. Taimiya* (Cairo, 1939), especially pp. 242–245; *Contribution . . . , op. cit.* See also Sirajul Haq, "Ibn Taimiyya's Conception of Analogy and Consensus," *Islamic Culture*, XVII (1943), 77–87.

> abused it to the point of using it without bothering to inform themselves of the existence of textual rulings, thereby being led to reject these texts.[48]

Despite this equation of the content of reason and revelation, in Ibn Taimiyya's view reason must rest on firm ground supplied by revelation in the form of a "causal link" or "middle term" (*amr jāmi'*) connecting the two analogous subjects, by which he appears to mean an *'illa.*

> This explanatory reason [says Laoust] may be immediately given by God; most often, however, it appears only through recourse to experimentation, analysis, and induction. The idea of a purely formal logic is altogether foreign to the thought of Ibn Taimiyya, who thus shows himself more Aristotelian than many scholastic theologians. Again, he is more Aristotelian when it comes to appreciating the value of syllogistic knowledge. Usually, as Ghazālī remarks, the *fuqahā'* are content with a simple (apparent) analogy, without going so far as to seek a causal link. Because of the uncertainty of this method, the jurists' *qiyās* does not offer a certain proof. . . . Ibn Taimiyya manages to identify the *qiyās* of jurists with the syllogism of the philosophers. The juridical syllogism founds knowledge on the natural order of causes; in striving "to reason as nature reasons," and penetrate the secret of things, he must essentially reproduce the causality which God willed and placed in the world.[49]

What this seems to mean is that while Ibn Taimiyya insisted on finding a principle (in effect, an *'illa*, or even an "act of wisdom") on which to base *qiyās*, so as to ensure that it be an extension of the moral content of revelation and not an irresponsible jumping at conclusions, at the same time he recognized that this principle could not often be known through entirely deductive means, and so relied instead on what amounted, in effect, to moral insight (though of a common sense rather than esoteric or inspirational type).[50] Since—as Ibn al-Qayyim recognizes—the search for the connecting principle is bound in most cases to involve considerations of utility or convenience, the dividing line between *qiyās* and *istiṣlāḥ* for Ibn Taimiyya was not clear-cut.[51]

---

[48] Laoust, *Essai*, pp. 242–243, quoting from *Majmū' min ar-Rasā' il wa 'l-Masā'il* (Cairo, 1349 H.), V, 22.

[49] Laoust, *Essai*, p. 244.

[50] *Ibid.*, p. 243: he rejected the claims of subjective intuition (*ilhām*).

[51] Laoust, *Contribution*, p. 15. The reference to Ibn Qayyim al-Jauziyya is from the *I'lām al-Muwaqqi'īn 'an Rabb al-'Ālamīn* (Cairo, n.d.).

But lest it appear that Ibn Taimiyya was not concerned with preserving the interpretation of the law from independent moral judgments, it should not be forgotten that he viewed the texts of the Qur'ān and Sunna as a constant limitation on such judgments. As a literalist in textual exegesis he was not willing to concede the existence of a "spirit" of the revelation antagonistic in any way to its letter, nor therefore ever to admit setting aside or restricting a text to make room for a *qiyās* or a *maṣlaḥa*. If his *qiyās* was more liberal than that of some jurists who relied more heavily on deductive logic, it was offset by the fact that the doctrine of *maṣlaḥa* into which it merged was strictly limited in scope. This is contrasted with the methodology, of for example, Al-Ghazālī whose adherence to formal deductive logic in *qiyās* Ibn Taimiyya regarded as sterile, yet whose view of *maṣlaḥa* provided a loophole for liberal judgments well beyond anything envisaged by Ibn Taimiyya. This will be apparent in the section below on *maṣlaḥa*.

C. *Ijmā'*

The principle of *ijmā'* or Community consensus, based on the Prophetic ḥadīth "My Community will never agree upon an error," needs no detailed analysis here because it is not related directly to the methodology of *istiṣlāḥ*, which is our primary concern. It is sufficient for the moment merely to observe that as a source of law or doctrine it should not be thought to represent a belief in the moral or epistemological soundness of human judgment, akin to the Western voluntarist proposition that the voice of the people is the voice of God. Like the other sources of law, it is a judicial rather than a legislative principle, a means (however inorganic and often unverifiable) of confirming rules of the law made through the accepted processes of interpretation.

It is true, of course, that it is inevitably *ijmā'* that sanctions the entire system of law and doctrine, but this is its positive rather than ideal function—not a principle but a fact.[52] In any event, it is essential to the traditional concept of *ijmā'* that it was not institutionalized but remained in the form of an inarticulate accumulation of conscience. This enabled it to preserve its claim to infallibility, for once *ijmā'* was reduced to the form of a specific institution, the positive function

[52] That is, by the same token, the statement that the law of the United States is whatever the Supreme Court says it is, does not tell us what shall be the criteria of the court's decision, or whether its reasoning in a particular case has been sound.

would assimilate the ideal function and subject it to the possibility of error. By remaining inorganic, *ijmā'* conserves its reputation as the means of authenticating the interpretive efforts of *ijtihād* rather than as a conscious process of judgment. *Ijtihād*—the effort of the individual jurist to deduce the law from the Qur'ān and Sunna with the aid of analogical reasoning—is always subject to error, and becomes authoritative only when acknowledged by the conscience of the Community.[53]

D. *Al-Maṣāliḥ al-Mursala*

Maṣāliḥ (sing. *maṣlaḥa*) means interests or welfare; *mursala* (when used with *maṣāliḥ*) means unrestricted, undefined, independently arrived at. For the jurist, a *maṣlaḥa mursala* denotes the textually unrevealed benefit or utility to man inherent in a principle of conduct or judgment. The method of *istiṣlāḥ* consists of a determination by the jurist of man's best interest and judging the case at hand in a manner calculated to promote it.

Carried to its extreme and freed of other possible conflicting considerations, *istiṣlāḥ* would amount to utilitarianism pure and simple. In Islam, of course, this is out of the question, since the jurist's first premise must be that the Sharī'a has been revealed to distinguish for man between good and evil, and therefore this revelation must be applied to the full extent that it can be understood. *Istiṣlāḥ*, therefore, can be no more than supplementary to the revealed sources, and can be considered no more than a tool of interpretation, not a substantive source in its own right.

Qiyās, as we have seen, is the primary method of deducing the implications of the textual sources beyond the scope of their immediate and literal rulings. *Istiṣlāḥ* represents an extension of the method of *qiyās*, progressing beyond the limits of *qiyās* to an extent that varies considerably with the various jurists resorting to it; the most extreme of these reach a point at which the original resemblance to *qiyās* virtually disappears.

In *qiyās* the chief problem is to determine the *'illa*, the attribute of the object on which a ruling already has been revealed that gives rise to the ruling; behind the *'illa* there is a *ḥikma* or moral evaluation on

---

[53] For penetrating studies of the doctrinal value of *ijmā'* see Gardet, *La Cité musulmane* (Paris, 1954), pp. 119–129; Kemal A. Faruki, *Ijma and the Gate of Ijtihad* (Karachi, 1954); Laoust, *Essai*, pp. 239–242 and *passim.*; 'Alī 'Abd ar-Rāziq, *Al-Ijmā' fī 'sh-Sharī'a 'l-Islāmiyya* (Cairo, 1947).

the part of the Lawgiver (God), which may perhaps be made known to man, but of which knowledge is not needed for drawing analogies. But determining the *'illa* is not always a hard and fast process, and often the jurist has to project a little of his own moral preference into his calculations. If this amounts to no more than common sense, it will be generally accepted, but if it goes beyond that, it leads into *istiṣlāḥ*.

To make a guess at the *'illa* on the basis of one's own moral judgment means, in effect, first making a guess at the *ḥikma*, and to suppose that this can be done accurately is to assume that every *ḥikma* rests on some principle that man can understand and discover through his own judgment. *Istiṣlāḥ* assumes that this intelligible principle is *maṣlaḥa*, or human welfare, and that all the revealed Law, or at least that part of it to which one proposes to apply this method of interpretation, is designed to promote tangible human interests, rather than some inscrutable purpose known only to God Himself.

The *maṣlaḥa* is therefore a more specific term for *ḥikma*, and since it is known in each case not by direct indications in the textual source but by the jurist's own judgment, it is a *maṣlaḥa mursala*.

That God's purpose in the Sharī'a is in fact to promote human welfare is assumed on several grounds. There are, first of all, Qur'ānic verses such as ii:29 ("It is He who created for you all that is in the Earth")[54] and x:58 ("O ye people! An exhortation has come to you from your Lord, and a balm for what troubles your breasts").[55] Then there are various ḥadīths such as "Do not inflict injury nor repay one injury with another"[56] and accounts of the practice of the Prophet's Companions in judging unprecedented cases on the basis of *maṣlaḥa*, sometimes even at the expense of textual rules.[57]

More than this, the general consensus—with the exception of the Ẓāhirites—confirmed on rational grounds that the Sharī'a promoted human welfare. Najm ad-Dīn Ṭaufī, the thirteenth-century Ḥanbalite, although his use of *maṣlaḥa* was far from orthodox as we shall see, nevertheless presents the rational argument for the existence of *maṣlaḥa* in a fairly typical manner. He argues first that all God's acts are motivated by particular considerations (*'ilal*):

> The argument for the affirmative is that an act without an *'illa* would be nonsense, and that the Qur'ān is full of attribu-

[54] Cited by Najm ad-Dīn Ṭaufī in his treatise on *maṣlaḥa* in Muṣṭafā Zaid, *Al-Maṣlaḥa fī 't-Tashrī' al-Islāmī wa Najm ad-Dīn at-Ṭaufī* (Cairo, 1954), Appendix, p. 24.

[55] *Ibid.*, Appendix, p. 19.

[56] "La ḍarar wa la ḍirār."

[57] See for example Zaid, *Maṣlaḥa*, p. 185; Khallāf, *Maṣādir*, p. 75.

> tions of *'ilal*, such as: "So that ye may count the years and make calculations" (Q. xvii: 12). The argument for the negative is that whoever commits an act for a particular reason (*'illa*) is seeking thereby to acquire something he did not have before the reason arose; therefore he is imperfect in himself and perfect only with the addition of something from outside himself; and imperfection in God is impossible.
>
> In reply to this the whole argument is denied, for what they have mentioned applies only to God's creatures, and the truth is that the acts of God are motivated by an ultimate judgment leading to the benefit and perfection of the Believers, not to God's own perfection and benefit; for He is sufficient unto Himself.[58]

Ṭaufī next establishes that this *'illa* or governing consideration is human welfare:

> Consideration for the *maṣlaḥa* is a grace from God to His creatures, according to the People of the Sunna, and incumbent upon Him, according to the Mu'tazila. The argument of the former is that God possesses sovereignty over His creatures and so nothing can be obligatory on Him. . . . The argument of the latter is that God obliges His creatures to worship Him, and therefore must consider their welfare, so as to remove their inability to perform their obligation. Otherwise that would be an obligation to do the impossible. To this the reply is that this argument is based on [human] judgment of what is good and bad, which is not considered valid by the great majority.
>
> The truth of the matter is that consideration of the *maṣāliḥ* is necessary on the part of God (*wājib min Allah*), not obligatory on Him (*wājib 'alaih*). In this sense we said elsewhere, in reference to the Qur'ānic verse iv: 17, "Forgiveness must come from God" (*innamā 't-tauba 'alā 'llah*), that forgiveness is necessary from Him, not obligatory on Him. . . .[59]

After giving examples from the Qur'ān and Sunna of *maṣlaḥa*, he continues:

> As for *ijmā'*, all the 'ulamā' have agreed—except the insignificant minority of the rigid Ẓāhirites—that the ordinances of the Law are motivated by concern for men's welfare and avoidance of corruption. The most steadfast of these was Mālik, who had recourse to the *maṣāliḥ mursala*. In actuality he was not

[58] Zaid, *Maṣlaḥa*, Appendix, p. 21.

[59] *Ibid.*, pp. 21–22.

> alone in this, indeed all had recourse to the *maṣāliḥ*, but it was he who was the most outspoken. Even the opponents of *ijmā'* as a source of law concurred in the *maṣāliḥ*. . . .
>
> As for rational inquiry, no thinking man can doubt that God takes into consideration the welfare of His creatures, in general and in particular. In general this is true of His creation of them and their means of sustenance. God brought them into being out of nothing, in a form which enables them to secure their own welfare in their earthly life. . . .
>
> As for their means of sustenance, the Creator of the Heavens and the Earth provided for them their food and comforts. "It is He who created for you all that is in the Earth" (Q. ii:39).[60]

It is noteworthy that these arguments, as well as the Qur'ānic verses cited, only assert that God is concerned with human welfare, not that man is himself capable of recognizing where his welfare lies. To establish the mere existence of human-welfare motives behind the revealed Law does not suggest that man can apply them through his own judgment; in fact, in one sense it implies the opposite, namely that God must have taken adequate care to incorporate all the valid *maṣāliḥ* into His revelation, so that by a scrupulous adherence to Qur'ān, Sunna, and perhaps *qiyās*, man is assured of securing his own welfare. Proponents of this view could cite the Qur'ānic verse v:3, which reads: "This day have I perfected your religion for you and completed My favor unto you. . . . " Therefore, if considerations other than those already inherent in the revealed sources are used, then extraneous matter is being introduced.[61] If, on the other hand, the *maṣlaḥa* in question does have a Sharī'a corroboration, then it is not *mursala* but only the occasion for *qiyās*.[62]

It appears, however, that the proponents of *istiṣlāḥ*, while beginning from the premise that the Sharī'a intends man's welfare, at least unconsciously assume that the Sharī'a is incomplete and does not allow for rulings in all conceivable cases, and that in the gaps that must arise, human value judgment must be the rule. These assumptions

---

[60] *Ibid.*, pp. 23–24.

[61] This criticism was leveled by Shāfi'ī, among others. See Vesey-Fitzgerald, "Nature and Sources of the Sharī'a," *in* Khadduri and Liebesny, eds., *Law in the Middle East*, p. 102; also Khallāf, *Maṣādir*, pp. 78–79.

[62] Khallāf, *Maṣādir*, p. 80. See also *ibid.*, p. 78, for a citation of the argument that whatever man's interests really are, God has provided for them in the texts, and where the texts say nothing, there is the presumption that no new ruling is to be given (*al-barā'a 'l-aṣliyya*).

seem implicit in the following abstraction of the résumé of their position given by ʿAbdalwahhāb Khallāf:

> 1. The Sharīʿa rules have been decreed for the benefit of man, to secure his interests and deter injuries. Therefore, if the particular case is dealt with by the texts and/or by *ijmāʿ*, the law is followed, since that is a dependable verification of the *maṣlaḥa*. Otherwise, the ruling that provides for the *maṣlaḥa* should be adduced. This ruling will enjoy Sharīʿa status because it follows the general spirit and pattern of God's explicit rulings. "Wherever the *maṣlaḥa* is found, there is God's Law."
>
> 2. Times change and new problems arise; what was once *maṣlaḥa* becomes an evil. Unless the *mujtahids* are allowed to use *istiṣlāḥ*, the Sharīʿa will fail to provide for the people's interests, which would clearly be contrary to its intent.
>
> 3. The *maṣāliḥ* on which the Sharʿī ordinances are based are amenable to reason, i.e., human intelligence can understand the goodness of what the Law demands and the evil which it forbids. God obliges us to do what our intelligence tells us is beneficial and forbids us to do what it tells us is harmful. So if a situation arises for which there is no Sharʿī provision, and the *mujtahid* bases his ruling on what his intelligence dictates, then his ruling will rest on firm ground approved by the Divine Lawgiver.
>
> The members of this general school of thought agree in principle with the "school of rational determination of good and bad" that whatever intelligence tells us is good must be good in the sight of God and must be followed. They also agree in principle with the "school of utility" (*madhhab al-manfaʿa*) who believe that "good is what produces the greatest utility for the greatest number." The advocates of *istiṣlāḥ*, however, are not pure rationalists, for "they do not believe that ruling by *istiṣlāḥ* is a rational ruling, but that it is a Sharʿī ruling to which the intelligence is guided by the light of the rulings of the Lawgiver and of His general principles and purposes in promulgating the Law."[63]

Thus, if Khallāf's summary is correct, *istiṣlāḥ* has overtones of natural law not unlike what we shall later find in Muḥammad ʿAbduh's writings: revelation and reason are mutually corroborative. But this is only the case to a very limited extent: reason is confined to cases where the revealed texts are silent,[64] and even here must seek to derive

---

[63] Khallāf, *Maṣādir*, pp. 74–76.

[64] The above résumé does not take account of *ḍarūra* (necessity) as a subcategory of *maṣlaḥa mursala*. Here, of course, textual rules are indeed overridden, but ostensibly on grounds implicit in the Sharīʿa as a whole. See below, pp. 90–102.

its moral assumptions from known rulings. By contrast, for the proponents of *istiṣlaḥ*, in such cases revelation speaks by its very silence, in accordance with the presumption of *al-barā'a 'l-aṣliyya* (basic exemption from judgment), so that there can be no such thing as a gap in the law, no matter how many new problems occur.

It is noteworthy that some definitions of *maṣlaḥa mursala*, however, go so far as to imply that the *maṣlaḥa* itself is something that is readily apparent to reason, but that it is *mursala* only in the sense that it is not known from the textual sources whether in a given case account is to be taken of it or not. In some instances, as we have seen, the Qur'ān or ḥadīth explicitly commands that it govern the decision; in such cases we have not a *maṣlaḥa mursala* but a *maṣlaḥa mu'tabara*, which constitutes an *'illa* suitable for *qiyās*. In other cases consideration of a particular *maṣlaḥa* is explicitly ruled out, in which instance it is "excluded" (*mulghāh*). It is in other cases, when the *maṣlaḥa* is neither enjoined nor excluded, that it is *mursala*.[65] But the texts that suggest this definition tend to equate it with our previous definition by also implying that if a given *maṣlaḥa* is not specified as applicable, then it is not really known whether it is a true *maṣlaḥa* or not. Ghazālī found it necessary, for example, to justify his definition of *maṣāliḥ mursala* as comprising protection of the well-known "five universals"—religion, life, property, family, and reason—on the ground that these interests were implicit in the Sharī'a.[66] But to the extent that there is convincing support for a given consideration in the revealed sources, whether in a general or a particular way, of course such a consideration is not *mursala*; and since it has been a practice common to both classical and modern proponents of *istiṣlāḥ* to claim such support, it would appear questionable that in its absolute and literal sense a conception of *maṣlaḥa mursala* really existed at all.

On the other hand, it was sometimes alleged by proponents of *istiṣlāḥ* that the method was at least unconsciously used by all jurists, even its opponents. Qarāfī denied that it was only a Mālikī device:

> It is commonly said that *maṣlaḥa mursala* is peculiar to us [i.e., the Mālikī school], but if you examine the other schools you will find that when they weigh the similarities and differences be-

[65] Cf. Maḥmaṣānī, *Falsafa*, p. 146; Ghazālī, *Al-Mustaṣfā min 'Ilm al-Uṣūl* (Cairo, 1937), I, 139; Khallāf, *Maṣādir*, pp. 72–73. The latter writes, "It is *mursala* because there is no indication from the Lawgiver that it should be considered or ignored."

[66] *Mustaṣfā*, I, 140; see above, p. 69. Maḥmaṣānī speaks of "considering the reasonable meaning which conforms to the public interest and to the intent of the Sharī'a" (*op. cit.*, p. 147; Ziadeh translation, p. 88).

> tween two matters, they do not seek [textual] corroboration for the consideration on the basis of which they compare and differentiate, but rather that they are content with sheer suitability (*munāsaba*), which is [none other than] *maṣlaḥa mursala*. Thus it is found in all the schools. [But] it is known that the [correct] meaning of *maṣlaḥa mursala* is more restricted than sheer suitability or sheer *maṣlaḥa*, for sheer *maṣlaḥa* might be ruled out, as we have seen. . . . [Here Qarāfī offers several examples.] Thus what is suitable belongs to a more general category than the *mursala*, for the *mursala* is characterized by silence regarding its use, and accordingly it is more restricted.[67]

The truth of this allegation should be evident in the following pages of this chapter as we examine the various types of *istiṣlāḥ*.

Istiṣlāḥ may be divided into two main categories: situations in which ruling on grounds of *maṣlaḥa mursala* does not contravene clear texts of Qur'ān or ḥadīth, and those in which it does. These are, respectively, situations of *munāsaba* and *ḍarūra* (overriding necessity).[68]

1. Munāsaba

This category, as already indicated, is an outgrowth of *qiyās*. As in the case of the latter, it overrides a presumption of permissiveness (the basic rule in the Sharī'a being that what is not specifically enjoined or

---

[67] *Sharḥ Tanqīḥ al-Fuṣūl*, pp. 346–347; a very loose translation also appears in Laoust, *Essai*, p. 245. Jamāl ad-Dīn al-Qāsimī, the modernist commentator on Najm ad-Dīn Ṭaufī (see below, pp. 97–102), writes: "Al-Qarāfī said that the *maṣlaḥa mursala* is found in all the schools, inasmuch as they draw analogies and distinctions between related situations without openly calling attention to it; and this is all that is meant by *maṣlaḥa mursala*" (*Manār*, IX, 747). But Qāsimī does not cite the latter part of the above passage, which makes it clear that *maṣlaḥa mursala* ought properly to mean more than this.

[68] Neither the traditional jurists nor their modern commentators formally classified *maṣlaḥa mursala* in this manner. The various discussions appear simply to accept one category or the other, but usually not both, as representing *istiṣlāḥ*. Where both are considered, the difference between them is only implicit from the examples given. Cf. Maḥmaṣānī, *Falsafa*, pp. 146 f.; Ziadeh translation, pp. 87 f.: his definition alternately includes and excludes *ḍarūra*, but does not use the term, reserving it instead for a separate chapter (pp. 245–55; translation, pp. 152–159). The difficulty is that all jurists recognize *ḍarūra* itself, in extreme circumstances, but do not commonly consider it a part of the methodology of *istiṣlāḥ* where it logically belongs, for fear of regularizing it. For most of them, *maṣlaḥa mursala* as a methodological concept refers only to what, for the sake of clarity, we have here termed *munāsaba*; and many jurists in theory reject the notion of *maṣlaḥa* altogether, however much they may resort to it in practice.

prohibited is open to private discretion) but does not challenge textual rulings. Thus what it involves is a preference of *maṣlaḥa* over *ibāḥa* (license). The following four subcategories are included:

(i) A loose analogy in which preference has played some part in determining the *'illa*, or in which no *'illa* is identified as such by the jurist, but a general resemblance is deemed sufficient grounds for analogy on grounds of desirability. This lies on the borderline between *qiyās* and *istiṣlāḥ*, and the term *munāsaba* is applicable to both.

(ii) Promotion of an established rule by the requirement that whatever action is necessary to aid its observance is itself obligatory, and conversely whatever leads to a prohibited end is itself prohibited. Such contributory action is sometimes referred to as *dharī'a* (pl. *dharā'i'*). The entire process of *istiṣlāḥ*, broadly speaking, is a question of *dharī'a*, in that *istiṣlāḥ* is supposedly a means of implementing the general purposes of the Sharī'a, while *dharī'a* in turn is logically related to *qiyās*. But these relationships are only general and can often prove misleading if the particular distinctions are ignored.

By use of the concept of *dharī'a* a large area of normally indifferent actions assume the quality of good or evil in particular circumstances. This procedure was Ibn Taimiyya's principal field for *istiṣlāḥ* and followed naturally from his cardinal doctrine that the revealed Sharī'a contains, explicitly or implicitly, a complete guide to proper behavior for all occasions.[69]

(iii) Preference for a *maṣlaḥa* over *ibāḥa* in a nonanalogous situation, not in order to promote a specific obligation (which would be *dharī'a*), but to promote a general consideration of utility. Or, what is virtually the same, in a situation of *ibāḥa* there may be two alternative *maṣlaḥas* to choose from, in which case the one that is decisively stronger is to be preferred. This method also was used by Ibn Taimiyya, with the condition that the utility involved must significantly outweigh all possible disadvantages. For if something appears to be beneficial and no justification is found for it in the Sharī'a, this is either because the Sharī'a is misinterpreted or because it is not really useful. The Qur'ān itself takes into account such conflicts of utility: for example, the harm in drinking wine outweighs its benefits.[70] The risk of mistaken judgment must therefore be accepted, but it will at least be

[69] Laoust, *Essai*, p. 249.

[70] Q. ii:219: "In both [wine and gambling] is great sin, and also utility for men; but the sin of them is greater than their usefulness."

minimized by insisting on the clear and decisive superiority of one consideration over another.[71]

This kind of *istiṣlāḥ* provides the moral basis for the general enterprise of statecraft in Islam, known as *siyāsa shar'iyya.* Thus Ibn Qayyim al-Jauziyya quotes approvingly from Ibn 'Aqīl:

> The permissibility of *siyāsa shar'iyya* in a sultanate has been generally accepted on grounds of its effectiveness. No imam has failed to hold this. Thus a Shāfi'ite has said, "no *siyāsa* except that which conforms to the Law," and we reply, "*siyāsa* is an act done which brings people closer to virtue and removes them from corruption, even though it was not prescribed by the Prophet nor by any revealed message. So if you mean by saying 'that which conforms to the Law' that nothing enunciated in the Law should contradict it, you are right; but if you mean that there is no *siyāsa* except that which the Law does enunciate, you are mistaken, and have [implicitly] ascribed error to the Companions of the Prophet themselves."

Ibn Qayyim al-Jauziyya then remarks that the difficulties in interpreting this question

> . . . lead some to abandon it, thereby rendering the prescribed criminal punishments (*ḥudūd*) inoperative and the specified rights (*ḥuqūq*) unredeemable. They have encouraged the impious in their corruption, and caused the Sharī'a to be restricted and incapable of serving the needs of men and in need of supplementation. They have barred themselves from sound paths to knowledge and implementation of the truth, and rendered these paths of no account, despite their own and others' awareness beyond doubt that these methods are proper and suitable for reality. Instead they imagine them to be contrary to the principles of the Law.[72]

The techniques in this category are not applied to matters of ritual and worship (*'ibādāt*), since these are assumed to bear benefits of a spiritual order rather than a material one, and whatever *maṣlaḥa,* if any, underlies the revealed rules in this field is not rationally discernible. The policy in relation to the *'ibādāt* is therefore one of *tauqīf* (re-

---

[71] Laoust, *Essai*, p. 247, citing *Majmū' min ar-Rasā'il wa 'l-Masā'il,* V, 22. Laoust characterizes these calculations as "an arithmetic of profits and risks." It is difficult to see how a purely quantitative or probabilistic judgment can be avoided.

[72] Ibn Qayyim al-Jauziyya, *Al-Ṭuruq al-Ḥukmiyya fī 's-Siyāsa 'sh-Shar'iyya* (Cairo, 1953), p. 13.

straint, abstinence), that is, restriction to what is specifically commanded by the texts. It is not always easy, however, to draw the line between *'ibādāt* and *mu'āmalāt*; which, for example, is *jihād* (holy war)?[73]

(iv) Finally among the *maṣāliḥ* that are not contradictory to the Qur'ān and Sunna there is the procedure known as *istiḥsān*. This technique, propounded by the Ḥanafī school, ostensibly involves giving preference to one *qiyās* over an alternative one for reasons that are not clearly defined but amount to consideration of *maṣlaḥa*. This in some cases took the form of preferring what was allegedly a "hidden *qiyās*" (*qiyās khafī*), derived from "an indication intuitively sensed by (lit., "sparked in the soul of") the *mujtahid*, which he cannot adequately express or demonstrate."[74] This was subjected to scathing criticism by Ghazālī, who observed that if the "indication" in question really defies expression, there is no way of knowing whether it is sound or not.[75]

In reality the "hidden *qiyās*" constitutes an appeal to a *maṣlaḥa* that is not only *mursala* (not textually specified), but not identified at all, and therefore particularly objectionable. Those jurists who recognized the consideration of *maṣlaḥa* generally did so on the assumption that the *maṣlaḥa* in each case, while not specified in the textual sources as applicable to that case, could nevertheless be clearly identified so that its consonance with the Law as a whole and its overriding circumstantial value could be examined and verified. This would have the effect of forcing the individual jurist to find persuasive justifications for the *maṣlaḥa* he had singled out for consideration, and thereby reduce the likelihood of personal whim or poor judgment. But if the *mujtahid*'s rationale is not expressed—let alone if it is incapable of expression—there is no check on irresponsible value judgments.

Therefore we find Ibn Taimiyya, for example, sometimes identifying the *maṣlaḥa* in his methodology as performance of a given legal duty, concluding thereby that another act contributing to such performance becomes obligatory also. Again, he rules that in a question of fulfillment of contract the *maṣlaḥa* is the implementation of the parties' original intent, on the grounds that in principle the subject matter of

---

[73] Laoust, *Essai*, p. 248.

[74] Ghazālī, *Mustaṣfā*, I, 138; Maḥmaṣānī, *Falsafa*, p. 125. The modernist Rashīd Riḍā offers the opinion that the claim of "hidden *qiyās*" was made merely to answer the critics who saw in *istiṣlāḥ* and *istiḥsān* an attempt to introduce an independent source of law (*Manār*, IV, 211, 860).

[75] Ghazālī, *Mustaṣfā*, I, 138–139.

contracts is left to the parties' discretion, and that therefore the intent rather than the letter of contracts should be enforced.[76] Ghazālī, as we have noted, reduced the *maṣāliḥ mursala* to the "five universals."

The assumption in these specifications is that the *maṣlaḥa* may be *mursala* only to the extent that it is not specified in the texts themselves as applicable to the particular case in question. But it may not be *mursala* to the extent of being subjected to no intelligible definition at all.

To return briefly to *istiḥsān*, besides the "hidden *qiyās*" there were other cases to which the term was sometimes applied in which nothing really more than an intelligent interpretation of the revealed sources was involved: when, for example, an analogy is avoided by restricting the application of the original rule by means of another text. This, as Ghazālī again objects, is not *istiḥsān* but simply a correct adjustment of two seemingly conflicting texts.[77]

The difficulty with *istiḥsān*, in short, is that it does not rest on any clear-cut method of reasoning, and hence appears to the more systematic jurists to represent no more than an arbitrary introduction of personal preferences. The appeal to utility, if it is to be made at all, is most congenial to the revealed-law concept of the Sharī'a when at least an attempt is made to show that the utility in question is an object of the law itself. The failure of the Ḥanafī proponents of *istiḥsān* to do this—to justify their avoidance of *qiyās* in each case by reference to a specific *maṣlaḥa*—exposed them to the charge of "legislating."[78]

The fact remains, however, that the method's proponents did not accept the premises of this criticism, but maintained that *istiḥsān* was quite within the confines of a revealed system of law, and despite any inadequacies in their defense, it cannot be said that *istiḥsān* represented a deliberate arrogation of the power of unrestricted value judgment. For the argument does not carry beyond the limits set by explicit rules of the Qur'ān and Sunna, which continue to be respected.

2. *Ḍarūra*

The doctrine of necessity, which held that extreme cases may arise

---

76 Ibn Taimiyya and Ibn Qayyim al-Jauziyya, *Qiyās*, p. 48; French translation in Laoust, *Contribution*, p. 174.

77 Ghazālī, *Mustaṣfā*, I, 139.

78 E.g., Shāfi'ī, *Risāla* (Cairo, 1321 H.), p. 70, in reference to *istiḥsān:* "God has not permitted any man since His messenger to present views unless from knowledge that was complete before him" (cited in R. Paret, article "Istiḥsān and Istiṣlāḥ," *SEI*).

in which the usual requirements of the law may be set aside, was in general currency among jurists, although not always directly associated with the technique of *istiṣlāḥ*, partly because it purports to deal only with exceptional cases and partly because it pertains to matters of *'ibādāt* as well as *mu'āmalāt*. The Qur'ānic justifications of "necessity" are numerous.[79]

From the rational point of view, the doctrine rests on the principle of general consequences, according to which the sequence of events to which a rigorous course of action gives rise may tend to defeat the purposes of the action.[80] In Ghazālī's expression, "Everything that exceeds its limit changes into its opposite."[81] Account of this principle is taken by the Ottoman *Mecelle* under the headings of lessening of hardship (Articles 17, 18) and necessity (Article 21). The *Mecelle*, however, sets the following limitations: (1) What is permitted by necessity is limited to the extent of the necessity (Article 22); (2) what is permitted is valid only so long as the necessity lasts (Article 23).[82]

In cases where the dictates of necessity are in opposition to a *maṣlaḥa* evident in the normal rule, the *Mecelle* calls for preference of the lesser of two evils in accordance with the following rules: (1) an individual injury is preferable to a general one (Article 26); (2) avoidance of an evil takes precedence over securing a benefit (Article 30); (3) the lesser evil, reckoned on a qualitative basis, is to be preferred (Articles 27, 28, 29).[83]

In Ghazālī's *Mustaṣfā* one finds one of the fullest classical treatments of the doctrine of necessity as a type of *maṣlaḥa mursala*. Indeed, it is only this type, and not the *maṣlaḥa* of suitability (*munāsaba*) which falls within textual limits, to which his definition of *maṣlaḥa mursala* really applies. The *maṣlaḥa* of mere suitability in his view does not

---

[79] Q. ii:173, v:3, vi:119, vi:145, and xvi:115 permit the eating of forbidden food in circumstances of extreme hunger, and all use the phrase "whosoever is compelled" (*fa-man iḍṭurra*) or a slight variation of it. Q.xxii:78 says: "He hath chosen you and hath not laid upon you in religion any hardship." The word *ḍarūra* itself does not appear in the Qur'ān.

[80] For a comparison of this doctrine with the Aristotelian doctrine of extremes in medieval Muslim philosopy see W. F. Thompson (tr.), *Practical Philosophy of the Muhammadan People* (London, 1839), pp. xxxvi–xxxix.

[81] Quoted in Maḥmaṣānī, *Falsafa*, p. 245, Ziadeh translation, p. 152.

[82] Cited in Maḥmaṣānī, *Falsafa*, pp. 246–250; translation, pp. 153–156. The full translated text of the *Mecelle* is found in Charles Hooper, *The Civil Law of Palestine and Transjordan* (Jerusalem, 1933), Vol. I.

[83] Maḥmaṣānī, *Falsafa*, pp. 252–253; translation, pp. 157–158.

properly speaking involve *istiṣlāḥ* at all, but only an exercise of the usual methods such as *qiyās*. Since the comprehensiveness and systematic reasoning of his analysis make it a classic statement of the doctrine of necessity, it deserves a detailed account.

Istiṣlāḥ, says Ghazālī, is one of the "imaginary" sources of law, of which he lists four.[84] It becomes clear, as his argument progresses, that this does not mean that the conclusions drawn from these sources are invalid, but that they are not truly independent sources of law in themselves; they are already incorporated, explicitly or implicitly, into the recognized *uṣūl* of Qur'ān, Sunna, *ijmā'*, and *qiyās*, or else serve to elucidate them.

In the case of *istiṣlāḥ*, three situations may arise: a *maṣlaḥa* will be specifically identified by the texts as the basis for decision, or it will be ruled out of consideration, or no clear indication will be given. An example of the first case is the drinking of wine, which is forbidden because intoxication prevents the individual from performing his religious duties properly. This specification of the *maṣlaḥa* gives grounds not for *istiṣlāḥ* but *qiyās*. As an example of the second case, we are told the story of a ruler who breaks the Ramaḍān fast, and instead of the prescribed penance of freeing a slave and distributing alms, a court jurist gives judgment that the ruler should fast for two consecutive months, since the usual penance would be no great sacrifice for a wealthy man. Ghazālī condemns this reasoning because it "opposes the words of the scripture with a *maṣlaḥa*. Opening this door will lead to changing all the legal penalties and their textual sources because of changed circumstances."[85] Here we have a clear example of what Qarāfī called an excluded *maṣlaḥa* (*maṣlaḥa mulghāt*).

If the Sharī'a is silent on the use of *maṣlaḥa* in a particular situation, continues Ghazālī, we must then distinguish between cases of necessity or need (*ḍarūrāt wa ḥājāt*) and cases in which only improvements and embellishments (*taḥsīnāt wa tazyīnāt*) are in question. Here again we find a formula later invoked by Qarāfī.

This distinction severely restricts the meaning of *maṣlaḥa*, for while it basically means "obtaining benefit and preventing injury," these are only

---

[84] The other three are the teachings of earlier prophets not abrogated by Muḥammad (Ghazālī, *Mustaṣfā*, I, 132–135), sayings of the Companions of the Prophet (*ibid.*, 135–137), and *istiḥṣān* (*ibid.*, 137–139).

[85] *Ibid.*, p. 139.

> . . . human aims, concerned with human welfare only in human terms, whereas what we mean by *maṣlaḥa* is conservation of the aims of the Sharī'a. The aim of the Sharī'a in regard to man is fivefold: to conserve his religion, life, reason, offspring, and material wealth. All, then, that secures conservation of these five elements is a *maṣlaḥa*, and all that jeopardizes them is *mafsada*, prevention of which is a *maṣlaḥa*.

The preservation of these five interests falls within the category of necessities and is amply exemplified in the revealed laws punishing heresy, murder, wine-drinking, adultery, and theft.[86]

But when only improvements and embellishments are at stake, in the absence of support from a text or *qiyās*, no ruling should be given. "If the Sharī'a offers no support for one's opinion, it is the same as *istiḥsān*, while if one of the sources does support it, then it is a case of *qiyās*, and the judgment is valid."[87]

The only example given by Ghazālī in which necessity overrules the texts is an odd one, but illustrates important principles:

> An example is the case of the unbelievers who shield themselves with a group of Muslim captives. If we hold back from them they will fall upon us, overwhelm the territory of Islam and kill all the Muslims. If, however, we strike at their shield, we should kill an innocent Muslim who has committed no wrong, and there is no allowance in the Sharī'a for such an action. But otherwise the unbelievers would gain mastery over all the Muslims and kill them, and then kill the prisoners as well, so that it may rightly be said that the captives will be killed in either case; and preserving the great body of Muslims is closer to the intent of the Law. For we know that the Law intends minimizing killing, just as it intends stopping it altogether if possible. If we cannot stop it altogether, we can at least minimize it. This would be a case of resorting to a *maṣlaḥa* known as necessity, since we know it to be an intent of the Law not by any particular indication or specific source, but by indications free of any restrictive definition.
>
> But securing the intent by this means, namely by killing an innocent person, is unusual (*gharīb*) and finds support in no particular source. Thus it is an example of a *maṣlaḥa* not determined by analogy from a particular source, but is inspired by three considerations: (1) it is a matter of vital necessity (*ḍarūra*),

---

[86] *Ibid.*, pp. 139–140.

[87] *Ibid.*, p. 141.

(2) it is a case of clear-cut certainty (*qaṭʿiyya*), and (3) its importance is universal (*kulliyya*)."[88]

By these limitations Ghazālī would prevent *istiṣlāḥ* from becoming a wide-open door for innovations of all kinds. They would rule out appeal to necessity in other cases that at first impression might seem similar. Should the unbelievers shielding themselves with a Muslim captive be shut up in a fortress, for instance, whose capture is not vitally necessary for the preservation of Islam and is not assured, then the considerations of necessity and certainty are absent. Again, in the case of a foundering ship, the lives of only a limited number of persons would be at stake and therefore it would not be lawful to throw one person overboard to save the rest. Nor may a group who are starving draw lots and practice cannibalism on one of their number,[89] since the *maṣlaḥa* would not be a universal one.[90]

Determining the *maṣlaḥa*, Ghazālī explains, is not a matter of sheer weight of numbers: the interests of the entire community may outweigh those of one or two individuals, but those of ten do not outweigh those of one. The objection is anticipated that in the case of the enemy shielding himself with Muslim captives, killing the latter contravenes clear prohibitions in the Qur'ān.[91] How can this be justified, when in the relatively trivial case of the ruler who broke the fast of Ramaḍān, Ghazālī insisted on following the prescribed penance, regardless of the *maṣlaḥa*? Ghazālī replies:

> We consider this a question of *ijtihād*. It would not be implausible to argue for a total prohibition [of *istiṣlāḥ*], reasoning

---

[88] *Ibid.*

[89] *Ibid.* Maḥmaṣānī (*Falsafa*, p. 254) recalls similar decisions in British and American courts refusing to condone cannibalism to keep the group from starving (Regina *v.* Dudley and Stephens, L. R. 14 Q. B. D. 273; United States *v.* Holmes, 1 Wallace 1).

[90] The meticulous Ghazālī pursues his lugubrious example to its conclusion: "Nor may they cut off only his hand to eat, preserving his life and thereby claiming license, for this would injure his *maṣlaḥa*. The Law allows injuring a person in his own interest, as for example by bleeding or cupping and such like. Thus a person in need might cut flesh for food from his own thigh, which would be like cutting off his hand. But it might be obvious that the amputation would cause his death, in which case it would be forbidden, for there would then be no assurance of saving himself, and it would not be a clear-cut and certain *maṣlaḥa*" (*Mustaṣfā*, p. 141).

[91] Q. iv:93: "Whoever intentionally slays a believer, his reward is everlasting hellfire"; Q. vi:151: "Slay not the life which God hath made sacred, save in the course of justice."

> from the example of the ship, which [if the interests of the majority were followed] would serve to justify killing a third of the Community in order to save two-thirds, by sheer preference of numbers. For there is no question but that if an unbeliever intended to kill a limited number of Muslims—ten, for example—and shielded himself with a single Muslim hostage, then the ten would not have the right to kill the hostage in self-defense. Rather, they would be judged in the same light as ten men compelled to kill—or, in case of starvation, to eat—a single man. Here we have a case of weight of numbers, not a principle of universality.
>
> But for an unlimited and universal number there is a different and stronger case than for the simple preference of the greater number. . . . In the case before us [in which all Muslims are in danger] . . . it must be said that shedding forbidden and innocent blood must be weighed against the fact that in abstaining, an unlimited amount of innocent blood will be shed. We know that the Law gives preference to the universal over the partial; therefore preserving the people of Islam from the onslaught of the unbelievers is more important in the intent of the Law than preserving the blood of a single Muslim. This is clearly indicated by the intent of the Law, and what is thus clearly indicated needs no support from a source.[92]

This last sentence is of great importance.[93] The principle of preference on which Ghazālī has relied is, he admits, not covered in a particular text in so many words so as to justify an ordinary *qiyās*, yet he insists that it is undeniably present in the clear intent of the law as a whole. Therefore, *istiṣlāḥ* is a sound procedure under certain circumstances, yet it is not an independent source of law. This is why he calls it an "imaginary source" (*aṣl mauhūm*): the definition of it as a "source," not the procedure, is imaginary.

> We have restricted use of it to implementation of the purposes of the Law as determined by the Qur'ān, Sunna, and *ijmā'*. Every *maṣlaḥa* that does not consist of implementing the understood intent of the Qur'ān, Sunna, and *ijmā'* is foreign and inappropriate to the operations of the Law. It is therefore void and rejected, and whoever has recourse to it is arrogating the

---

[92] Ghazālī, *Mustaṣfā*, p. 142.

[93] The Arabic reads: "Fa-hādhā maqṭū'un bihi min maqṣūdi 'sh-shar' wa 'l-maqṭū'u bihi lā yaḥtāju ilā shahādati aṣl."

> power of legislation, just as whoever uses *istiḥsān* is legislating. Every valid *maṣlaḥa* is based on implementing the intent of the Law, which must be determined by the Qur'ān, Sunna, and *ijmā'* and must not fall outside the scope of these sources. But it is not called *qiyās* but rather *maṣlaḥa mursala*, because *qiyās* is a well-defined source in itself, while we know that the Law intends application of the *maṣlaḥa* not by one single indication, by by unlimited indications in the Qur'ān, the Sunna, and the context of circumstances; and because of this diversity of indications, it is called *maṣlaḥa mursala*. As long as *maṣlaḥa* is interpreted to mean conservation of the intent of the Law, then there is no room for argument in following it; rather it should be accepted as a basis for judgment without dispute. Insofar as we have acknowledged disagreement, that has been in cases of two opposing *maṣlaḥas* and intents, in which case preference must be given to the stronger.[94]

But how, the questioner persists, does he know that the universal interest is decisive while that of a limited number is not? He replies:

> We do not know this by virtue of any specific single text, but by a variety of judgments and a concurrence of indications which leave no doubt that preservation of the continuance of Islam and the lives of the Muslims is more important in the intent of the Law than preservation of a particular individual for another hour or a day, when the unbelievers are going to kill him in any case.[95]

Ghazālī is firm in insisting that the absence of specific textual proof does not mean the absence of any textual backing at all, and that it cannot be said that he has had recourse in his examples to his own moral assumptions or preferences. While he distinguishes his process from *qiyās*, it is clear that he claims to be deriving conclusions from unassailable principles, which place his reasoning on the same circumspect level as *qiyās*. Whether his claim is justified is another matter. It might easily be argued, of course, that his conception of what constitutes a vitally necessary, certain, and universal *maṣlaḥa* is inevitably somewhat subjective. But the significant fact is that he thought it necessary to allay such fears and defend his position as being textually sound, arguing that he only contravened revealed principles on the strength of other revealed principles.

---

[94] Ghazālī, *Mustaṣfā*, pp. 143–144.

[95] *Ibid.*, p. 144.

One final observation must be made about Ghazālī. While applying the term *istiṣlāḥ* to contraventions of textual rules on grounds of necessity, he has denied the applicability of the term to more ordinary cases in which it is only proposed to override the presumption of the absence of a ruling (*al-barā'a 'l-aṣliyya*) with a *maṣlaḥa.* In the latter class of cases, what is thought to be *istiṣlāḥ* is either a misunderstood case of *qiyās* or an unjustified resort to ill-defined subjective preferences. In this sense Ghazālī's argument permits much less amplification of the sources than that envisaged by such jurists as Ibn Taimiyya, despite the fact that the latter left no room in his definition of *maṣlaḥa* for contravening the texts. This difference reminds us once again of the essential conservatism of Ghazālī's position.

In contrast to Ghazālī, one medieval jurist stands out who not only used the concept of *maṣlaḥa* to justify setting aside the texts but went to the lengths of making this a general rule. Najm ad-Dīn Ṭaufī (d. 716 H.), the most radical of all champions of *istiṣlāḥ*, asserted in effect that every *maṣlaḥa* is a necessity and must therefore take precedence over everything else.

Ṭaufī's doctrine is set forth in his commentary on the thirty-second of forty ḥadīths listed by the Shāfi'ite jurist al-Nawawī (d. 676 H.).[96] Ḥadīth No. 32 is the admonition, "Do not inflict injury nor repay one injury with another" (*lā ḍarar wa lā ḍirār*). Ṭaufī takes this to be the first principle of the Sharī'a, enabling *maṣlaḥa* to take precedence over every other consideration. It is no argument to say that God is the best judge of the *maṣlaḥa*, for the Sharī'a orders man to judge for himself.

As for the texts and *ijmā'*, writes Ṭaufī, if they should happen to conform to the *maṣlaḥa* in a particular case, they should be applied forthwith. But if they oppose it, then "consideration of the *maṣlaḥa* must take precedence over them. This is done through the process of restriction (*takhṣīṣ*) and clarification (*bayān*)—not by the process of attacking them or suspending them—just as the Sunna is sometimes given preference over the Qur'ān by serving as a means of clarifying it."[97]

---

[96] The text is published in *Majmū' ar-Rasā'il fī Uṣūl al-Fiqh* (Beirut, 1324 H.); *Al-Manār*, IX, 745–770 with some omissions, with commentary by Jamāl ad-Dīn al-Qāsimī; Zaid, *Maṣlaḥa*, Appendix, pp. 14–48; Khallāf, *Maṣādir*, pp. 87–122. Subsequent page references will be to the Zaid text (cited in note 54).

[97] Zaid, *Maṣlaḥa*, Appendix, p. 17. It will be assumed in this case, Ṭaufī means, that the textual rule does not properly extend to the circumstances under consideration.

In some cases, Ṭaufī grants, what is called for by the texts or *ijmāʿ* will intrinsically involve an injury (*ḍarar*): for example, criminal penalties. In this case they "can only be viewed as exceptions to the Prophet's formula, '*lā ḍarar wa lā ḍirār*.' " But if the injurious element is only incidental, then—barring special indications to the contrary—it must be eliminated by the process of restrictive interpretation, "in order to achieve conformity among the sources."[98]

Ṭaufī then proceeds to establish that *maṣlaḥa* is the fundamental intent of the Law, following in this case a conventional point of view. Like all other jurists, he restricts consideration to the *muʿāmalāt* and excludes the *ʿibādāt*, "for which the law has its own justification and whose foundation cannot be analyzed beyond its support by the texts and *ijmāʿ*."[99]

Three reasons are given by Ṭaufī forjthe precedence of *maṣlaḥa* over the texts and *ijmāʿ*:

(1) As for *ijmāʿ*, even the opponents of that method support the concept of *maṣlaḥa*; therefore it has more universal backing and is more worthy of use as a criterion of decision.[100]

(2) "The textual sources are diverse and mutually contradictory, which is the reason for the difference among the schools in the rules they follow; this difference is condemned by the Law. Consideration of the *maṣlaḥa*, on the other hand, is a matter consistent within itself and brings about the agreement demanded by the Law."[101]

(3) Examples can be found in the Sunna of the Prophet and his Companions of cases in which the textual sources contradicted considerations of *maṣlaḥa*, and the latter was preferred. In one such example, the Prophet ordered Abū Bakr and ʿUmar to immediately put to death a man whose behavior in the mosque was offensive; they refused to do so because he was praying, and Muḥammad approved their disobedience.[102]

These arguments are open to severe criticisms which have been

---

[98] Zaid, *Maṣlaḥa*, Appendix, p. 18. The suggestion is implicit that *ḍarar* signifies an injury of a physical or material kind, and that *maṣlaḥa* signifies no more than the avoidance of this. Criminal penalties are an "exception" to the requirements of *maṣlaḥa*; he does not refer to a greater *maṣlaḥa* of public security, overriding that of the criminal's physical well-being.

[99] Zaid, *Maṣlaḥa*, Appendix, p. 21.

[100] *Ibid.*, Appendix, p. 35.

[101] *Ibid.*

[102] *Ibid.*, Appendix, pp. 39–40.

made by a number of modern writers. The first argument, for example, is entirely misleading if it means to suggest that *maṣlaḥa* enjoys universal support in the manner in which Ṭaufī proposes to use it. At most, he can claim an *ijmāʻ* in support of the belief that the Sharīʻa was revealed in man's material and moral interest; but most jurists would draw from this the presumption that the *maṣāliḥ* are already incorporated into the Law as it was revealed, so that Ṭaufī's methods are unnecessary and even blasphemous.[103]

Taufī, anticipating such an objection, replies:

> If it is said, the Law knows best what are the true interests of the people . . . and it is fanciful and presumptuous to determine the *maṣaliḥ* by other means, then we say: Indeed the Law does know best what are the true interests of mankind. But what we said does not amount to discarding the proofs of the Law in favor of other means, which would be forbidden. Rather, some proofs are set aside in favor of another preferred proof, on the authority of the ḥadīth *lā ḍarār wa lā ḍirār*, just as you sometimes give precedence to *ijmāʻ* over other proofs. Furthermore, God provided us with a means to determine our interests in all but exceptional cases, so we shall not forsake it for a doubtful method which may or may not lead us to the *maṣlaḥa*.[104]

On the second argument—that the textual sources are inconsistent—it may be recalled that the same argument was marshalled against *qiyās* and refuted by Ibn Qayyim al Jauziyya, who insisted that any apparent inconsistencies in the texts were merely the result of inadequate interpretation.[105] There the allegation served the argument that the motivation behind revealed laws could not be known. Ṭaufī makes the same allegation, but assumes that the motivation can be known, and concludes that therefore we must apply the motivation, which is consistent, rather than the revealed form, which contradicts itself. It is true that he adds that an attempt should be made to reconcile the sources if this is possible without "manipulating" them (*talāʻub bi'l-adilla*); but otherwise the *maṣlaḥa* must take precedence. "For the

[103] Zaid writes (*ibid.*, p. 188): "As long as the Lawgiver is so entirely moved by consideration of the *maṣlaḥa* [as Ṭaufī claims Him to be], there is no possibility of His decrees being contrary to it, in such a way as to necessitate giving it precedence over them."

[104] *Ibid.*, p. 41.

[105] Ibn Qayyim al-Jauziyya and Ibn Taimiyya, *Qiyās*, quoted above in the discussion on *qiyās*, p. 77.

maṣlaḥa is what was intended in establishing the laws for the direction of mankind's affairs, while the sources are only means to this end; and ends must take precedence over means."[106]

But the reply of Ibn Qayyim al-Jauziyya to his critics applies to Ṭaufī as well. The disagreement among the *madhāhib* on various points is no logical indication of contradiction among the textual sources, but only of the imperfect degree of understanding on the part of each *madhhab*.[107] Or it may indicate the change in the *maṣāliḥ* themselves from one time or place to another.[108]

Ṭaufī, however, does not anticipate such objections and confines himself to rejecting the view that just as differences among the Schools are a blessing, so are disagreements between the sources of the Law, and therefore do not need to be resolved by *istiṣlāḥ*. If that were the case, he argues, everyone could do as he pleased, finding one authority or another to support him.[109] In this we are reminded of his underlying assumption: the *maṣāliḥ* are by nature sufficiently clear to be known with certainty in any given case, and are a more reliable guarantee of a unified and systematic application of law than strict adherence to the revealed sources would be. This is indeed an unusual assumption among medieval jurists, for the great mass of whom it was a matter of dogma that the Sharī'a was revealed precisely for the purpose of rescuing man from the uncertainties and failings of his own diverse inclinations. But that is not Ṭaufī's view. For him the Sharī'a is essentially a call to utilitarianism:

> And let it not be said that the Law knows better what are man's interests and that therefore his interests can be deduced from the Law's indications. For we have established that regard for these interests is itself one of the indications of the Law, and in fact the strongest and most specific of them. Let us then give it precedence in order to achieve these interests.[110]

---

[106] Zaid, *Maṣlaḥa*, Appendix, p. 46.

[107] This is also Ibn Taimiyya's view. See Laoust, *Essai*, p. 250.

[108] Zaid's view. (*Maṣlaḥa*, pp. 188–189). Furthermore, observes Zaid, given Ṭaufī's logic on this point, there is no justification for separating *mu'āmalāt* from *'ibādāt* and using *maṣlaḥa* only in the former; are the *'ibādāt* then not contradictory too? (*ibid.*). 'Abdalwahhāb Khallāf makes the same objection (*Maṣādir*, p. 84).

[109] Zaid, *Maṣlaḥa*, Appendix, p. 42. He quotes a satiric verse of poetry: "Indulge in drink, sodomy, fornication, and gambling, and justify thyself in each case by the dictum of an imam."

[110] *Ibid.*, Appendix p. 48.

His third argument for *istiṣlāḥ*—that the Sunna gives examples in which the texts contradicted *maṣlaḥa* and the latter was preferred—is also subjected to criticism. The Sunna is itself a textual source, and therefore the contradictions he cites amount only to the restriction or suspension of one text by another.[111]

On one further point Ṭaufī unwittingly leaves the door wide open for criticism of his claim that *istiṣlāḥ* is a means of bringing order out of the chaos found in the traditional sources. He admits the possibility—which indeed would have been hard to deny—that conflicts may arise among the *maṣāliḥ* themselves. In seeking a method of selection, he first gives preference to the ruling that would secure "as many benefits as possible . . . or the most important one." But if there are no clear grounds for preference, Taufī is driven to advocate a random choice or the drawing of lots.[112] This undignified procedure is scarcely congenial to his assumption that the *maṣāliḥ* have greater inner consistency than the revealed texts and *ijmā'*.

Taken as a whole, Ṭaufī's theory of *maṣlaḥa* can only be considered an extreme exception to the traditional view. While insisting that his method is securely grounded in a ḥadīth and that therefore he cannot be accused of disrespect toward the revealed Law, it seems questionable whether this claim was made entirely in good faith. The ḥadīth was not one generally in use, and by Ṭaufī's own implied admission[113] was considered a weak one; other writers on *maṣlaḥa* do not base their arguments on it. In making it the basis of his entire structure of legal reasoning, Ṭaufī declares in effect, "All ḥadīths may be restricted or explained away except this one." His method enables him to choose the legal judgment in a given case that most appeals to his utilitarian sense of values and then bend the normal sources of law to conform to his preference. If they will not bend, they are simply "restricted." It is

---

[111] Zaid's criticism in *ibid.*, pp. 189–190; also Khallāf, *Maṣādir*, p. 84. Ṭaufī's argument is revived by Rashīd Riḍā (*Manār* IV, 209–210).

[112] Zaid, *Maṣlaḥa*, Appendix, p. 46. This passage in particular attracts Zaid's ridicule (*ibid.*, p. 189). It should be remembered that the drawing of lots is objectionable in itself to Muslim jurists because of its suggestion of frivolity and because of the Qur'ānic ban on gambling. Cf. Ghazālī, *Mustaṣfā*, I, 141, for a refusal, partially on these grounds, to accept a decision to throw a passenger overboard in the hypothetical case of the foundering ship.

[113] Zaid, *Maṣlaḥa*, Appendix, p. 18: Ṭaufī anticipates an objection that "consideration of the *maṣlaḥa* is not decisive, for it rests on a ḥadīth that is not decisive." He does not refute this allegation but only answers by reiteration of his position.

this license that leads 'Abdalwahhāb Khallāf to object that Ṭaufī "opened the door to suppression of the revealed texts, and made the judgments of the texts and *ijmā'* liable to cancellation by opinion. For consideration of the *maṣlaḥa* is no more than naked opinion and arbitrary speculation."[114]

The fact remains that sincere or not, Ṭaufī found himself compelled to defend himself on orthodox grounds by claiming textual support, and it is this defense that makes him the exception that demonstrates the rule.

---

[114] Khallāf, *Maṣādir*, p. 84.

IV

MUḤAMMAD ʿABDUH AND NATURAL LAW

Having outlined in the past two chapters some of the fundamental elements in the idealist tradition of Muslim legal and constitutional theory, and having tried to show that these elements were outgrowths of a conservative theology, we now turn our attention to the late nineteenth and early twentieth centuries to consider the manner in which this tradition was reformulated by two representative reformist intellectuals, Muḥammad ʿAbduh and Muḥammad Rashīd Riḍā. Of these two, the former is much the more important historical figure, although we shall have less to say about him of direct relevance to matters of law and government. So much has been written about ʿAbduh by both orientalists and Muslims that it may seem redundant to say anything more.[1] Nonetheless we shall do so, if only to emphasize a certain perspective. For it was ʿAbduh's reformist theology that Rashīd Riḍā took as the basis for his reformist theories of jurisprudence and constitutionalism. The shakiness of this basis underlay the incoherence of Riḍā's ideology, and thus appears to have contributed something to its failure as a political program. While this would not matter very much

[1] The most extensive record of information on ʿAbduh's life and work remains Rashīd Riḍā's three-volume *Tārīkh al-Ustādh al-Imām ash-Shaikh Muḥammad ʿAbduh* (Cairo, 1931). Volume I is an 1100-page biography, Volume II is an anthology of ʿAbduh's articles, and Volume III reproduces the texts of eulogies and appreciations of ʿAbduh in the press and by friends and official personages after his death. A number of Egyptian scholars have championed ʿAbduh's ideas in western-language studies, most notably Moustapha Abdel Razik (Muṣṭafā ʿAbd ar-Rāziq) and Osman Amin (ʿUthmān Amīn); these works are cited in the bibliography. Among western scholars the leading studies of ʿAbduh are by Max Horten, I. Goldziher, C. C. Adams, J. Jomier, R. Caspar, and A. H. Hourani, also listed in the bibliography. Shorter studies of note are in the cited works of P. J. Vatikiotis, J. M. Ahmed, and N. Safran, and in L. Binder, *The Ideological Revolution in the Middle East* (New York, 1964).

if Riḍā were only an isolated figure, the fact is that his theories have been substantially shared by a large number of educated Muslims, at one ideological level or another, up to the present day.

'Abduh's life and career have been described at length in many works. He was born in 1849 in a village in the Nile Delta, into a family of modest means. As a boy he attended the mosque school in the city of Ṭanṭā; he then moved on to Al-Azhar University in Cairo where in 1877 he received the degree of *'ālim*. For two years he taught at the Azhar and at the new college of Dār al-'Ulūm. During his period at the Azhar he came under the influence of Jamāl ad-Dīn al-Afghānī, the legendary Afghan then visiting Cairo who traveled up and down the Muslim world and Europe preaching his revolutionary message of religious revival and pan-Islamic political activism. When Afghānī was expelled from Egypt in 1879 'Abduh, as his disciple, was sent back to his village, only to be recalled to Cairo a year later to become editor of the official gazette, *Al-Waqā'i' al-Miṣriyya* ("Egyptian Events"), in which he published a number of articles calling for various political, religious, and social reforms. For a time he became involved with 'Arābī and his group of nationalist army officers who resisted the British occupation of Egypt in 1882, and for this was sentenced to three years of exile from the country. After a short stay in Beirut he rejoined his old mentor Jamāl ad-Dīn al-Afghānī in Paris, helping him produce the famous journal *Al-'Urwa 'l-Wuthqā* ("The Firmest Bond") until it expired after 18 issues in 1884. After another sojourn in Beirut, where he taught in an Islamic school, 'Abduh returned to Cairo in 1888 and soon was appointed a judge in the "native courts" (*al-maḥākim al-ahliyya*) created to apply the newly established (and essentially non-Islamic) codes of law enacted by the Khedive. In 1895 he became a member of the newly formed administrative council of Al-Azhar University, and in 1899 the Khedive appointed him Grand Muftī of Egypt and a member of the Legislative Council, an advisory quasi-parliamentary body. As Muftī he was responsible for supervision of the system of religious courts—into which he managed to introduce some reforms—as well as giving formal advisory opinions to the Government on matters involving Islamic law. In addition to this, he revived a moribund practice of granting opinions to private individuals on their problems of personal belief and practice, and in this regard he issued a number of controversial *fatwās*. He died in 1905.

In our perspective in the following pages the degree of consistency, clarity, depth, and sustained intellectual commitment in 'Abduh's thought assumes an importance not always conceded by his commentators. All of them duly record the fact that these were not the qualities for which 'Abduh was noted, and many of them see this as a virtue, as of course in a way it was. In seeking to reconcile Islamic belief to the scientific age, they point out, 'Abduh was prudent and pragmatic, avoiding sharp breaks with traditional dogmatic formulas and elaborating what was novel in his thought only to the extent demanded by clear and present needs. By doing this he made his message more palatable to the orthodox and established a common ground of discourse between them and the products of modern secular education. Alternatively, it has been possible simply to note on how wide a front 'Abduh departed at least a little from tradition, even if he did not do so in a systematically thought-out way, and consequently to credit him with being, in his own indirect manner, a kind of radical. For example, as one very able study shows clearly, his theological departures amounted implicitly to a revival of Mu'tazilism, the systematically rationalist theological school of the early centuries of Islam, even though it is pointed out in the study that 'Abduh carefully avoided calling himself a Mu'tazilite and refrained from pursuing the implications in question to their logical conclusions.[2]

Both these observations are valid. 'Abduh was a conservative by language and manner and a radical by the implication of many of his teachings. For a reformer to be doctrinaire or systematic is not always a virtue, and one can admire the humane, tolerant, practical, conciliatory spirit that prevented 'Abduh from so being. It is not surprising that both 'Abduh's own generation and later ones have revered him as a great teacher.

Nonetheless, the limitations of his theology are historically no less important than the nobility of his character. While it would be unjust to speak of his failure, it needs to be recognized that his ideas provided a better basis for apologetics and polemics than for social reform and cultural rebirth.[3] Yet his theology, with all its limitations, was ac-

---

[2] Robert Caspar, "Le Renouveau du mo'tazilisme," Institut Dominicain d'Études Orientales du Caire, *Mélanges* IV (1957), 57–72.

[3] Three of the most recent studies of 'Abduh both establish this point convincingly. It is emphasized most strongly by Nadav Safran, *Egypt in Search of Political Community* (Cambridge, Mass., 1961), pp. 62–75. See also Binder, *The Ideological Revolution*, pp. 60–72, 95–106. Albert Hourani, in describing 'Abduh's debates with Gabriel Hanotaux and Faraḥ Anṭūn, writes: "But polemics have their danger: in defending oneself, one may draw closer to one's adversary than one thinks. It is significant that both his con-

cepted as a starting point where a more solid one might not have been. No one has dared, or seen the need, or enjoyed the necessary prestige, to improve on it.

The legal and constitutional doctrines of the classic Islamic tradition, exhumed and reformulated by Riḍā and other modernists, had been solidly grounded in an Ash'arite theology whose relevant characteristic in our concerns was its emphasis on divine voluntarism and rejection of naturalist concepts of authority and justice. Among modernists typified by Riḍā, an essential assumption has been that the "true" Islamic system of law and government of the age of the Founding Fathers, properly understood, was really based on natural principles, such as would seem to be required by the modern age. The rigid formalism and quietism commonly associated with the traditional dogmas must be the results of ignorance and error. Muḥammad 'Abduh's theology, and his occasional ventures into political and legal questions, encouraged this path of explanation but failed to provide a satisfactory intellectual framework that might enable it to succeed. In the first place the effort required a certain amount of historical distortion; in the second place one may wonder whether either 'Abduh or Riḍā really believed in all they said, or appreciated what it must mean. It was the reservations with which 'Abduh surrounded his own innovations that gave Riḍā reason in the first place to choose such unpromising models of traditional doctrine for modern revival, and in the second place to revive them in such an ambiguous and confused way that they could not possibly be given practical effect if taken at face value. It was possible for Riḍā to insist in abstract principle on the naturalism of Islamic legal and constitutional doctrines, without consistently interpreting their processes in the ways that naturalism would demand, because the theology introduced by 'Abduh to which Riḍā

---

troversies were concerned, not with the truth or falsity of Islam, but with its being compatible with the supposed requirements of the modern mind; and in the process, it may be that 'Abduh's view of Islam was itself affected by his view of what the modern mind needs. . . . It was, of course, easy in this way to distort if not destroy the precise meaning of the Islamic concepts, to lose that which distinguished Islam from other religions and even from non-religious humanism. . . . Once the traditional interpretation of Islam was abandoned, and the way open to private judgment, it was difficult if not impossible to say what was in accordance with Islam and what was not. . . . It was not an accident that, as we shall see, one group of his disciples were later to carry his doctrines in the direction of complete secularism" (*Arabic Thought in the Liberal Age* [London, 1962], pp. 144–145).

subscribed was not so thoroughly naturalist as it purported to be. It was only intermittently and incidentally naturalist on certain salient points while still marked with traditional nominalism on others. The naturalist elements are thus the impetus to reinterpretation in Islamic legal and constitutional doctrine, and for this reason need to be identified; likewise, their limits became the limits of the reinterpretation.

In searching for a religious and social doctrine in keeping with their efforts to lift Islamic society out of its tradition-bound inertia, Muslim reformers could consider the merits of two alternative natural law conceptions. The first would be to assign separate spheres of competence to reason and revelation, along lines roughly similar to the Thomist tradition in Catholicism. According to this view, God's creation of the world of nature, including human nature, in keeping with an Eternal Law, provides human reason with the necessary basis for determining the principles of social morality, while revelation addresses itself to spiritual questions of personal devotion and redemption.

Islamic thought has not inclined in this direction because of its own primary image of God as ever-present, ever-willing, and ever-creating. God is "wholly other" than His creation, but He cannot have withdrawn or detached Himself from it.

The second possibility is to recognize the parallel competence of both reason and revelation within the same sphere, denying that there is either a separation or a conflict between them. Specific divine commands may exist in matters immediately concerning ordinary social life, without the competence of reason thereby being devalued. Similarly, reason may be capable of reaching certain conclusions regarding the nature of the Deity or of the after-life. There are gaps, to be sure, but only random ones, in the subject matter of each kind of knowledge. Thus reason can discover the existence of God and identify His most important qualities, but can not determine the correct forms of worship; revelation prescribes all the details of the law of inheritance, but omits mention of the details of governmental organization. It was this approach, in which reason and revelation form an integrated combination, and which is more congenial to the Islamic religious outlook, that Muḥammad 'Abduh and many other modernists adopted.[4]

---

[4] An admirable statement of this position is given by Khalifa Abdul Hakim, "The Natural Law in the Muslim Tradition," University of Notre Dame Institute of Natural Law, *Proceedings*, V (1951), 29–65.

This type of naturalism departs from the long-established Ashʿarite tradition by its promotion of the potential of human faculties beyond the secondary role of merely elaborating the circumstantial applications of revealed commands. It adopts the position central to all natural law theories—that sound reason is capable of identifying right and wrong in their true forms, not merely as distorted images. Where Christianity saw original sin, Islam saw original inadequacy. Now this is changed. If reason falls short, it is only because it has been hampered by some other influence.

ʿAbduh himself described the main objects of his career as follows:

> I spoke out on behalf of two great causes. The first of these was the liberation of thought from the chains of imitation and the understanding of religious faith as the members of the early Community understood it before dissension arose, and the return of religious learning to its original sources, and consideration of religion in the scales of human intelligence that God created to repel the excesses of faith and diminish its errors and stumblings, so that the human social order prescribed by God in His wisdom may be attained. In this way religion may be counted the true friend of science, a stimulus for inquiry into the secrets of the universe, and an appeal to respect established truths and rely upon them in cultivating our spirits and reforming our actions. All this I have considered to be a single matter. In appealing on its behalf I found myself in opposition to the views of the two great groups of which the Community is composed: the devotees of the religious sciences and others of their type, and the devotees of modern techniques and their partisans.
>
> The second cause I adopted was the reform of the Arabic language. . . .
>
> I also made an appeal on behalf of another reform that people ignored and whose importance they did not seem to understand; nevertheless this reform is at the very basis of social life, and the Egyptians have fallen into decadence and have been humiliated by their neighbors only because they neglected it. This consisted of drawing the distinction between the government's right to the obedience of the people and the people's right to justice on the part of the government. I was among those persons who called upon the Egyptian population to recognize their right over their ruler—a notion which had not occurred to them for over twenty centuries. We preached the belief that the ruler, although he must be obeyed, is only a human being,

subject to error and prey to his passions, and that he can be deterred from these errors and passions only by the counsel that the Community gives him in word and deed.

But I later abandoned this question of political authority for fate to determine and for the hand of God to settle, for I realized that in such matters nations reap the fruits of what has been planted and cultivated over a long period of years, and that it is this planting with which we must now concern ourselves, with God's help.[5]

A. *General Attitude toward Reason and Revelation*

One of 'Abduh's most constantly stressed themes in his theological and apologetic writings is the essential harmony of reason, revelation, and individual moral temperament. When properly expressed and understood, there can be no conflict between them, although the fact that men often understand them in distorted form leads them to suppose that there are contradictions.

'Abduh's two leading works in this field of thought are the *Risālat at-Tauḥīd*,[6] which is a concise expression of his theology, and *Al-Islām wa 'n-Naṣrāniyya ma' al-'Ilm wa 'l-Madaniyya*,[7] which is a defense of Islam's attitude to reason and science as compared to that of Christianity. In the latter work he argues that certain problems in Muslim history, particularly the rigidity (*jumūd*) of the various sciences after the first four or five centuries of Islam, have been due to the accumulated crust of custom and habit superimposed on "true" human moral instinct (*al-wijdān aṣ-ṣādiq*), artificially making the latter appear to be in conflict with reason. There is no fundamental antagonism between the two so long as moral instinct is freely expressed and reason stays within its proper bounds (which are defined elsewhere). Each has its proper function. That of reason is to examine means and ends; that of temperament (heart, disposition, emotion) is to ascertain pain, pleasure, and other feelings. The two are the "eyes" of the human spirit: one for distant objects, the other for close ones; both are essential and are mutually supporting. "Complete religion is both knowledge and taste, heart and mind, evidence and acknowledgment, thought and

[5] Riḍā, *Tārīkh*, I, 11–12.

[6] The edition used is that of Cairo, 1351 H.; French translation by B. Michel and M. Abdel Razik, *Rissalat al-Tawhid*; *exposé de la religion musulmane* (Paris, 1925). Page citations below are to translation/original.

[7] Cairo, n.d.

temperament." Whenever there appears to be conflict between reason and temperament it is only because what is thought to be one or the other is really something else.[8]

This is a convenient loophole by which any contradiction of ʿAbduh's thesis can be explained away. The same sort of relationship, often with the same loophole, is conceived for reason and revelation.

Reason and revelation are different paths to truth and fulfill differing functions, but cannot contradict each other. "The Muslims are agreed," says ʿAbduh, "that if religion can reveal certain things to us that exceed our comprehension, it cannot teach us anything that is in contradiction with our reason."[9] If there appears to be a contradiction one or the other has been incorrectly understood. According to Rashīd Riḍā, ʿAbduh explained that the conclusions of both reason and revelation may be either decisive (*qaṭʿī*) or suppositional (*ẓannī*), with the decisive conclusion always taking precedence. What is decisive cannot be false, and therefore all decisive conclusions, whether revealed or rational, must always be in agreement; but most of the indications from both sources are of the suppositional kind, and therefore are subject to interpretation (*taʾwīl*).[10] It is reason, continues ʿAbduh, that confirms the validity and coherence of religious doctrine. Logical inconsistencies need not be accepted at face value. Still, when further rational investigation fails to reconcile the contradiction, the matter should be "committed to God in His omniscience"[11]—that is, a rational explanation exists although man has not discovered it.

The limits to the use of reason as conceived by ʿAbduh appear to fall within two categories. Sometimes they are inherent in the subject matter. At other times they are imposed not on the validity of reason itself but on the ability of individuals to make sufficient use of reason, so that rational conclusions must be guided or confirmed. The latter category applies to value judgments, and will be dealt with in the next section of this chapter. The first category includes such questions as free will and predestination, God's essence, and certain of His attributes.[12]

---

[8] *Al-Islām wa'n-Naṣrāniyya*, 142–144.

[9] *Risāla*, 6–7/8.

[10] Shakīb Arslān, *As-Sayyid Rashīd Riḍā au Ikhāʾ Arbaʿīn Sana* (Damascus, 1937), p. 690.

[11] *Risāla*, 88–89/129–130.

[12] He cites the ḥadīth, "Reflect on what God has created, but not on His essence, or you will perish." They are "rational" attributes which are part of the "Necessary Be-

ʿAbduh's position on free will is of interest not only because of his conclusion but also because of the process of reasoning by which he arrives at it. The process is a pragmatic one, in which conflicting rational arguments are weighed on the scale of utility. ʿAbduh's main concern in the free-will puzzle is on a psychological level, with the individual's consciousness of his ability or inability to determine his own actions and their consequences, rather than with a complete and systematic philosophy of causality. He finds it desirable to promote an assumption of free will, and had he wished to do so he could have adopted the full Muʿtazilite rationale in support of this assumption. But this would have violated his essential conservatism, by which he remained faithful to certain fundamental Ashʿarite formulas: in this case, God's transcendent and unique role as Creator of all things. The term *khalq* (creation), or *khāliq* (creator), belongs to God alone. Some Muʿtazilites had scrupulously avoided applying these terms to men's actions for fear of being charged with the blasphemy of *shirk* (derogation of the uniqueness of God), and instead used the term *mukhtariʿ* (producer, inventor); but most Muʿtazilites did speak of men as *khāliq*, explaining that men create their actions by a power implanted in them by God.[13] ʿAbduh appears to accept the spirit of the Muʿtazilite rationale but carefully eschews Muʿtazilite terminology, using neither *khāliq* nor *mukhtariʿ* and speaking only of *kasb*. *Kasb* was a term used by some of the more cautious Muʿtazilites to denote acquisition of the power of transitive action, but in ʿAbduh's own time it was a hoary symbol of Ashʿarite conservatism, denoting acquisition of no more than an illusion of authorship of acts for which the individual is nonetheless morally responsible. ʿAbduh interprets *kasb* in substantially the Muʿtazilite way, but the term is inevitably ambiguous, and connotes a link with orthodoxy which he has not entirely broken. He neither invokes the name of the Muʿtazilites nor acknowledges that his position is at variance with that of Ashʿarī, Ghazālī, and the other great masters of the Sunnī tradition.

In the *Risāla* ʿAbduh partially clears the ground for a free-will theory by carefully distinguishing between natural forces that are

---

ing" and are discernible through a type of first-cause reasoning; other attributes, notably the fact that God addresses Himself to man through prophets, are nonrational. But even knowledge gained through revelation is limited to the external forms. (*Risāla*, 32–37/44–52.)

[13] L. Gardet, *La Mesure de notre liberté* (Tunis, 1946), p. 21; Caspar, "Le Renouveau du mo'tazilisme, *op. cit.*, 168.

beyond men's control and limit their options, and men's own voluntary acts of choice. Limitations on freedom of action are not limitations on the will itself.[14] To claim free will for men is not to commit the heresy of *shirk*. *Shirk* would be implicit only in the attribution to anyone but God of freedom of action unrestrained by natural forces.[15] Here we find ʿAbduh adopting (but not acknowledging) the Muʿtazilite concept of "engendered" (*mutawallid*) acts, which are the unintended results of previous acts; these were distinguished by the Muʿtazilites from acts of volition, which enjoy the status of immediate causes (*asbāb*) and cannot be "engendered" because they can be modified by the will of the actor.[16]

Again, he draws a distinction between God's omniscience and the idea of predestination:

> God's omniscience encompasses what man accomplishes by his will. He knows that at such-and-such a moment man will perform an action that will be good and for which he will be rewarded, or some other action that will be evil and for which he will be punished. In all cases the actions follow from human effort and free choice, and nothing in God's omniscience prevents man from choosing to make the effort. The fact, on the other hand, that what God knows will happen inevitably does happen, is only because what is known to God is none other than reality, and reality does not change.[17]

But these considerations are no proof in themselves, and ʿAbduh admits that no firm proof is possible. There are, first of all, conflicting considerations:

> Consciousness and the senses testify that certain acts of a man are his own. . . . The Qur'ān also speaks of "what ye do," and "what your hands have acquired." . . . All the requirements of the Divine Law are based on the principle that a man is responsible for what he does. There would be no justice in holding a man responsible for something not within his power nor his will. . . . At the same time, there is no question that all things

---

[14] *Risāla*, 42–43/59–60.

[15] *Ibid.*, 43/61.

[16] Albert Nader, *Le Système philosophique des Muʿtazila* (Beirut, 1956), p. 198.

[17] *Risāla*, 45/64. The term "human effort" (*effort humain*) is used by Michel and Abdel Razik as a free translation of ʿAbduh's Arabic word *kasb*—a rendering justified in the context of ʿAbduh's meaning. Cf. the observation on this point by Osman Amin, *Muhammad Abduh: Essai sur ses idées philosophiques et religieuses* (Cairo, 1944), p. 82.

> originate with God and are attributable to Him. This is practically an instinctive recognition. . . . His power is also unquestionable. If He wished, He could rob us of the ability and will which He has given us. . . .[18]

Elsewhere he writes that

> Belief in predestination is supported by decisive arguments; indeed, man's natural disposition leads him to it. . . . The human will is but one of the links of the chain [of causality]. Will itself is an effect of perception, which stems from sensory feelings; ultimately all is to be traced back to the Supreme Being.[19]

But how to reconcile the conflicting possibilities is a problem that 'Abduh is content to leave unsolved. To seek an ultimate explanation would be "to seek to penetrate the secrets of Destiny, and it is forbidden to us to plunge into this abyss and occupy ourselves with what reason is virtually incapable of attaining."[20] Discussion of the free will issue has always proved fruitless in Christianity and Islam alike, and the alternative arguments only lead to "destruction of the Sharī'a, obliteration of obligations, and invalidation of that unpremeditated rational judgment which is fundamental to religious faith."[21]

Therefore 'Abduh arrives at his belief in free will by other means than examining the arguments for and against it on their own rational merits. This other method is to consider the question pragmatically in relation to other articles of belief, choosing the alternative most compatible with them. The belief that is evidently uppermost in his mind in this regard is faith in the destiny of the true Muslim Community.

---

[18] *Manār*, VI, 589–590, from 'Abduh's commentary on Sūra ciii of the Qur'ān ("Al-'Aṣr"). This translation is that of C. C. Adams, *Islam and Modernism in Egypt* (London, 1933), p. 154.

[19] "Al-Qadā' wa 'l-qadar," *in* 'Abduh and Jamāl ad-Dīn al-Afghānī, *Al-'Urwa 'l-Wuthqā* (Cairo, 1927), p. 107. In much of the '*Urwā* [as it will hereafter be cited] it is fruitless to try to separate the ideas of 'Abduh from those of Jamāl ad-Dīn. We are told that 'Abduh's function was to supply the language for his master's thought (Riḍā, *Tārīkh*, I, 289; Hourani, *Arabic Thought*, p. 110). The language, however, is crucial to the expression of the ideas that concern us here; they are substantially similar to those found in 'Abduh's own *Risālat at-Tauḥīd*, and in this instance there is no reason to abstain from associating 'Abduh fully with them. On certain other occasions the case is somewhat different (see below, pp. 138–141).

[20] *Risāla*, 43/61.

[21] *Ibid.*, This maintenance of contradictory positions without seeking final solutions is characteristic of Māturīdite theology. (See D. B. Macdonald, "Al-Māturīdī," *Shorter Encyclopedia of Islam* [*SEI*], p. 383.)

He comes to the conclusion that this faith in destiny cannot be effectively maintained, and indeed scarcely makes sense, unless accompanied by an assumption of free will.

This faith in destiny is a salient attitude in traditional Sunnī Islam. The Sharī'a is designed by God to bring worldly as well as spiritual success to man. Its social prescriptions are assumed to assure the best and most prosperous of earthly communities, provided that they are properly observed.[22] The demands of Sunnī apologetics against Shī'ite criticisms in Abbasid times made it fashionable for juristic writers to try to prove that the main body of Muslims had indeed observed the Sharī'a. This was done by systematically justifying, through legal fictions and otherwise, the political record of the Sunnī Caliphate to date. What this amounted to was an implicit defense of *ijmā'*. But at that time it could still be believed that Islam was enjoying the prosperous place in history that true belief was supposed to bring. Hence it was plausible to argue that the Community had in fact followed the correct path, even if it did require a rather tortured and artificial interpretation of certain procedures and events.

By the time of Muḥammad 'Abduh the historical picture is very different on two counts. First, the cleavage between Sunnism and Shī'ism on matters of political doctrine has long since lost its practical importance, so that the question of *ijmā'* is no longer a burning issue between them. Secondly, the social and political fortunes of the Community are in an evident state of decline, so that it is no longer plausible to suppose that the Community is enjoying the material rewards of righteousness. Either one must cease to believe that upright belief and conduct are rewarded in history or he must change his view of *ijmā'* according to which the Community as a whole is divinely protected from error. Between these alternatives it is clearly less painful and radical to suppress or revise the principle of *ijmā'*, imperceptibly at least, since this would not strike at the heart of the concept of God's justice, as the first alternative would do.

'Abduh, who wholeheartedly believed in the promise of worldly success for the righteous,[23] could only conclude that conditions in

---

[22] The virtual fatalism with which Ibn Khaldūn describes the rise and fall of empires has been ascribed to a belief on his part that human sin and pride and failure to follow the true path of faith as dictated by the Sharī'a are what condemn man to continuance of the cycle. (H. A. R. Gibb, "The Islamic Background of Ibn Khaldūn's Political Theory," *Bulletin of the School of Oriental Studies*, VII [1933], 31.)

[23] See *Risāla*, 100/144, where it is stated that the Qur'ān established laws for man's

society that are evidently good or bad must stem from correct or incorrect religious belief and practice.[24] There is, then, an empirical or pragmatic check on doctrines drawn by purely deductive reasoning from the primary sources of revelation: if history has not rewarded the Muslims, somehow in their beliefs they must have gone astray.[25]

But it would be a distortion of this position to suppose that this pragmatic check can be built up into a direct source of doctrine in its own right, to the point where a particular religious belief (e.g., on the question of free will) is determined inductively by deciding what theoretical position will produce the best results. For then belief ceases to be a matter of faith and becomes only a working hypothesis or simply a mere device. Faith in destiny does not mean submitting individual beliefs to the test of their immediate results. Rather, it involves trust that over a long period of time, the natural forces by which God limits human freedom of action will help devout men achieve their worldly purposes rather than frustrate them. The faith in question is religious faith, not faith in nature. An investigation of natural forces in order to calculate what course of action is most expedient to accomplish practical goals is one thing; such an investigation in order to decide what religious belief is most expedient is quite another.

It would be a suspect approach, therefore, to assume that since belief in predestination of the individual's will seems to have an undesirable social effect, the belief must be discarded, regardless of the logical arguments for or against it. On the other hand, ʿAbduh found the arguments themselves inconclusive on both sides. What appears to have led him to an espousal of free will was not simple utilitarianism but the consideration that religious belief was itself undermined by the idea of predestination.

---

interest which bring prosperity and justice when followed, and calamities when ignored.

24 For a detailed study of the influence of the Muslim faith in historical destiny on Egyptian modernists, see Wilfred Cantwell Smith, *Islam in Modern History* (Princeton, 1957), chap. i: "Islam and History," and chap. iii: "The Arabs: Islamic Crisis."

25 Religious beliefs, write ʿAbduh and Afghānī in *Al-ʿUrwa ʾl-Wuthqā*, determine actions; therefore bad actions can only be the result of false beliefs. If doctrines are improperly transmitted or grasped, the result will be an unwitting deviation by the believer from the true principles of the faith, and eventually religion itself will be discredited and innovations and corruption will appear. This, they say, is what has happened in the case of the doctrine of free will and predestination. (*ʿUrwa*, pp. 102–103).

This connection is spelled out in one of 'Abduh's earlier writings on predestination—an article in the journal *Al-'Urwa 'l-Wuthqā*—in which the implication is clear that the true meaning of the phrase *al-qaḍā' wa' l-qadar* is not predestination but destiny. Faith in this concept, he says, has been the impulse in Muslim history to courage and action. He who trusts in God has the sense of observing God's will without fear of the consequences of possible failure. This is the meaning of the Qur'ānic verse, "Those who, when they were told, 'The people are gathered against you,' were only increased in faith and replied, 'God is sufficient for us, and most excellent is He in whom we trust!' "[26]

This faith, the article continues, is the antithesis of the doctrine of the Jabriyya ("compulsionists") of early Islam that "there is no difference between an individual moving his jaw to eat and its being moved by shivering from cold."[27] It is the Jabriyya doctrine that has a weakening psychological influence and leads men to accept tyranny and lack social conscience.[28] Eventually, it is suggested, false belief can only lead to the discredit of religion itself.[29]

The apparent implication is that it is not sheer material utility that is at stake but the religious attitude and religious ethics, with which faith in destiny is associated. 'Abduh and Afghānī have judged the doctrine of predestination not in the light of its apparent material effects but in the light of the religious attitudes that must accompany or follow from it.

A full rationalization of free will in relation to God's omnipotence remains absent, and this is unavoidable; but the way is clear in 'Abduh's mind for a wholehearted presumption in its favor. In his commentary on the Sūrat al-'Aṣr he concludes:

> It is therefore the duty of every Muslim to believe that God is the Creator of everything, in the manner He knows; and to acknowledge that his own deeds are to be attributed to himself, as his own instinct tells him; and to act . . . [righteously] by exercising that power of choice which he finds within himself. And beyond that, he is not required to lift up his vision to what lies beyond all this.[30]

---

[26] Q. iii:173, quoted in *'Urwa*, p. 109.

[27] *Ibid.*, p. 106.

[28] *Ibid.*, pp. 104–105, 107–109.

[29] *Ibid.*, pp. 102–103 (cited above).

[30] *Manār*, VI, 589–590; trans. Adams, *Islam and Modernism*, p. 154.

In the sense that he has chosen between two equally plausible doctrinal positions, his procedure might be called a theological version of *istiḥsān*. In the sense that his choice of doctrine is made on grounds of promoting an already established desideratum, it is comparable to the type of *istiṣlāḥ* known in legal terminology as *dharī'a*.

These methods, signifying a mild and cautious pragmatism in the domain of jurisprudence, might appear to constitute a more striking innovation when applied to theology. Insofar as Islamic theological schools—including both the Ash'arite and the Mu'tazilite—had been characterized by the systematic elaboration of dogma, tempered by the mysticism of the Ṣūfīs on the one side and the "illumination" (*ishrāq*) of the philosophers on the other, rather than by any tradition of pragmatism, this appearance is borne out. In another sense, however, what passes here for pragmatism is simply 'Abduh's distaste for pure speculation and his reluctance to probe the roots of fundamental theological problems when their direct relevance to the needs of the individual believer is not established.[31] This is a conservative position not unlike that of those medieval theologians (e.g., Ibn Ḥanbal, al-Ash'arī, al-Ghazālī, Ibn Taimiyya) who had inveighed against the speculations of the philosophers. As 'Abduh enjoined Muslims "to believe that God is the Creator of everything, in the manner He knows," and "not lift up their vision to what lies beyond," so al-Ash'arī had insisted, almost nine centuries earlier, on enumerating God's attributes *bilā kaif*, that is, without seeking explanation.

It is characteristic of 'Abduh's concern for the social effects of religious belief that he takes pains to show that Islam gives due regard to man's material needs. "In Islam, life takes precedence over religion," he writes. Islam does not impose physical hardships on men by requiring asceticism or abstinence. In the rules governing prayer, fasting, and the like, exceptions are always made when necessitated by consideration for the individual's welfare. "The health of bodies takes precedence over the health of religions." Various Qur'ānic verses are cited to show that God created the Earth for man's use.[32]

---

[31] Caspar notes 'Abduh's practice of "covering his most audacious positions with names as venerated as those of Ash'ari and Ghazali. . . . He systematically avoided taking a position in controversies involving ideas that had no direct influence on the reforms he propounded; he repeated in these cases that one must avoid scrutinizing these problems—an attitude that caused him to be accused of agnosticism" (Caspar, "Le Renouveau du mo'tazilisme," *op. cit.*, p. 161).

[32] *Al-Islām wa 'n-Naṣrāniyya*, pp. 74–76.

Furthermore, according to 'Abduh, Islam forbids excess of religious zeal (*al-ghulūw fī 'd-dīn*). Man should not be overly concerned with the afterlife to the detriment of this one. "God reminds us that the Hereafter can be achieved while enjoying God's blessings in this world." The Muslim's best way to show gratitude to God, then, is to use his mind in quest of material progress.[33]

It is interesting to compare this presentation with the following passage by al-Ghāzalī, whom 'Abduh generally considered one of his sources of inspiration:

> We say that the right ordering of religion is only accomplished by the right ordering of the mundane world. . . . If it should be said, "Why do you say this? . . . Nay, it is accomplished only by the ruin of this world, for the religious and the mundane are mutually antagonistic, and working to cultivate the one is to ruin the other"—we should reply, "These are the words of one who fails to understand. What do you mean by 'the world'? It is an expression of several meanings. In one sense it may refer to an excess of easy living and pleasure, and more than what is necessary and essential; in another sense it may refer to all that one needs before his death. One of these meanings is contrary to religion and the other is of prime importance to it." Thus he errs who fails to distinguish between the various meanings of ambiguous expressions. When we speak of the right ordering of religion we mean that state of knowledge and piety which are only attained with a healthy body, preservation of life, and assurance of the necessities of life, such as clothing, shelter, food, and security. . . . In truth, he who is secure in his heart, is sound in body, and has his daily bread, may as well have the whole world given to him. . . . The Faith could not be firmly established without the attainment of security in these essential necessities.[34]

There is a marked difference in emphasis between the two writers. 'Abduh describes material well-being as having an importance of its own which even "takes precedence" over acts or expressions of devotion. What he seeks to show is that religion is no impediment to worldly prosperity. For Ghazālī, the need is to show that worldly prosperity is no impediment to religion, and is in fact necessary for it as a means to an end; and the end is faith.

---

[33] *Ibid.*, pp. 77–79.
[34] *Al-Iqtiṣād fī 'l-I'tiqād* (Cairo, 1320 H.), p. 105.

B. *The Elements of a Natural Law Theory*

It was observed in chapter ii that Ash'arite theology, with its assumption that the workings of nature were the result not of a regular system of physical laws but rather God's custom, was not well suited to a concept of natural law. It was also observed that the Ash'arites did, however, assume that God's custom was unchanging and dependable. If that assumption should be strongly enough emphasized, the difference between God's custom and physical laws would be of less significance and in many minds might virtually disappear. This appears to have been the case with 'Abduh: he seized upon the notion of *sunnat Allāh* and, disdaining to split hairs, went on practically to equate it with an ordered system of nature. The shift from Ash'arism was for 'Abduh not one of doctrine but of emphasis and attitude. He continues to use traditional terminology, and one feels at times that he has arrived at new conclusions without quite coming to grips with some questions that should be fundamental to the subject.

This seems to be the case in his attitude on miracles. He takes pains to show that Islam rejects the idea of miracles, and that it is Christianity that has been so unscientific and credulous as to make them an article of faith.[35]

A miracle, in 'Abduh's writings as well as in traditional terminology, is called *khāriq al-'āda:* literally, the infringement of what is usual or customary. The expression is better suited to the Ash'arites than to 'Abduh, for what it suggests is that what God habitually causes to happen (*sunnat Allāh*) does not happen on a particular occasion. The Ash'arites taught that God customarily causes the sun to rise in the morning and set in the evening, and therefore could appropriately apply the words *khāriq al-'āda* to irregularities, with no more than the outward meaning of the words implied. But the natural-law theorist, while he might refer to physical laws as God's customs, necessarily means much more, and miracles for him are much more than unusual events: they are outright contradictions of established, fixed principles, and therefore irrational. 'Abduh's reason rebels against miracles in this way, and so he denies that they have any place in Islam, and yet he continues to use the expressions *sunnat Allāh* and *khāriq al-'āda,*[36] and apparently does so not simply as a matter of respecting

---

[35] See especially *Al-Islām wa 'n-Naṣrāniyya,* pp. 19–20, 52–53, 58.

[36] Instead of coining more appropriate expressions such as *aḥkām al-khalīqa* and *khāriq al-ma'qūl* respectively.

traditional usage but because he has not entirely discarded the idea of the immediate presence of God's will in natural events.[37] But he refuses to see any issue implied in the words themselves:

> The *sunan* are those well-established paths along which all things take their course and in accordance with which effect follows cause; they are what are also called *sharā'i'* or *nawāmīs*, and some people call them *qawānīn*. But what difference does it make to us, in view of the variety of expressions in which the Qur'ān declares that the order of human society, whatever may happen in it, is a single order, unaltered and unchanging, and that whoever seeks happiness in this society must look to the sources of the order . . . ?[38]

'Abduh's position here is not fundamentally different from that of the Ash'arites, although there is an important shift in emphasis. God adheres to His custom without change, not out of physical necessity but out of moral necessity implicit in His essence: it is unthinkable that He would engage in imperfection after willing what is perfect (i.e., the laws of nature). 'Abduh writes: "Islam has shown that the great phenomena of the universe follow a custom which God has fixed in His eternal knowledge and which no accident can modify."[39] God's custom, then, as 'Abduh conceives it, is equivalent from the practical point of view to the physical laws of nature. But this is true only from the practical point of view; by *sunnat Allāh* 'Abduh literally means custom and nothing more.

'Abduh admits one exceptional miracle recognized by Islam: the Qur'ān. The miracle of the Qur'ān was necessary to establish proof of the prophecy of Muḥammad. Significantly, the miraculous element according to 'Abduh was not in logical contravention to the processes of nature, but only lay in the fact that the Qur'ān is superhuman in eloquence and spiritual insight. Hence the customary term for "miracle" in this instance is *i'jāz al-Qur'ān* ("the surpassingness of the Qur'ān"), although 'Abduh also uses the term *khāriq al-'āda*, which in this case is equally appropriate from the Ash'arite and naturalist points of view.[40]

Despite the limitations in 'Abduh's naturalism in the subject of

---

[37] E.g., *Risāla*, 43/61: The sin of *shirk* is defined as ascribing to anyone but God freedom unconstrained by natural forces, above the level of apparent causes.

[38] *Al-Islām wa 'n-Naṣrāniyya*, p. 58.

[39] *Risāla*, 118/175. Cf. Michel and Razik, *Rissalat*, pp. lxii–lxiii.

[40] For 'Abduh's position see *Al-Islām wa 'n-Naṣrāniyya*, pp. 53–55.

miracles, there is no doubt of his intention: to render Muslim religious doctrine harmonious with the modern scientific spirit by denying any contradiction between the two. Recognizing that ʿAbduh was a reformer and apologist rather than a metaphysician, one can only accept his rejection of miracles as a first step toward a general position of natural law, and proceed to examine his particular views on the normative and epistemological issues set forth in the preceding chapter.[41]

His treatment of these questions follows one course for individuals and another for groups. For the individual the starting point of ʿAbduh's thinking is man's ability to distinguish for himself between good and evil—to determine the norm of right behavior—through a combination of esthetic instinct and rational calculation of utility. The obligatory character of the norm is then supplied by religious consciousness, which informs him that it is God's will that the norm be adhered to on pain of punishment in the afterlife. The norm, in other words, is inherent in what man perceives in his environment and is determined by proper use of natural human faculties, while the sanction is beyond nature and rational perception.

For the group, the starting point is perception not of the norm but of the sanction, from which the norm can be inferred. The sanction in the case of the group is material and worldly, and can therefore be rationally perceived, whereas for the individual this is not the case. Groups are rewarded and punished on earth for their deeds and misdeeds. By taking heed of the fate of other groups—that is, by the study of history and sociology—they are led to seek the patterns of conduct that will bring them success. These they then discover through collective reason.

The norm prescribed for the individual, then, is natural in the sense that his natural faculties discover it from natural data. But his adherence to it is an act of religious faith, since he has no assurance of material reward for his adherence, and the utility of his actions is not necessarily utility in his own interest. The group's norm is natural in all senses, but primarily in the sanction. It is discovered by natural human faculties (though only in their collective form), with the aid of the natural data of the sanction. The group's adherence, unlike the individual's, is motivated not by religion but by material self-interest. Therefore it does not really matter whether the group determines the norm inductively by studying past history or deductively by calculat-

[41] See above, pp. 57–58.

ing the long-term expediency of alternative future courses of behavior, except that perhaps the first is more reliable since it is empirical.[42] There is of course a certain overlap with the natural ethic of individuals, in that articulate individual members of society possessing a strong moral sense may succeed in bringing the group as a whole to accept the religious imperative in certain situations; but this is not ʿAbduh's dominant note.[43] For if societies and individuals bear moral obligations that are ultimately similar in substance, the modes of perception and implementation are different. We need see nothing esoteric, or even peculiarly Islamic, in ʿAbduh's view of the matter. As every politician and social thinker knows, large groups tend to respond most readily to considerations of collective self-interest rather than collective moral duty, and the surest path to public acceptance of the latter is through appeals to the former.

Religion is thus logically essential to ʿAbduh's conception of natural law in relation to individuals but not to groups. The distinction was not altogether new in Islamic thought, though ʿAbduh came to it in his own way and for his own purposes. The point was later to be reiterated by ʿAbduh's disciple Rashīd Riḍā, who asserted that a nation that behaves justly receives its reward in history whether its people are Muslims or unbelievers,[44] while individuals are recompensed on the Day of Judgment not simply for outward behavior but in accordance with the sincerity of their devotion. Furthermore, ʿAbduh held that the role of prophecy and religion differs in relation to individuals and groups. To individuals, prophets bring religious awareness and knowl-

---

[42] Possibly ʿAbduh speaks only in terms of the first method because it is susceptible to religious overtones: the record of nations of the past is referred to as *sunan Allāh fī 'l-umam* ("God's customs toward nations")— a good classical expression which it was natural for ʿAbduh to use, whatever his intent, but which suggests the immanence of divine will in a manner convenient to ʿAbduh's theological interest.

[43] See, for instance, *Risāla* 85–86/125–127.

[44] *Manār*, IX, 56, citing Q.iii:117: "And whatever good they do, they will not be denied the meed thereof." This indicates "that God will not destroy a nation on account of its idolatry, if otherwise it does justice and observes the rules of progress," according to Riḍā (see Adams, *Islam and Modernism*, p. 141). Ibn Taimiyya, of whom Riḍā was an enthusiastic student, wrote that "God supports the just state even if it be non-believing but does not support the unjust state even if it be Muslim" (*Al-Ḥisba fī 'l-Islām* [Medina, n.d.], 82). Niẓām al-Mulk cites the ḥadīth, "A government may subsist with impiety, but it cannot last with oppression and tyranny" (C. Schefer, tr., *Siasset Nameh* [Paris, 1893], pp. 9–10). Ghazālī cites the same in the *Naṣīḥat al-Mulūk* (see Ann K. S. Lambton, "The Theory of Kingship in the Naṣīḥat al-Mulūk of Ghazālī," *Islamic Quarterly*, I [1954], 54).

edge of the spiritual sanction; to groups, they bring not knowledge so much as the religious spirit of love and brotherhood, without which no group succeeds in practicing justice.

We come now to a more detailed examination of 'Abduh's treatment of individuals and groups respectively.

1. Individual natural law

'Abduh's theory of the good is expressed concisely in a few pages of the *Risāla*.[45] An admirable résumé of the essential ideas in the light of classical theology and philosophy is given by Osman Amin,[46] whose analysis seems to suggest that 'Abduh's liberalism here, as elsewhere, finds its antecedents in Mu'tazilite doctrine, resurrected to fit certain contemporary needs.

In the *Risāla* 'Abduh uses the terms *ḥasan* and *qabīḥ* to describe good and bad not only in the moral sense but also in the sense of esthetic or intellectual perfection or imperfection, and in the sense of utility of harmfulness. This ambiguity is inherent in the usage of the Arabic terms. While 'Abduh is careful to make the necessary distinctions, he is apparently quite content that the ambiguity should exist and that concepts of esthetic beauty, utility, and moral desirability should all be expressed by the single word *ḥasan* and be discussed as distinct but inseparable parts of the same whole.[47]

'Abduh first discusses esthetics. Material objects are judged beautiful or ugly according to their completeness, harmony of color and form, and so on, and while individual tastes may vary, they do so only in degree. Everyone finds certain flowers beautiful, or certain mutilations of natural forms repulsive. "So although tastes may differ, things are beautiful or ugly in themselves."[48]

The same is true of ideas: all men tend to be attracted to ideas of a certain quality, involving concepts of completeness, perfection, moral elevation, or strength of character. The only difference here is that the

---

[45] *Risāla*, 46–50/66–73. A summary without critique is found in Adams, *Islam and Modernism*, pp. 165–166.

[46] Osman Amin, *Muhammad 'Abduh*, pp. 92–99.

[47] Osman Amin, who also refers to the ambiguity of the term *ḥasan* (*ibid.*, p. 92), notes that the three categories in which 'Abduh uses the term are familiar in medieval speculation: perfection, suitability, and praiseworthiness or meritoriousness (*ibid.*, p. 95). The last of these categories, which signifies moral or religious virtue, becomes known only through revelation, as we shall see presently.

[48] *Risāla*, 47/67.

medium of perception is intellectual rather than sensory; we are still dealing with esthetics.[49]

Third, human actions have a certain esthetic value commonly attached to them, just as objects and ideas do. Examples are found in athletic coordination and musical virtuosity.[50]

These types of esthetic value constitute what ʿAbduh calls things that are "good in themselves." A second category includes those things that are good or beautiful not in themselves but by virtue of their effects and consequences. This may be true of material objects—for example, bitter medicine—or, more important, of voluntary human actions. (Nothing is said for the moment of the consequences of ideas.) An action is beautiful or ugly according to its direct consequences of pain or pleasure, or, more subtly, according to its more indirect utility or harmfulness.

> The harm, in this case, proceeds from the brevity of the pleasure compared with the duration of the sufferings that follow . . . and from the disproportion between the intensity of the pleasure and the force of the pain.[51]

Such a lack of proportion between immediate pleasure and ultimate utility leads us to regard with distaste such actions as robbery and manslaughter, no matter how unpopular the victim, because "these acts carry the germ of a general insecurity that extends even to the person committing the violence."[52]

It is apparent that this second class of actions—those that are good or bad according to their effects rather than in themselves—is not entirely removed from the field of esthetics, although it is clear that it depends on intelligence rather than mere sensitivity for its value determination. The esthetic appreciation is only transferred by one step: from the thing itself to the thing it leads to. We weigh—esthetically—the action or the object together with its effect and compare the two. When we picture to ourselves something that is distasteful in itself but whose effects are clearly desirable, these effects "change our psychological condition, and the beauty (*jamāl*) of the effect casts the rays of its splendor on the subject" (which produced the effect).[53]

---

[49] *Ibid.*

[50] *Ibid.*, 48/68.

[51] *Ibid.*, 49/70.

[52] *Ibid.*, 50/71.

[53] *Ibid.*, 48/68.

Utility and esthetic beauty, then, are inseparable, and what is useful is determined by man's intelligence in accordance with the dictates of his apparently instinctive esthetic appreciation. ʿAbduh continues:

> The human mind has known these things [i.e., consequences] for a long time. It has divided them into harmful and useful, and has called the former bad actions and the latter good actions. It is on this division that the distinction rests between virtue and vice [*faḍīla wa radhīla*]. Human thought has defined them more or less precisely according to the degree of intelligence of the thinker, and has made dependent on them the happiness or misery of man in this life . . . although those persons who have been able to do so with any degree of correctness have been few in number.
>
> Voluntary actions are beautiful or ugly [*ḥasan wa qabīḥ*] either in themselves, or by their particular or general consequences. Man's reason, together with his senses, can distinguish beautiful actions from ugly ones, according to the different significations we ascribed to them above, without need to find support in revelation [*simʿ*: lit., what he hears, i.e., what he is told by God].[54]

But the fact that reason and esthetic instinct are suitable to determine what is naturally good (beautiful) or bad (ugly) does not mean that they always succeed in doing so. Very few persons, according to ʿAbduh, are able to use their reason with complete success in determining the utility or esthetic perfection of actions or in reaching essential ethical truths. The great mass of men are held back by imbalance in their psychological makeup, by false hopes and desires, by distorted perceptions, by a sense of rivalry, and so forth. Consequently, few persons reach by rational means an understanding of the true principles of utility in this life, not to mention the principles of preparation for the hereafter.[55]

This explains one function of revelation: the Divine Law makes up for the deficiencies in human nature. It confirms reason and lends certainty to its conclusions when reason is right, and corrects and supplements it where it has been misguided. It also enumerates certain special duties which cannot be determined by reason, such as ritual exercises. Only revelation can give man any certainty as to the substance of his beliefs and principles.[56]

[54] *Ibid.*, 50/71–72.
[55] *Ibid.*, 52–54/73–77.
[56] *Ibid.*, 55–57/80–82.

But revelation has another function that is still more important. If human faculties need confirmation from revelation in determining what the true ethical norms are, they need still more help in providing man with a decisive impulsion to follow these norms. For this impulsion must be primarily religious, coming from consideration of the prospects of the afterlife. If it were true, says ʿAbduh, that reason could discern these prospects, revelation would again be only supplementary:

> If then a thinker succeeds in demonstrating the existence of God and His rational attributes by the sole force of his reason, without benefit of revelation, as has been the case for certain peoples; if after that he deduces, in a correct or incorrect manner, that the survival of the human soul after death involves felicity or hellfire; if he establishes that this felicity after death is obtained from acknowledgment of God and the practice of virtues, and that the soul is given over to hellfire when it ignores God and indulges in vice; if, finally, he concludes that among actions there are those that are useful for the soul to gain felicity after death, and others which are harmful to it and expose it to hellfire—if he can deduce all this, what rational or dogmatic impediment can forbid him to say, relying only on reason, that acknowledgment of God, the virtues, and all the acts that follow from this acknowledgment are obligatory for us, while vice and all that it entails are forbidden to us? Who is to prevent him from setting forth the rules that he judges good and calling other men to share his beliefs and to act as he does? All this is permissible, so long as there is no provision in the revealed Law to contradict it.[57]

Knowledge of the existence of God and His major attributes can indeed be deduced by reason, as ʿAbduh has explained earlier in the *Risāla*.[58] But all the rest, involving rational discovery of the afterlife, is pure hypothesis, and ʿAbduh goes on to indicate that he does not believe that it is possible.[59] What the above passage does make clear is that the norms of religious virtue and the norms of utility and esthetics are the same in substance. The possibilities of hellfire and salvation are not norms but sanctions, which lend the character of obligation (as

[57] *Ibid.*, 51/73.

[58] *Ibid.*, 34/48 f.

[59] Osman Amin is apparently mistaken in citing this passage as evidence of the wide extent of ʿAbduh's rationalism and assuming that ʿAbduh does think it conceivable for reason to detect the nature of the afterlife. (*Muhammad ʿAbduh*, p. 96.)

distinct from mere desirability) to the norms. The Māturīdite school of medieval theology taught that good and evil could be known by right reason, but that the obligatory character of virtue could only be known from revelation. This is 'Abduh's position as well:

> The obligation to perform actions that are commanded or simply recommended, and to avoid or disapprove actions that are forbidden, in the manner prescribed by the Sharī'a, which determines the appropriate rewards and penalties—all this reason cannot attain to by itself. The only way to know, then, is by revelation. This is not to deny that what is commanded is already good, in the sense that it leads to worldy or other-wordly benefit. . . .[60]

Revelation, then, does not endow actions with the quality of good or evil, but only defines the obligation. What is commanded is "already good" (*ḥasan fī dhātih*) for reasons man can understand; the basis of value is not in God's will but in the essence of His creation. This is good Mu'tazilite doctrine; the Māturīdite element lies in the revelationary nature of the obligation.[61]

This Māturīdite qualification by 'Abduh is crucial to his whole discussion of ethics. It means that reason can tell men *what* they should or should not do,[62] and revelation tells them the most compelling reason *why* they should or should not do it.[63]

But since reason is often obscured or distorted in its operation by other human qualities, it seldom proves adequate even for its own primary role, and therefore most men need the confirmation of revelation to help them decide *what* they should or should not do. And furthermore, although reason, together with the senses, can provide limited, practical, instinctive reasons why one should behave a certain way in a certain situation, these reasons lack psychologically compelling force, and therefore the religious imperative becomes neces-

[60] *Risāla* 56–57/82.

[61] Cf. J. N. D. Anderson, "Reflections on Law: Natural, Divine, and Positive," *Proceedings* of the 940th Ordinary General Meeting of the Victoria Institute (December, 1956), p. 15. D. B. Macdonald writes that 'Abduh in the *Risāla* "showed himself a Māturīdite with no mention of Māturīdī" (article "Al-Māturīdī," *SEI*, p. 363).

[62] With certain exceptions such as ritual duties.

[63] Elsewhere 'Abduh maintains that human nature is naturally attracted by good rather than evil, so that revelation only recalls man to his own inclinations. (*Tafsīr Juz' 'Amma* [Cairo, 1922], pp. 17–18, 90; cited by Amin, *Muhammad 'Abduh*, p. 109.) But these human inclinations are not the same as obligations, and they are less effective because they are subject to misguidance.

sary. Very few men, observes 'Abduh, have any understanding of Plato or Aristotle, and were they given a simple explanation of their philosophies, most men still would not be led to improve their character or conduct. The only effective way to impress the need for virtuous conduct on them is by appealing to their sense of religious awe and mystery.

> When have we ever heard that a class of people have made the good triumph in their actions solely on the grounds of the utility that this good offered for the masses or the elite, or that it prevented evil simply because it would have led to corruption and ruin? This has never occurred in human history and is not in accord with human nature. The foundation of good habits rests only in dogmas and tradition, and these things themselves have no other basis than religion. Therefore . . . religion's power over men's minds is greater than the power of reason that is peculiar to them.[64]

But this, of course, is only a psychological argument, and does not mean that reason has no role in examining the truth of religious doctrines.[65] While religious and rational experience differ from each other, representing respectively the knowledge of the philosopher and that of the believer, the substance is the same. "The Sacred Law came only to indicate what [already] exists, and does not itself create goodness."[66] And prophecy only makes obligatory duties that are rationally comprehensible to all.[67]

It is consistent with this point of view for 'Abduh to remark, in his commentary on the Qur'ān, that what is good is called ***ma'rūf*** (lit., "recognized" or "known") and what is bad is called ***munkar*** (lit., "denied") in the classical phrase ***al-amr bi 'l-ma'rūf wa 'n-nahy 'an al-munkar*** (commanding good and forbidding evil) because good and evil are "recognized" or "denied" by rational judgment. God orders virtue because it is naturally good; it does not become good only with

---

[64] *Risāla*, 85–86/125–127. It should be noted that for 'Abduh, revelation is a type of of intuition, and therefore—since here he speaks of the specifically religious intuition of personal conscience—there is no need in this case to distinguish between the substance of the two. (See *Risāla*, 73–76/108–111: Revelation [*al-waḥy*] is "knowledge that a man finds within himself, with the certainty that it comes from God. . . ." It is received by prophets and passed on to others. Intuition [*al-ilhām*], by contrast, is a general feeling whose origin is not clearly sensed.)

[65] *Ibid.*, 89/130.

[66] *Ibid.*, 56/80. Se also Amin, *Muhammad 'Abduh*, p. 97.

[67] *Risāla*, 55/80; Amin, *Muhammad 'Abduh*, p. 98.

His command.[68] "God has sent down two books: one created, which is nature, and one revealed, which is the Qur'ān. The latter leads us to investigate the former by means of the intelligence which was given us."[69] And still more explicitly: "The Qur'ān itself is too elevated in character to be in opposition to science."[70]

This means that for 'Abduh, though intuition or revelation may be the most effective path to spiritual devotion,[71] the claims of reason as regards the substance of its attainments are fully recognized: rational knowledge is as full a representation of Truth as intuitive or revelationary knowledge in practical matters. Accordingly, in the practical field of social ethics and politics, as well as in science, reason must be granted a wide role, and needs to be guided by revelation or intuition only in its general moral orientation. This becomes apparent in 'Abduh's writings on political and social questions.

2. *Group natural law as an approach to politics*

"The Qur'ān speaks of creation," writes 'Abduh, "in such manner as to stimulate men's minds to follow the course natural to them and discover the original character of things and the rules that regulate them. . . . In many verses the Qur'ān calls us to take heed of the signs of God in nature."[72]

Elsewhere he writes:

> The universe has laws [*sunan*] in the composition of precious stones and the rocks, in the growing of plants, in the life of animals, in the assembling of bodies and their scattering, in their composition and dissolution. This is what we designate as the secondary origin.[73]

More important than the physical laws governing things, however,

[68] 'Abduh, *Tafsīr Sūrat al-'Aṣr* (Cairo, 1926), p. 19; cited in Amin, *Muhammad 'Abduh*, p. 99.

[69] *Manār*, VII, 292, cited in Adams *Islam and Modernism*, p. 136; see also Goldziher, *Die Richtungen der islamischen Koranauslegung* (Leiden, 1920), pp. 352–353, for fuller quotation.

[70] *Manār*, IX, 334–335, cited in Adams, *Islam and Modernism*, p. 138; Goldziher, *Koranauslegung*, pp. 356 ff.

[71] Abdel Razik and Michel, in the introduction to their translation of the *Risāla*, remark that in this respect 'Abduh is closer to such modern philosophers and theologians as Harnack and William James than to the Mu'tazilites, but that in practical questions he is unquestionably rationalist. (*Rissalat al-Tawhid*, p. xlix.)

[72] *Al-Islām wa 'n-Naṣrāniyya*, pp. 49–50.

[73] Adams, *Islam and Modernism*, p. 140 (no source given).

are the laws governing the destinies of human groups. Although more often than not these laws are expressed by ʿAbduh in religious terms that refer to God's punishment, reward, warning and so forth, what we have in effect is an acknowledgment of historical and sociological principles that might have been phrased in nonreligious terms without destroying the content.

There is, for example, an effort on ʿAbduh's part to read the Darwinian theory of evolution into interpretation of the Qur'ān.[74] The pertinent verse is Q. ii:251: "Had God not repelled some of the people by means of others, the earth would have been corrupted." This, says ʿAbduh in his Commentary, is a general custom of God and is today commonly referred to as the struggle for survival (*tanāzuʿ al-baqā'*).

> Some intruders into the science of God's custom with societies suppose that the struggle for survival is only an effect of the materialism of the present age and that it is the materialists who instituted and pronounced this idea, which is contrary to the teaching of the Faith. But if those who say this understood the meaning of human nature or understood themselves, they would not say what they do.[75]

The verse confirms God's custom known today among sociologists and biologists as "natural selection" (*al-intikhāb aṭ-ṭabīʿī*) or "survival of the fittest" (*baqā' al-amthal*), explains ʿAbduh; the earth would have been corrupted were it not for this process of elimination.[76]

Given ʿAbduh's purpose of stimulating a spirit of moral responsibility in Muslim society, it is natural that he should repeatedly cite the Qur'ānic verse (xiii:11): "God will not change the state of a people until they change what is in their hearts. . . . " These words taken alone are easily misinterpreted, for in their full context they refer not to change for the better but for the worse. It has been alleged that ʿAbduh's failure to cite the remainder of the verse (" . . . and if God willeth misfortune for a people there is none who can repel it, nor have they a defender beside Him") represents a deliberate evasion by him of its deterministic implications.[77] The surrounding passages in the

---

[74] ʿAbduh was an acquaintance and an admirer of the social Darwinist Herbert Spencer, whose work on education he translated into Arabic from the French version, but did not publish.

[75] *Manār*, VIII, 929–930.

[76] *Ibid.*

[77] P. J. Vatikiotis, "Muhammad ʿAbduh and the Quest for a Muslim Humanism," *Islamic Culture*, XXXI (1957), 115.

Sūra make it clear, however, that the verse in question emphasises not divine capriciousness but the inexorability with which the retribution of history is visited upon those societies that deserve it. This theme is amplified as follows:

> Nations have not fallen from their greatness, nor have their names been wiped off the slate of existence, except after they have departed from those laws which God prescribed with supreme wisdom. God will not change the state of a people from might and power and wealth and peace, until that people change their own state of intellectual knowledge and correctness of thinking and perception, and consideration for the works of God toward previous nations who went astray from the path of God and therefore perished. Ruin overtook them because they turned aside from the law of justice and the path of insight and wisdom . . . and chose to live in falsehood rather than die in the aid of truth.[78]

There are two ideas in this passage that can, each in its own sense, be called "law." First there is the moral law prescribed in revelation which mankind is warned to follow. Second, there is the inexorable law of history, which decrees that ruin shall overtake those groups who do not follow the moral law. The moral law, being in keeping with sound human judgments and instincts and being dictated by considerations of long-range advantage for the group, is comparable to the Western concept of natural law. The law of history—God's custom, or *sunnat Allāh*—belongs in a class with the physical laws of nature. It is not a moral code in itself but only its sanction. It is misleading, therefore, to equate *sunnat Allāh* with natural law, as some writers have done.[79] Natural law is the moral code prescribed by the Sharī'a and by sound human faculties; God's custom constitutes the promise and threat of the historical process, of which men are advised to take account.

'Abduh has relatively little to say about the norm itself. Knowledge of it is apparently more or less presupposed, derived from other indications applying to individuals (the group then being a collection of individuals), or vague reference is made to the imperative of "justice," or—more extensively—to the conclusions of the nation's representa-

---

[78] "Sunan Allāh fī 'l-Umam," in *'Urwa*, pp. 222–223; also published in Rashīd Riḍā's compilation of 'Abduh's writings in the second volume of *Tārīkh*, pp. 323–324. Translation here is that of Adams, *Islam and Modernism*, p. 141.

[79] E.g., Adams, *Islam and Modernism*, p. 140; Michel and Rāzik, *Rissalat, op. cit.*, p. lxii.

tives in consultation.[80] We find considerably more references to the lessons of history and sociology, including both an exposition of group patterns of behavior and identification of the factors influencing group success or failure; of the latter the most important is religion. Since it is on this earth that societies reap their punishments and rewards, this course of study enables those who follow it to profit from the trials and errors of past generations and thereby learn the path to the good life. The norm, in other words, is learned from the sanction.

A detailed account of some of these sociological principles is given in one of 'Abduh's early articles, "*Ash-Shūrā wa 'l-Qānūn*" (consultation and statutory law), written in 1881.[81]

> The social structure of a nation, in the beginning, has no motivating force except chance or other compelling causes such as misfortunes which overtake man and drive him to seek a refuge. . . . Once the society is set in order and its members feel secure . . . they fall to rivalry and disputation of all kinds imaginable . . . so that though they live together in one place they become separated in their purposes . . . unwilling to sacrifice their own interests for the sake of others. . . . Finally the one with the strongest support among them seizes power over the rest . . . without controls or restraints. At such a time no two men will share common opinions or related goals . . . For the causes of their troubles have led each of them to restrict his attention to his own immediate concerns, and never to think of the rights of the society and the kinship of its ties. . . .
>
> But if with the succession of events they learn something of the conduct of other nations they will recall that they once had rights as a group which would lead them to a prosperous life. . . . Then they will resolve to redress their society in accordance with those principles that its nature demands. They will be held back by their acqiured qualities of character, but as their social impulses grow in strength they will become increasingly impatient of delay, and they will set to work to clear away the dross of their corrupted qualities. Their impulses to activity grow and their intentions come to be directed toward a single goal, namely, the maintenance of the society . . . . They have not learned this at the feet of a teacher, for it is necessity that is the master whose teachings are remembered and unfailing.[82]

---

[80] See "Ash-Shūrā wa 'l-Qānūn," *Tārīkh*, II, 213–218 (from *Al-Waqā'i' al-Miṣriyya*, Dec. 25, 1881).

[81] *Ibid.*

[82] *Tārīkh*, II, 213–215.

ʿAbduh continues by suggesting that once this natural spirit is regained it is the collective intelligence in the form of public opinion (*ar-ra'y al-ʿāmm*) that determines the proper norms of behavior. This enlightened public opinion is the "focal point on which all types of diverse ideas converge and by which personal aims are erased, since in truth they are not personal aims, though they may appear as such; rather they are varying paths to the same end. . . . [This is] the most expeditious and natural course."[83] In these words ʿAbduh refuses to admit the existence of any real conflict of interests within society, not only between subjects but presumably also between subjects and rulers. An enlightened public will

> . . . only be satisfied by a just law worthy of their condition, in accordance with their character and habits. . . . [But] they are unwilling to confide the task of instituting this law to a single one of their number, since a single individual is unable to interpret the [seemingly] divergent interests of all.[84]

Then follows a plea for representative government,[85] which we may by now suppose is "naturally" the best form once the population is enlightened.[86]

The particular content of the laws should vary with the circumstances. What is important is to establish a unity of concern and outlook within the society.

> It is enough for individuals to set themselves to aspire to the truth and to seek to arrange their interests in a way compatible with those of the country and the circumstances of people. And let it not be imagined that the just law based on liberty is that which is modeled entirely on the civil principles and political foundations of other countries. . . . Many a law is suited to the interests of one people but not to those of others. . . .[87]

In this article ʿAbduh has arrived at his conclusions without refer-

---

[83] *Ibid.*, 215.

[84] *Ibid.*

[85] *Ibid.*, 215–216. But this does not mean democracy: "There is no harm in some of the population being uninformed, such as the lowest class and the workers, even if they are large in number, for they perform the function of deaf instruments, limited to bodily activities alone" (*ibid.*, 216).

[86] "From what we have said, it is clear that the best and most beneficial of laws is that emanating from public opinion." (*Ibid.*).

[87] *Ibid.*, 216–217.

ence to religious teachings. It is by virtue of the *nature of human society* that men are well advised to apply their collective intelligence to the circumstances in which they find themselves, and this fact they can discover simply by examining the record of other nations. On purely rational grounds he seeks to establish that laws should be based on the interests of the group and that collective reason, when freed from the "dross of [acquired] corrupt qualities," finds individual and group interests to be one and the same. Collective intelligence corrects the errors of individual reasoning. For the individual cannot rise above the desires, ambitions, and personal inclinations with which he is surrounded, even should he have the will to do so, except through cooperation with others. This is true for ruler and subject alike.[88]

This assumption of the community of the interests of all enables Muḥammad 'Abduh to view the principle of consultation (*shūrā*) as a genuine restriction on the ruler's power.[89] The Western political theorist, accustomed to drawing a sharp distinction between benevolent dictatorship and formally limited authority, can only be skeptical of the enthusiasm with which modern Muslim apologists have so often claimed that the *shūrā* represents an indigenous principle of representative or constitutional government in Islam. As long as the ruler appears free to accept or reject the advice he receives, the Western student refuses to see any real limitation of authority at all.

But this skepticism ignores a vital assumption in 'Abduh's case: that in the light of right reason conflicts of interest simply dissolve away. Since consultation supplies a check on the ruler's reason and rectifies any apparent divergence in his interests from the nation's, consultation becomes in practice a check on his exercise of authority, and thus the virtual equivalent of a check on his authority itself. What for the Western thinker is perhaps the assumption of original sin, according to which politics is the process of adjustment of inevitably selfish and conflicting interests, is for Muḥammad 'Abduh no more than the handicap of the isolated individual intelligence, naturally surmountable by consultation. *Shūrā* is thus to be contrasted not simply to isolated judgment but even to unilateral decision. The sincere desire on the ruler's part to benefit from the wisdom of his counsellors is implicit. It is a time-honored assumption in traditional

[88] See the article "Ash-Shūrā," *Tārīkh*, II, 210–213 (from *Al-Waqā'i' al-Miṣriyya*, Dec. 24, 1881).

[89] See "Ash-Shūrā wa 'l-Istibdād," *Tārīkh*, II, 203–210 (from *Al-Waqā'i' al-Miṣriyya*, Dec. 12, 1881).

Islamic political literature that wide knowledge of the Law and consultation with the 'ulamā' by the ruler would serve to assure just rule.[90] What 'Abduh gives us is essentially a modern version of this assumption.

All this, however, presupposes that the nation has reached a mature stage of intellectual development, and until it has done so the quality of government cannot rise above that permitted by the attitudes of society.

> The ruling power is dependent on that of its subjects, and takes no steps unless on the latter's part there is some directing impulse to do so. We do not deny that the ruling power must be depended on to take the actual steps and compel or persuade the subjects to accept them; but only insofar as the subjects will tolerate it. The diversity of forms of governments and changes in their laws are dependent on the dictates of the national spirit, which means, in reality, the condition of the subjects. . . .[91]

This means that the changes in social outlook must precede sweeping reforms. 'Abduh continues:

> In sum, the form of civil order in a society is only the image of the substance of the characteristics its members have acquired through the habits and customs that have grown in them, whether praiseworthy or reprehensible. The different laws they have had in their periods of rise and decline cannot be detached from these characteristics, no matter how much those laws may have changed in form or subject matter. This has been recognized by those wise persons who have striven first of all to change people's characteristics and manners, whenever they wanted to to establish a well-defined order in the society. They therefore gave priority to good education. . . .[92]

It is therefore not surprising that, together with his pleas for representative government, 'Abduh could equally assert that "only a just dictator can cause the East to progress." Fifteen years under such a

---

[90] See Niẓām al-Mulk, *Siasset Nameh* (French trans.), 82–83, 124–126. This idea appears closely related to what Leonard Binder calls the "pious Sultan theory" according to which government receives religious sanction from the justice of its performance rather than the legitimacy of its origins (*Religion and Politics in Pakistan* [Berkeley and Los Angeles, 1961], pp. 35–38).

[91] "Ikhtilāf al-Qawānīn bi 'khtilāf Aḥwāl al-Umam." *Tārīkh,* II, 171–172 (from *Al-Waqā'i' al-Miṣriyya,* June 19, 1881).

[92] *Ibid.,* 172.

ruler, he estimated, would enable the Muslim East to prepare itself for the first steps in representative government.[93]

The concept of historical development is further spelled out by 'Abduh and Afghānī in the '*Urwa*, in psychological terms:

> Intellectual concepts, religious beliefs, and other spiritual phenomena and perceptions, although the inspiration of actual behavior . . . are in turn confirmed, strengthened, and imprinted in men's minds by such behavior. . . .
>
> To be sure, man is man by virtue of his thought and belief, although those of his perceptions that are reflected in his mind have the strongest effect upon him. Every perception occasions a thought, every thought gives rise to an impulse, and out of every impulse arises an action; then the process reverts in turn from action to thought. And so thought and action continuously act and react on each other as long as the spirit remains in the body, each side reinforcing the other.[94]

This psychological principle of reinforcement serves to explain Muslim political lethargy: long accustomed to quietism and acceptance of tradition, the Muslims are naturally the slower to accept active reform, for the higher ideals of Muslim brotherhood and political supremacy are mere mental images not reinforced by action.[95]

> If any of them realizes the truth and perceives what would bring honor to his nation and return its past glory to it, this will be considered foolishness and delirium. Or it is supposed that should he respond to an appeal to his conscience, this would only bring down destruction and catastrophe upon him. . . .[96]

Thus the individual is overwhelmed by his environment.

The theme of unity of spirit and outlook in society is brought out in 'Abduh's earlier writings, especially those composed under Afghānī's inspiration in the '*Urwa*, again and again. This message is carried in God's custom (i.e., the lessons of history). God punishes man only with just cause—for his failure to use his God-given ability to distinguish between right and wrong by collective judgment and to follow the course he recognizes as best for his material and spiritual interests.[97]

---

[93] "Innamā yanhaḍ bi 'sh-sharq mustabidd 'ādil," *Tārīkh*, II, 450–451 (from first issue of *Al-Jāmi'a 'l-'Uthmāniyya*; no date given).

[94] "Inḥiṭāt al-Muslimīn wa Sukūnuhum wa Sabab Dhālik," '*Urwa*, pp. 74–75.

[95] *Ibid.*, pp. 76–79.

[96] "Māḍī 'l-Umma wa Ḥāḍiruhā wa 'Ilāj 'Ilalihā," '*Urwa*, p. 46.

[97] "Asbāb Ḥifẓ al-Mulk," '*Urwa*, pp. 202–203.

Although reason alone indicates the evils of social disunity, the Qur'ān itself adds further warnings; for example: "Do not quarrel, else you shall fail and your strength shall leave you."[98]

Cooperation is necessary because the isolated individual is weak and shortsighted even in discerning his own best interests, let alone those of the group. Thus the extent of consultation necessary is commensurate with one's responsibilities and authority.[99] "No king is overthrown, no throne overturned, except because of division and controversy [within the society]," or because of exclusive use of one's own judgment, misplaced confidence, or allowing the intrusion of foreign elements.[100]

The influence of Ibn Khaldūn,[101] as well as that of Jamāl ad-Dīn al-Afghānī, strongly suggests itself in a statement in the *'Urwa* that unity and political supremacy are mutually interdependent. No nation, the reader is told, can prosper without a cohesive and aggressive spirit. "This is God's custom with human societies. Their lot in history depends on the extent of their share of unity, and their measure of greatness is in accordance with their perseverance in aggressive competition (*al-ghalba*)."[102] A united spirit is only to be achieved through the selflessness of individuals in the interests of the group.[103]

The potential strength of such unity must be directed to the advantage of Islam. The decline of Muslim political fortunes from their glorious past has been due chiefly to "rivalry of the seekers of power among themselves," which has led to dependence on foreign sponsors and consequently the loss of Muslim independence in certain territories.[104]

This united and aggressive spirit is reminiscent of Ibn Khaldūn's repeated reference to "group solidarity" (*'aṣabiyya*) as the indispensable source of political success for society. In the *'Urwa* the terms *'aṣabiyya* and *ta'aṣṣub* are used as synonymous and attention is called to the relatedness of their respective usual meanings of "group solidarity" and "fanaticism" or "zealotry": the distinction is only one of

---

[98] *Ibid.*, p. 203 (Q. viii:46).

[99] "Asbāb Ḥifẓ al-Mulk," *'Urwa*, pp. 205–206.

[100] *Ibid.*, p. 208.

[101] 'Abduh delivered a course of lectures on Ibn Khaldūn at the Dar al-'Ulūm college in Cairo in 1878. Although prepared in book form under the title *Falsafat al-Ijtimā' wa 'l-Tārīkh* ("Philosophy of Society and History"), they were never published (see Adams, *Islam and Modernism*, pp. 41, 121).

[102] "Al-Waḥda wa 's-Siyāda," *'Urwa*, p. 142.

[103] *Ibid.*, pp. 142–143.

[104] "Al-Waḥda 'l-Islāmiyya," *'Urwa*, pp. 134–135.

degree, regardless of which term is used. In the former (more moderate) sense, it is a desirable quality, for much the same reasons as those adduced by Ibn Khaldūn:

> If *'aṣabiyya* is weakened in a people, God casts failure upon them, and they become heedless of one another. The result of such heedlessness is severance of the bonds between them, and dispersion follows, which facilitates infiltration among them by foreigners. Thereafter they will never rise again until God once more causes the spirit of *ta'aṣṣub* to descend upon them.[105]

But it also has its excesses, in which case it becomes a curse rather than a blessing, leading to the abandonment of justice in the community. It was in this sense that the Prophet said, "He who appeals to *'aṣabiyya* is not one of us" (i.e., is not one of the Community of believers).[106]

The *'Urwa* article goes on to declare that although it is fashionable in the modern age to blame religious *ta'aṣṣub* (in the sense of fanaticism) for the ills of ignorance, lack of social conscience, and backwardness, the truth is that the *ta'aṣṣub* of believers (in the sense of unity in purpose and action) is the greatest of blessings when tempered with the spirit of moderation and tolerance.[107]

There is a sharp distinction to be drawn, however, between religious and secular-nationalist *ta'aṣṣub.* The former is "purer, more sacred, and of more general benefit;"[108] the "foreigners" have encouraged suspicion of religious solidarity because they know that it is the Muslims' strength, while by vaunting secular nationalism they create divisions among the Muslims. "All intelligent persons know that the Muslims know no [true] nationality other than their religion and belief."[109]

In this article the predominant voice appears to be that of Jamāl

---

105 "At-Ta'aṣṣub," *'Urwa*, pp. 89.

106 *Ibid.*, pp. 89–90.

107 *Ibid.*, pp. 91–92.

108 *Ibid.*, p. 95.

109 *Ibid.*, 96. Ibn Khaldūn's treatment differs on this point. While affirming that religion is the only sound and lasting basis of empire (chap iii, sec. 4–6), he maintains that *'aṣabiyya* in the sense of clan solidarity is also necessary. "A religious appeal without solidarity will not succeed" (chap. iii, sec. 6; Rosenthal, p. 322.). He cites the ḥadīth, "God never sends a prophet except with protectors from among his people" (*ibid.*). Religious kinship in Ibn Khaldūn's terminology is not treated as a type of *'aṣabiyya*, though its effectiveness is not denied. But it would be stretching a point to equate Ibn Khaldūn's *'aṣabiyya* with modern nationalism.

ad-Dīn al-Afghānī rather than Muḥammad 'Abduh's. This applies even more to another article in the *'Urwa* on "Nationality and the Islamic Faith," which declares that a proper religious attitude removes the psychological origins of nationalism (*ta'aṣṣub al-jinsiyya*) which lie in the necessity of self-protection amidst the conflicts caused by competing material interests. A nationality is an evolved group dedicated to the defense of common interests. But "we cannot say that nationalism is natural [i.e., inborn], although it may be a characteristic common to all mankind, inscribed in their souls by the force of necessity. . . . Were the need for this type of group spirit to cease, the spirit would also cease. . . . "[110]

In this article we see nationalism conceived as a divisive rather than a unifying spirit—a cover, in fact, for tyranny and injustice. With the substitution of religious for nationalist loyalties, say the authors, there would no longer be a need to endure tyrannical government, for the ruler would join the people in submission to the "highest ruler" (God), whose law he would enforce, and would thereby win the people's confidence. "They would dispense with national spirit for lack of need for it, and its traces would be erased from men's souls."[111] But if the ruler fails in his duty to rule according to the Sharī'a without selfishness or discrimination, the people will inevitably fall back on *'aṣabiyya* and nationalism, and the ruler's power will be reduced as a result.[112] On the other hand, a ruler who does rule according to the dictates of Islam is assured of success without the need to spend large sums, maintain a large army, and so forth. "He can dispense with all this by following the path of the Rāshidūn caliphs and returning to the primary sources of the righteous Islamic faith."[113]

All this suggests something very different from the general line of 'Abduh's thought as we have traced it in the preceding pages. This article from the *'Urwa* announces, in effect, that the general principles of social behavior which we usually suppose to be "natural"—not only grouping together for self-protection in the struggle for survival, but the struggle itself—dissolve into nothing when men have been given a taste of Sharī'a rule by their leaders. The religious kinship will then be

---

110 "Al-Jinsiyya wa 'd-Diyāna 'l-Islāmiyya," *'Urwa*, pp. 38–39.

111 *Ibid.*, pp. 39–40.

112 *Ibid.*, pp. 41–42.

113 *Ibid.*, p. 43. This is another facet of the "pious Sultan" tradition: virtue in the ruler assures the virtue and welfare of society.

accepted by man as the basis for government without need of constraint, and hence can be said to be ultimately more "natural."

What, then, does Islam prescribe in the way of political relationships? The authors of the article give us only a general answer:

> The foundations of the Islamic religion are not limited to calling mankind to the truth and to the realization that the nature of their souls is spiritual, summoned away from this base world; rather, it ensures this by setting forth the limits of transactions among men and clarifying their rights, in both a general and a particular way, and by setting limits to the enforcing authority that undertakes to give effect to the revealed laws, apply the prescribed penalties, and define their circumstances of application.

This ensures that government will be neither tyrannical, hereditary, nor based on power, privilege, or wealth. "Rather it will derive only from dependence on the ordinances of the Sharīʿa, the necessary power to enforce it, and the satisfaction of the Community."[114]

It is, then, the revealed Law that defines the correct relationships in society, "in both a general and a particular way." Yet since application of this Law finds a ready and willing response among men, it is apparently "natural" in the sense of being in harmony with human nature and human needs.

By contrast, in the previously cited writings authored by ʿAbduh alone[115] and even in a number of other pieces in the *ʿUrwa* penned by ʿAbduh even if inspired to a greater or lesser extent by Afghānī, the moral is pointed in another direction: revealed law either goes unmentioned altogether or assumes no central importance, and the suggestion is made that the remedy for social and political ills could be found through the process of consultation, and that in fact societies are normally impelled to this by the study of history (i.e., "God's custom").

The conclusions are not contradictory, but the paths leading to them are strikingly different: one pragmatic and rational, the other religious and messianic. ʿAbduh's instinctive preference for the pragmatic and rational path of argument, which emerges in so much of his writing, even early in his career when he wrote for *Al-Waqāʾiʿ al-Miṣriyya*, did not preclude his readiness to express in *Al-ʿUrwa*

---

[114] *Ibid.*, p. 40.

[115] See especially "Ash-Shūrā wa 'l-Qānūn," *Tārīkh*, II, 213–218.

'l-Wuthqā the messianic notions of his mentor Jamāl ad-Dīn. For it was characteristic of his thought that the revealed principles of Islam should be seen as corroborating those of rational observation and consultation. In both cases similar formulas emerge: protection of individual rights, limitation of the executive power, and abolition of privilege. We might expect to find an acknowledgment of this mutual corroboration somewhere in the '*Urwa*, but in fact we do not, and the presumption that here 'Abduh was speaking more for Jamāl ad-Dīn than for himself seems particularly strong. Much later, in his theological work *Risālat at-Tauḥīd*, 'Abduh was to explain the point implicitly, by saying (in another context) that "prophets play the same role in relation to peoples that intelligence does in relation to individuals."[116]

Nonetheless, the two paths of rational observation and consultation on the one hand, and revelation on the other, are less susceptible of harmonious interpretation than might at first appear. The general burden of most of 'Abduh's writings on social, political, and historical matters—including his contributions to the '*Urwa*—is in his acceptance of the idea of evolution, development, and variation in society.[117] By this is meant not the straight-line evolution spoken of in the Qur'ān—according to which mankind received a series of prophecies culminating once and for all with the final and authoritative message of Muḥammad, so that the final stage of social progress became accessible to all the world almost overnight—but rather the notion of constant change and adaptation within society, in which progress is relative to circumstances of tradition and environment and is always to be measured in terms of human achievement rather than cataclysmic enlightenment. It was only in terms of those assumptions that he could argue that the Community can best regulate its interests by collectively counseling with itself to determine those interests, that systems of law and government vary from people to people in suitability, and that history rewards those groups who show a spirit of initiative in improving their lot. The idea of Muslim society becoming suddenly transformed by a new attitude of piety and enforcement of the detailed provisions of the Sharī'a law by the ruler seems, in the

---

[116] *Risāla* 81/118.

[117] Vatikiotis, "Muhammad 'Abduh and the Quest for a Muslim Humanism," *op. cit.*, 125: "Throughout his active teaching and writing, Muhammad 'Abduh actually came very close to introducing into Islamic thought an evolutionary concept of historical development."

light of the bulk of 'Abduh's writings, as much an "infringement of custom" (*khāriq al-'āda*) as the miraculous contraventions of physical nature which he so adamantly rejected.

Further suggestions that 'Abduh did not consider revelation a sufficient path to knowledge in the social and political field are found in his chapters on prophecy in the *Risāla*. In establishing the second of his "proofs of the necessity of prophecy," 'Abduh argues that society needs as a binding tie not only a community of material interests but also love (*maḥabba*). Such love is purest when it does not depend on material interests but is self-sustained. Only men with unusual moral insight have a clear conception of this love in its pure form and are able to distinguish it from mere equity or justice (*'adl*), which depend only on widespread reasonableness, and to recognize that men too frequently are not guided by reason.[118]

The role of the prophet is to infuse the spirit of love into society by so using his moral qualities as to win the confidence of his fellow men and then enlighten them in the mysteries of God's nature, of which man is aware but whose substance only exceptional individuals can rationally understand. Thus by sending prophets, God compensates for the spiritual (rather than intellectual) deficiencies of human nature in society.[119]

Prophets play the same role in relation to groups as intelligence does in relation to individuals: to "purify the mind of the blemishes of passions that lead it astray, to discipline its faculties, and to instill in it what will bring it happiness in this world and the next."[120] This is a purely spiritual function. Prophets do not come to explain the practical details of material welfare but leave this to man's ingenuity, within the broad and tolerant limits of sound religious faith. The social rules enunciated by prophets are no more than the most general principles of fraternal love and mutual respect of rights, by which the common interests will be assured.[121] But prophets are not bearers of practical or scientific knowledge. "All these are among the means of acquiring prosperity and reaching contentment, to which God has led man by the faculties with which He has endowed him. . . . But the laws of the prophets did generally encourage man to strive by his own

[118] *Risāla*, 65–70/96–103.
[119] *Ibid.*, 70–73/103–107.
[120] *Ibid.*, 81/118; see also *Tafsīr al-Qur'ān*, ii, 287.
[121] *Risāla*, 82/119–120.

efforts for the means to achieve that degree of perfection for which God prepared human nature."[122]

Prophets and the revelation they bring, then, are conveyors in the social sphere not primarily of knowledge but rather of spirit and motivation, by which reason is guided in the right path.

Even in the *Risāla*, however, 'Abduh's break with the tradition of the millennial view of history and his espousal of evolution were incomplete and equivocal. Having in effect dismissed the legislative role of prophecy with one hand, he summoned it back on the stage with the other:

> The Qur'ān established for men laws conforming to their interests; the utility of observing them and applying them has been proved. Justice is established by them and the whole social order has been organized by them as long as their limits are respected. But great harm resulted from neglect or avoidance of them and from men's estrangement from the spirit they promoted.[123]

Is this again the revivalism of Jamāl ad-Dīn, still coexistent in 'Abduh's mind with the influence of Herbert Spencer? So it would seem. Here as elsewhere in the full range of his thought, 'Abduh hedged his espousal of secular notions and avoided a clear-cut rejection of orthodox conceptions, with ambiguous results.

Despite such survivals of traditional doctrine, on the whole it is the natural law approach that is dominant in 'Abduh's attitude. It is thus not surprising that the principle of *ijmā'* should represent a very different thing to him than to the orthodox jurists and theologians. The orthodox idea of *ijmā'* referred to the agreement of the Islamic Community on certain hitherto unresolved questions and in certain circumstances, as an infallible source of law and doctrine, in keeping with the ḥadīth "My Community will never agree upon an error." Since the limitations were severe—only unanimity on points of fact and interpretation, not subject to review by later generations, was recognized—it was possible to regard *ijmā'* as an indirect, inspired kind of revelation, and therefore much more than a mere aggregate of personal opinions; it enjoyed a value equal to Qur'ān and Sunna, or even superior to them according to some scholars.[124] It was in reaction to this

---

[122] *Ibid.*, 83/122.
[123] *Ibid.*, 100/144.
[124] See for instance the quotation from the Ḥanbalī jurist Ibn Qudāma (d. 1223) given

that Ibn Taimiyya had restricted the validity of *ijmā'* to the consensus of the very first generation of Muslims in matters concerning the implementation of statements and actions of the Prophet. Questions undecided by them, according to this conception, would be left not to later *ijmā'* but to individual or collective conscience.

For 'Abduh *ijmā'* appears to be a much more informal principle, being only the expression of collective rational judgment and conscience, not too different perhaps from what Ibn Taimiyya had in mind for the later Community but preferred not to call *ijmā'*. When the jurists are in voluntary agreement, says 'Abduh, with the interests of the Community in mind, they should be obeyed, "for it can be said that they are free of error in their consensus"; but this is so not as a matter of dogma but only of reasonable expectation.[125]

Ijmā' defined in this way loses its revelationary infallibility and no longer posses the classic problem of how it can be institutionalized without corrupting its special character. It is no longer necessary to distinguish between reason and *ijmā'*, for the latter is now only the collective aspect of the former. This new approach, of course, has been made possible by the fact that 'Abduh has first of all raised the value of reason to a higher status than was traditionally assigned to it, so that any exercise of judgment, whether in the traditionally recognized form of *ijmā'* or otherwise, is valid and true, so long as it is indeed based on sound reason and not a distortion of it.[126] But since men are usually imperfect in their mastery of reason and do not submit exclusively to its dictates, their image of the truth—collectively or individually reached—is often distorted unless guided by revelation. Therefore it was only natural for 'Abduh to ignore certain traditional

in H. Laoust, *Essai sur les doctrines sociales et politiques de Taḳī-d-Dīn Aḥmad b. Taimiya* (Cairo, 1939), pp. 241–242, for a sweeping declaration of the supremacy and infallibility of *ijmā'* as a legal source.

[125] See J. Jomier, *Le Commentaire coranique du Manâr* (Paris, 1954), p. 193; Laoust, *Essai*, p. 551.

[126] Laoust writes that for 'Abduh, "reason is, after the Qur'ān, the essential source of doctrine, although its relation to revelation does not appear clearly in a doctrine ['Abduh's] that seems to have been so unconscious of contradictions. *Naṣṣ* and *'aql* were, for Ibn Taimiyya, different manifestations of the same reality. For Muḥammad 'Abduh religion . . . is a brake which God has given us to avoid the exaggerations of human reason and diminish its errors" (*Essai*, p. 551).

But there is nothing in Laoust's words here to show why—as he seems to imply—it should not be said that to 'Abduh, as well as to Ibn Taimiyya, revelation and reason are "different manifestations of the same reality."

dogmas, supposedly sanctified by *ijmā'*, in some of his pronouncements, since *ijmā'* as he conceived it was always subject to review.

Here once again, we find 'Abduh's manner of proceeding to be discreet and inexplicit. Among the handful of *fatwās* he issued to private petitioners as Muftī of Egypt, a number caused a considerable stir because they seemed to contravene the established conservative consensus. Yet in each case, 'Abduh managed to make his point in such a way as to avoid any overt confrontation of principle. The most famous of his *fatwās*, the so-called Transvaal *fatwā*, offers an illustration of this. A member of the small Muslim community in the Transvaal sought guidance on the following questions: (1) Is it permissible for a Muslim in a predominantly Christian country to wear a European-style hat? (2) Is it permissible for him to eat meat slaughtered by Christians according to their own manner, without assurance of conformity to the stipulations of the Qur'ān concerning the method of slaughtering? (3) Is it permissible for Ḥanafīs and Shāfi'īs to hold public prayer together, led by a single imam, despite the differences in ritual between the two schools?

'Abduh answered all three questions in the affirmative. Here we need concern ourselves only with the first two. In the first case the underlying issue was whether the adoption of European headdress constituted "conformity" (*tashabbuh*) and consequently a reprehensible sign of disloyalty to Islam, perhaps even making the wearer of the hat formally an unbeliever. 'Abduh avoided becoming involved in complexities by simply stating that as long as the intention was not to abandon Islam, the question of *tashabbuh* did not arise, and that as long as some consideration of social convenience was at stake, the act could not be considered reprehensible (*makrūh*). He could have overtly raised the question of *ijmā'* had he wished, and discussed the traditional view of such matters, even if only to reject it. Or he could have declared the whole issue meaningless, on the ground that the true Islamic religion leaves a man to follow his own judgment in such mundane situations; indeed, in making the individual's intention the decisive element, he may seem to have implied as much. But he did neither of these things, and in fact his friends among the Egyptian '*ulama*' made haste to support his judgment by that most conservative of devices, an appeal to ḥadīth, in noting that the Prophet on several occasions had worn foreign garb as a matter of convenience.[127]

---

[127] C. C. Adams, "Muḥammad 'Abduh and the Transvaal Fatwā," *The Macdonald*

On the question of slaughtering meat, the essential conditions laid down for Muslims by the Qur'ān (verses ii:168, v:4, v:6) are that the victim should not die of itself or from a blow but by its throat being cut, and that the name of God should be pronounced over it at the time of slaughtering. There was doubt in the case at hand as to whether the Christians of the Transvaal met the first of these conditions: after striking the victim with an ax they cut its throat, but whether they did so before or after the extinction of life was unknown. Again, whether they met the second condition could not be known. Presumably they did not; but in any event the four orthodox rites of Sunni Islam differ over the necessity for Christians and Jews to do so in order to render the meat lawful to Muslims. Muḥammad 'Abduh declared both these issues of detail irrelevant to the case by invoking the verse v:7: "Lawful for you today are good things, and the food of those to whom the Book has been given is lawful for you and your food is lawful for them." Whatever Christians accepted as food for themselves, in other words, was acceptable for Muslims; and as assurance of this condition, 'Abduh stipulated that the Christian clergy, as well as the laity, should consider the meat lawful for themselves.

On this question, in short, 'Abduh was careful to respect the religious relevance of the problem put to him, and to base his permissive conclusion on a Qur'ānic verse, avoiding such questions as, for example, whether meat slaughtered by pagans would be lawful food for Muslims, or whether the Transvaal Christians did or did not conform to the stipulations of the preceding Qur'ānic verses. It is noteworthy that Rashīd Riḍā found it desirable to provide cover for his master by elaborating an affirmative answer of his own to the latter question.[128]

C. *'Abduh as a Political Thinker*

It would be fruitless to try to present 'Abduh's political ideas as a systematic structure. After taking much interest in politics in his early years he underwent a change in attitude and confined his writings to social, religious, and judicial matters. Even his early articles in *Al-'Urwa 'l-Wuthqā* and *Al-Waqā'i' al-Miṣriyya* dealing with political

---

Presentation Volume (London, 1933), pp. 17–20. Many years later 'Alī 'Abd ar-Rāziq, a graduate of the Azhar, was to be castigated by Rashīd Riḍā for wearing a hat, in an article entitled "Monsieur 'Alī 'Abd ar-Rāziq Removes his Turban" (*Manār*, XXVII, 715–717; see below, p. 205).

[128] Adams, "Transvaal Fatwā," *op. cit.*, pp. 23–28; Riḍā, *Tārīkh*, I, 681–689.

topics consisted chiefly of appeals for moral reform and cultural advancement, or else discussions of the Eastern policies of the European powers, rather than attempts to resolve questions of the role of political authority in Islamic society. When he did express his views on constitutional questions he made little reference to the religious issues involved.

As for general questions of the role of society in history, the preceding pages of this chapter show that he had much to say. We know that he believed that social cohesion, or a spirit of solidarity, was essential to the order and prosperity of the group; that the group is called upon in its history to face religiously significant moral problems, and that it is the moral level of the group's conduct in the sight of God that determines its success or failure; that this standard of morality can only be dependably ascertained through the collective intelligence with the aid of revelation; and that human societies in their quest for a prosperous order of political relationships are subject to the natural historical laws of evolution, according to which a given stage of development or decline is always liable to change.

But these are only very general observations. When the more specific issues of constitutional organization and the source of political authority were at stake, 'Abduh's views were fragmentary and changing. Early in his career he wrote of the need for representative government and limited powers of the executive; later he declared that fifteen years under a benevolent dictator would be necessary before such institutions could succeed. Almost never did he make reference to the Caliphate or call for a constitutional system based on the classical doctrines. Rashīd Riḍā records remarks on the Ottoman Caliphate privately made by 'Abduh in 1897, in which 'Abduh declared that he gave no credence to Sultan 'Abd al-Ḥamīd's claim to the title of caliph because the claim was motivated only by his personal ambitions and desire to increase his prestige in European eyes. 'Abd al-Ḥamīd, said 'Abduh, had no conception of the true meaning and function of the Caliphate; Islam no longer had any imam but the Qur'ān.[129]

In reply to an inquiry from Wilfrid Scawen Blunt, the English writer and partisan of the Egyptian cause, in 1904 'Abduh set forth his views on the form of constitution desirable for Egypt under the British

---

[129] *Tārīkh,* I, 913. But 'Abduh opposed the idea of an Arab attempt to withdraw from the Ottoman Empire, and wished the Empire political success, on the grounds that it represented the strongest existing Muslim power. Its dissolution, he feared, would only subject Muslim lands to further European penetration (*ibid.*, 911–915).

occupation. In substance he proposed a parliamentary system on the British model, with the Khedive reduced to a figurehead, legislative powers confided to a chamber of representatives, and the executive ministries answerable to the chamber. The only references to religious matters were the proposal that the prime minister should be a Muslim and that British supervisors and other officials be barred from authority in all matters touching on religion.[130]

As Rashīd Riḍā remarks in discussing these proposals, they represented the best that 'Abduh hoped for under the occupation, and were not a final declaration on his part of the ideal political organization for Egypt.[131] It is noteworthy, however, that 'Abduh proposed removing the effective authority of the Khedive, who was the viceroy of the Ottoman Sultan, and granting legislative authority to a parliament on the European model. It is a plea for Egyptian representative government, not for an Islamic state.

This at most can only corroborate indications in his other writings that political organization is not a matter specifically determined by Islamic doctrine but is rather to be determined from time to time according to circumstances, by general consultation within the Community.[132] But occasionally he spoke of the Sharī'a as prescribing social laws both in general and in detail, and these laws he extended on occasion to constitutional questions in a manner reminiscent of the medieval jurists, specifically in terms of the institution of the Caliphate.

A noteworthy example of this is found in 'Abduh's apologetic work *Al-Islām wa 'n-Naṣrāniyya ma' al-'Ilm wa 'l-Madaniyya*.[133] Here he seeks to prove that political powers in the Islamic constitutional

[130] The text of two letters containing these and other proposals is published in Blunt, *The Secret History of the English Occupation of Egypt* (London, 1907), pp. 624–628 (but not in the 1922 edition). An Arabic retranslation of this English translation appears in *Tārīkh,* I, 899–902.

[131] *Tārīkh* I, 903–907.

[132] A noteworthy exception is found in a letter from 'Abduh in 1886, during his exile in Beirut, to the Shaikh al-Islām in Constantinople, in which he acknowledges that loyalty to the Ottoman State is the "third article of faith after belief in God and His messenger," since it was the chief bulwark of Islamic sovereignty. "Whoever thinks that the idea of the homeland, national welfare, and other such resounding phrases can replace religion in stirring up people's concern and lead them to the desired goals, is badly misguided" (*Tārīkh* I, 909). But these words must be evaluated in their proper context: first, that the letter was addressed to the Shaikh al-Islām, and second, that its subject was a plea for better religious education in Ottoman territories. In these circumstances the above quotations must be interpreted cautiously.

[133] Pp. 61–67.

organization are not "religious" or "theocratic" but purely civil. The distinction he draws is essentially that between theocracy and divine-law nomocracy:[134] the ruler and his subordinates exercise their authority within the confines of a law over which they have no exclusive power of interpretation, let alone formulation; as *mujtahids* they are on the same level as other *mujtahids* not holding office. The Caliphate must not be confused with what Europeans term "theocracy," which would signify that the caliph receives the Law directly from God and that he is

> . . . entitled to obedience from the people not by virtue of the *bay'a*, with its requirement of justice and protection, but by virtue of religious faith, so that the believer can never oppose him even if he believes him to be an enemy of God's religion . . . for the deeds of a ruler with religious authority, in whatever manifestation, are religion and law.[135]

There is in Islam "no obedience in sin," and if the ruler's actions are persistently contrary to the foundations of the Law, the Muslims must replace him as long as the public interest permits it. "It is the nation or its deputies that installs him in office, and the nation that possesses the right to supervise him. It deposes him when it considers this in its interest. Thus he is a civil ruler [*ḥākim madanī*] in all respects."[136]

In reality, then, there is no such thing as religious power in Islam. The sultan or caliph, the *muftīs*, *qāḍīs*, and other officials are only civil officials, though it is the religious law that confirms their powers and duties.[137]

This passage is interesting in two respects. First there is the apologetic aspect: 'Abduh seeks to show—and does so convincingly—that the traditional constitutional theory of the Caliphate in Islam, in its positive manifestations as distinct from its religious origins, is as much a system of civil law as the Western secular type, and that if one confines his attention to one level at a time—in this case, the legal level—he must consider the subject of discussion on its own merits. Constitutional provisions must be distinguished from their religious or secular origins as long as matters of a specifically religious or spiritual nature are not dealt with by these provisions, and as long as political powers

[134] See Khadduri, *War and Peace in the Law of Islam* (Baltimore, 1955), pp. 14–18, for the same distinction.

[135] *Al-Islām wa 'n-Naṣrāniyya*, p. 65.

[136] *Ibid.*, pp. 64–65.

[137] *Ibid.*, p. 67.

are not at the same time spiritual powers. By drawing this entirely valid distinction, ʿAbduh manages to suggest that the Islamic system, being a civil one, is of the same general species as modern secular systems, and therefore presumably open to the same speculation, critical examination, and progressive development as the latter. Furthermore, by emphasizing that true Islamic government contains those virtues that are commonly recognized in the modern world—national sovereignty over the ruler, the conditional nature of authority, and regard for the public interest; virtues that are supposedly of proven and universal validity—he hints, almost imperceptibly, that the Islamic theory coincides with natural law.

This brings us to the second significance of the passage. Regardless of the validity of his distinction, and regardless of the "natural" worth of the classical theory of the Caliphate, the fact remains that ʿAbduh is speaking of the theory as one dictated by revelation. It is not right reason or the lessons of history that lays down the rules; it is Islam. The system he describes is explicitly Islamic. We have therefore at most a coincidence of religious and rational dictates, and not a delegation by religion to reason of the authority to make political judgments. This conception is similar to the one implicit in the references to *sunnat Allāh:* God's hand remains present in human affairs, although it has always followed a recognizable and unchanging course.

Even ʿAbduh's distinction between the religious and the civil appears to be only a tentative step in the light of other passages. In the same book he denies that there can really be any separation of religious and temporal powers, such as Christianity claims to maintain. The effectiveness of civil and temporal rule is always dependent on what religion will allow. Therefore it cannot be said, for example, that separation of religious and political authority provides an atmosphere of greater tolerance toward intellectual freedom:

> This separation would facilitate tolerance if it were the case that the subjects could perform their bodily functions independently of the souls by which they live, and that the souls could similarly perform their spiritual functions without the bodies which provide their strength.[138]

The separation of secular and religious powers in Europe, ʿAbduh claims, has only resulted in a struggle for power between the ecclesias-

[138] *Ibid.*, p. 46.

tical and temporal authorities, since their jurisdictions cannot entirely be separated.[139]

He is not arguing, of course, in favor of placing political power in the hands of religious authorities, but of abolishing religious powers altogether, which is what Islam claims to do. But if it is true that religious and political matters are inseparable—that political freedom is nothing without religious freedom and vice versa—then is it not also true that any political authority tends to restrict religious freedom, since souls cannot "perform their spiritual functions without the bodies which provide their strength"? Both the classical theorists and 'Abduh could say quite rightly that religiously sanctioned political authority is not the same as authority in religious matters. But he implies that they are only one step removed.

The question is liable to considerable sophistry, and it would be pointless to project 'Abduh's remarks beyond the immediate point he seeks to make. He has not attempted a systematic analysis of the role of politics in Islam. At times, in fact, he shows a certain aversion to politics which helps to explain his lack of enthusiasm for comprehensive doctrines in that field. He speaks of politics as if of the inevitably distasteful manifestation of the weaknesses of human nature. Politics is apparently synonymous with partisanship, rivalry, self-seeking, and *'aṣabiyya* (in the strictly pejorative sense);[140] therefore there is no place for it in the structure of Islamic social ethics with which he is so concerned. In politics he seems to find the disunity and destructive competition that is opposed to his notion of the coincidence of revelation, moral temperament, and reason, and the natural cohesion and consistency of human activities and interests when rightly guided. He may be said to have a definable political ideal, namely a Muslim community bound together by a fraternal spirit and a sense of common fortunes, interests, and goals. But this ideal is not a theory or a program. It is only a hope, realizable after other reforms of a social and

---

[139] *Ibid.*, p. 45.

[140] See for example *ibid.*, pp. 111–112: "If you wish to say that politics persecutes thought or religion or knowledge, then I agree with you." See also *ibid.*, p. 121: *Taqlīd* (blind imitation) in earlier Islam reinforced partisanship and sectarianism; this was "the role of politics" (*daur as-siyāsa*) in Muslim history. See also *ibid.*, pp. 114–115; it was out of political considerations that medieval Muslim despots, uninfluenced by Islamic precepts of government, naturally tended to discourage free thought and inquiry, and distorted Islam into a religion of compliance.

educational nature have taken place. And it is in this light that his infrequent references to the "Islamic" structure of government must be understood: the structure did exist in the Golden Age of early Islam, and can exist again when Muslim society is again transformed, but it is this transformation and not the political system it will facilitate that is his real concern.

V

MUḤAMMAD RASHĪD RIḌĀ: A REVIVED DOCTRINE OF THE CALIPHATE

Muḥammad Rashīd Riḍā (1865–1935) was a Syrian scholar who, under the attraction of Muḥammad 'Abduh, emigrated to Cairo and established himself as 'Abduh's most direct disciple, to the extent that anyone could claim such a title. As 'Abduh's leading biographer and as the founder and editor of the journal *Al-Manār*[1] ("The Lighthouse"), he devoted most of his career to propagating a revivalist interpretation of the Islamic faith and institutions which he proclaimed to be the reflection of 'Abduh's teachings. He wrote much more voluminously than his master, discussing a thousand subjects of mostly religious significance in the *Manār*, and he elaborated a doctrine of Islamic law and politics much more systematic and specific than anything 'Abduh had attempted. In terms of his historical importance and his overt influence on modern Muslim thought, however, he is a comparatively minor figure who since his death has received more attention from Orientalists than from his own coreligionists.[2]

---

[1] Thirty-five volumes appeared between 1898, soon after his arrival in Cairo, and hi death in 1935. After 1935 the journal was published for a few more years by Ḥasan al-Bannā' of the Muslim Brethren and then expired.

[2] The most detailed biography of Rashīd Riḍā is the volume entitled *As-Sayyid Rashīd Riḍā au Ikhā' Arba'īn Sana* (Damascus, 1937) by his friend Shakīb Arslān, the Syrian nationalist exile who, though of Druze family, championed the cause of Islamic regeneration and also made a fervent contribution to Muslim apologetics: *Li-mādhā ta'akhkhara 'l-Muslimūn wa li-mādhā Taqaddama Ghairuhum* (Cairo, 1358 H.; English translation by M. A. Shakoor, *Our Decline and Its Causes* [Lahore, 1944]). Riḍā tells tells much about himself in his biography of 'Abduh, and describes his education and religious development in a book published shortly before his death, *Al-Manār wa 'l-Azhar* (Cairo, 1353 H./1934–1935). The leading western-language accounts of his life and work are in C. C. Adams, *Islam and Modernism in Egypt* (London, 1933); J. Jomier, *Le Commentaire coranique du Manâr* (Paris, 1954); A. H. Hourani, *Arabic Thought in the Liberal Age* (London, 1962), pp. 222–244, 298–306; and H. Laoust, "Le Reformisme

The interest of the Orientalists is nonetheless merited, particularly inasmuch as Riḍā's ideas present an unacknowledged but substantial rationale for such movements as Wahhābism in Saudi Arabia and the Muslim Brethren in Egypt. His closeness to 'Abduh has not made his interpretations of 'Abduh's ideas the most widely accepted, or even necessarily the most authoritative. Yet they constitute one of the major alternative paths of 'Abduh's mixed legacy, and the intellectual snarls in which they became entangled, and which contributed to the eventual obscurity of Riḍā's reputation, are representative of a wider problem.

Rashīd Riḍā's formal education was broader and more modern than 'Abduh's. He first attended a local mosque school of the traditional type in his native village of Qalamūn, and then moved on to a Turkish government school in nearby Tripoli. After a year he left because, as he later explained, "I did not want to work for the government." He then entered a "National Islamic school" opened by an enlightened and moderately progressive shaikh of Tripoli, Ḥusain al-Jisr, and remained there until it closed several years later because of the refusal of the authorities to consider it a religious institution and thereby exempt its students from military service. Riḍā stayed in Tripoli to finish his education at a recognized religious school.[3] At the Turkish government school and at Shaikh Ḥusain's school, he was exposed to such subjects as logic, mathematics, natural sciences, Turkish, and French, as well as Arabic and the traditional religious sciences. But not all of this had much appeal for him. By his own account he considered his language instruction superfluous,[4] while 'Abduh, by contrast, took pains to master French, beginning at the age of 44, and considered that "no one can claim any knowledge enabling him to serve his country . . . unless he knows a European language."[5] 'Abduh thereafter read widely in French and traveled repeatedly to Europe; Riḍā's only visit was to Geneva in 1921, as a member of a Syrian-Palestinian delegation protesting the imposition of the French and British man-

---

orthodoxe des 'Salafiyya' et les caractères généraux de son organisation actuelle," *Revue des Études Islamiques*, VI (1932), 175–224. Cf. also the appendix to Gardet, *La cité musulmane* (Paris, 1954); the chapter on modernism in Laoust's *Essai sur les doctrines sociales et politiques de Taḳī-d-Dīn Aḥmad b. Taimiya* (Cairo, 1939); and Marcel Colombe, *L'Évolution de l'Égypte, 1924–1950* (Paris, 1954).

[3] Arslān, *As-Sayyid Rashīd Riḍā*, pp. 35–36.

[4] Riḍā, *Tārīkh*, I, 84.

[5] *Ibid.*, I, 104–105.

dates at the League of Nations. Unlike 'Abduh after the first few years of his career, Riḍā was politically active as a Syrian nationalist on a series of occasions over many years, most notably as President of the Syrian National Congress in Damascus that proclaimed Faiṣal as King in 1920.

Our concern here, however, is not with his career as a politician but with his efforts to spell out a systematic theoretical framework for the revival of the Caliphate and of the Sharī'a. 'Abduh had given little attention to classical doctrines of the Caliphate or of technical aspects of legal methodology. But by asserting that Muslims must look back to their earliest history to discover the true principles of their faith, he encouraged others to reëxamine traditional institutions of government and law as they had presumably existed in the great days of the Rāshidūn and to explain in what respects they had become corrupted. 'Abduh's stimulus thus made the almost-forgotten classical theory of the Caliphate and the resurrection of the Sharī'a as a comprehensive legal system live options for such men as Rashīd Riḍā. At the same time 'Abduh's espousal of concepts of natural law provided an intellectual starting point for Riḍā's reinterpretations.

We have seen that 'Abduh's approach to social ethics called for recognition of the natural sanctions of history under the Qur'ānic name of *sunnat Allāh* and assumed that by a study of historical and sociological principles and by use of their own innate moral sense, even without religious piety, men could determine for themselves the forms of behavior that would lead to worldly prosperity or failure.

Riḍā adopted these assumptions as his own. The teachings of revelation for him, as for 'Abduh, were largely supplementary confirmations of moral truths that right reason could discover for itself, and were necessary because human reason was often incomplete or distorted. In the first volume of his journal *Al-Manār* (1898) he suggested that the social message of Islam and the lessons of history were two aspects of the same reality. Seeking an explanation of the rise and fall of the fortunes of societies, he wrote:

> The Muslims say that it is religion that was the cause of their sovereignty and well-being, and that turning away from it was what landed them in misery and caused misfortune to descend on them. . . . But most of them say this without understanding, imagining that there is an irrational secret in religion which enables the believers to attain victory and power and gives them success by miracles and special blessings.

> On the other hand, students of human behavior in their own time or of the history of the past say that the weakness of the nations, their occupation by foreigners . . . and the exaltation of other states all takes place according to natural laws and divine customs which do not change in any way. God by His grace guided man's attention to two paths. Whoever followed the path to progress and sovereignty, taking into consideration God's customs, arrived at his destination, whether he was a Muslim or an unbeliever, while whoever followed the path to dependence on and mental service of others, and allowed himself to be subject to their laws, arrived at that destination, whether he was a Muslim or an unbeliever. For religion has no effect on the power or weakness of nations. . . . Indeed, civilized nations believe that religion is an obscuring veil which would eliminate progress where it not rent asunder by . . . knowledge. . . . These people think that the greatest obstacle in the path of Muslim progress is the Islamic religion itself, and that if they abandon it they can hope to follow in the footsteps of Europe and progress as she did.[6]

Shorn of their exaggerations, comments Riḍā, both arguments have an element of truth. The Muslims have owed their temporal success to their religion and their failure to their turning away from it, and yet God does have all-wise customs by which He exalts and abases whom He will, whatever a person's religion. The Muslims err when they suppose that adherence to religion involves irrational secrets giving them unseen powers; the other party errs in denying that religion has any effect other than to bring misfortune to its followers. In short,

> The Islamic religion is the religion of natural disposition in that it guides toward happiness in this world and the next together and makes it clear to the people that God has all-wise customs toward His creatures which do not change, that He leads them to behavior based on these customs, and that He has prescribed laws for them which, when followed, will keep them from ever going astray from the ways of happiness. . . .[7]
>
> The Islamic religion guided men toward the divine customs and commanded observation of the created world and reflection and consideration. It distinguished the requirements of necessity and indicated to us that every action has its effect without exception, that causes are linked with their effects, that every cause

[6] *Manār*, I, 586–587.
[7] *Ibid.*, 589.

> leads to an end, and that God does not bar worldly affairs from those seeking to engage in them, provided only that they make their approach and seek their objectives in the proper way, whether they be believers or unbelievers, although faith is indispensable for reward in the hereafter and perfect happiness on earth.[8]

Knowledge of God's physical creation, furthermore, is declared to be the means of worldly success for man:

> Whoever is most knowledgeable of existence and the order of nature is most knowledgeable of truth. . . . This is self-evident, and the supremacy of those who know the truths of existence and the customs of God in existing things, over those who do not know them, is an attested fact not denied by those who are mastered and overcome in their ignorance and emptiness, even if they may be unaware that the knowledge of their masters is the truth, and the reason for their supremacy. . . . If a nation is ignorant and is destroyed, then it has been rewarded for what it earned; it wronged itself, and was not wronged by others.[9]

There is no contradiction, evidently, between religion and reason, either in the rules of behavior that they indicate to us or in the material ends to which they lead. For, as Riḍā says elsewhere, "Islam is the religion of natural disposition and cannot possibly contradict the laws of creation, nor can its customs contradict those of nature, for everything is from God."[10] Riḍā prefers, with 'Abduh, to say that the Islamic revelation commands men to act justly, rather than that justice is to be defined as what conforms to the particular rules of behavior found in the Sharī'a.[11] Justice, in other words, is an eternal value implicit in Creation itself, intelligible to normal human faculties, rather than an outright creation of the Islamic message, determined without reference to already existing nature.

The humanist, almost secular implications of these general ideas found their way into Rashīd Riḍā's reformist adaptation of the classical theory of the Caliphate, where they coexisted uncomfortably with surviving elements of the formal structure and theological preoccupation of the ancient doctrine. The classical writers had not, after all,

---

[8] *Ibid.*, 591.

[9] *Ibid.*, IX, 54–55.

[10] *Ibid.*, IV, 216.

[11] *Ibid.*, 864–865. This of course is the Mu'tazilite position; Riḍā was often attacked by his conservative critics as a "Mu'tazilite or Wahhābī" (Adams, *Islam and Modernism*, p. 204, quoting *Manār*, I, 425).

attempted to devise institutions, or really even to describe them, but only to justify them. Yet they did so by reference to the presumed precedents of the Rāshidūn, and this gave their writings a natural appeal to an idealist like Riḍā. Together with 'Abduh's naturalism, therefore, but without much compatibility, the doctrine of the Caliphate could serve as the framework for Riḍā's political thought and as a model for the program of action he advocated.

The thought and program are summed up in Riḍā's book *Al-Khilāfa au al-Imāma 'l-'Uẓmā* ("The Caliphate, or Supreme Imamate").[12] This was written in response to the action of the Turkish Grand National Assembly in 1922 in stripping the Ottoman Caliphate of all temporal authority and leaving in its place an entirely ceremonial office. In reaction to this step his concern was to reassert the temporal as well as religious significance of the true office, to show the fitness of the institution for the political requirements of the modern age (i.e., by demonstrating that the attractions of fashionable Western political ideologies such as national sovereignty, parliamentarianism, and progressive legislation are matched and even surpassed by the system of the Caliphate if the latter is correctly interpreted), and to give coherent form to his appeals for the rejuvenation and reintegration of Muslim society.

In pursuing these aims Rashīd Riḍā appears at an intermediate stage of his development as a polemicist and apologist, in transition from his earlier emphasis on convincing the 'ulamā' and other orthodox Muslims of the need for reforms to his later preoccupation with the threat of Westernization and secularization. In the *Khilāfa* one can still find certain propositions advanced which are not entirely different from those of 'Alī 'Abd ar-Rāziq condemned by Riḍā with such fury in 1925; yet nothing in the *Khilāfa* is quite so radical as the thirteenth-century treatise on *maṣlaḥa* by Najm ad-Dīn aṭ-Ṭaufī, published in *Al-Manār* and commended to its readers in 1905.[13]

The contents of the *Khilāfa* can be suitably discussed under three headings: (1) Community sovereignty; (2) power, authority and necessity; (3) spiritual and temporal authority.

---

[12] Cairo, 1341 H./1923. The work first appeared as a series of articles in *Manār*, XXIII, 729–752; XXIV, 33–64, 98–120, 185–200, 257–272, 345–373 (Dec., 1922–May, 1923). French translation with notes by Henri Laoust, *Le Califat dans la doctrine de Raşid Rida* (Cairo, 1938). (Henceforth cited as *Khilāfa*, with page references to translation/original.)

[13] *Manār*, IX, 745–770.

A. *Community Sovereignty*

Riḍā sets out, in the first 57 pages of the *Khilāfa,* to review the traditional juristic presentation of the constitutional theory of the Caliphate and, by his own *ijtihād,* to define more clearly certain vague principles or correct what he considers mistaken ones. In the latter part of the book he seeks to apply his interpretations to the contemporary political situation and to determine to what extent it is possible to restore the institution in its proper form, and what role it should play in the general Islamic renaissance for which he hopes.[14]

"*Khilāfa, imāma 'uẓmā,* and *imārat al-mu'minīn* are three terms with the same meaning," Riḍā begins. "They signify the leadership of Islamic government combining the interests of religion and worldly life." Furthermore, as Fakhr ad-Dīn ar-Rāzī (d. 1209 A.D.) stipulated, the office must be confided to a single individual as "a safeguard for the entire Community in case they should have to remove the imam for evildoing."[15] By this is apparently meant that a single individual is more easily held accountable.

The obligatory nature of the office is sustained by traditional arguments: principally, the *ijmā'* of the Companions, but also the rational consideration that without the caliph the law cannot be enforced nor the welfare of the Community protected.[16] Also, the legally established obligation to obey the imam is meaningless without the assumption that the imam exists.[17] Lastly, ḥadīths are cited.[18] The familiar Qur'ānic verse, "O ye who believe! Obey God, the Prophet, and those in authority among you" (Q. iv:58) is not mentioned.

Rashīd Riḍā next turns to the subject of the *ahl al-ḥall wa 'l-'aqd.* It is traditionally agreed that the caliph is installed in office by their

---

[14] It is certainly misleading for Tyan to describe Riḍā's book as the "scrupulously faithful reproduction of the [traditional] doctrine, with the same formulas that had been taught for more than eight centuries" (*Institutions du droit public musulman.* Vol. II: *Sultanat et califat* [Paris, 1957], p. 264).

[15] *Khilāfa,* 14–15/10.

[16] *Khilāfa,* 16/10. This argument, of course, serves only to justify the need for authority in general and not the Caliphate in particular. It is criticized on these grounds by 'Alī 'Abd ar-Rāziq, *Al-Islām wa Uṣūl al-Ḥukm* (Cairo, 1925), pp. 13–15. It is, however, a traditional argument.

[17] *Khilāfa,* 16/11. See Aḍud ad-Dīn al-Ījī, *Kitāb al-Mawāqif,* ed. T. Sorensen (Leipzig, 1848), p. 304, for the same argument.

[18] *Khilāfa,* 16/11. E.g., "He who dies without being bound by a *bay'a* dies the death of an unbeliever."

bay'a, he says,[19] but they have never been clearly identified. The phrase itself, however, suggests to him "the chiefs of the Community and those prominent in rank, in whom the great majority have placed their confidence, so that whomever they choose will be assured of their submission and serve to organize their affairs, secure from their disobedience or rebellion."[20]

Various writers have characterized the *ahl al-ḥall wa 'l-'aqd* as "men of learning, leadership, and prominence"; "those who can easily meet together"; "those possessed of the sovereign power of decision, whom the other people follow."[21] For Rashīd Riḍā, the quality of effective influence is essential. With an overwhelming acknowledgment of their leadership, "it is easy for the Community to use its force of constraint to exact obedience and docility from those who would refuse to accept its decisions voluntarily."[22]

Riḍā draws the conclusion from his examination of the Caliph 'Umar's appointment of a conclave (*shūrā*) that the principle of consultation prior to selection of the imam had already been established by *ijmā'*, but denies any implication that the electors must be in any particular number.[23]

But in any case, he continues, it is not the selection of a candidate that concludes the contract of the Imamate in a constitutive sense, but the ratification of the selection by the Community. 'Umar's nomination of Abū Bakr and 'Abdarraḥmān b. 'Auf's choice of 'Uthmān were inconclusive until the adhesion of the Community took place. He concludes that "the *bay'a* is given only when the body of Muslims have been consulted and when the *ahl al-ḥall wa 'l-'aqd* have made their choice." If 'Umar's act of proclaiming Abū Bakr caliph is taken as an exception, as admittedly it might conceivably be, this was done in unusual circumstances and cannot set a precedent. It would be inadmissible to think of imitating him by swearing allegiance to a random individual without the proper qualifications being present in either party.[24]

---

[19] He ignores, of course, testamentary designation, which was historically the more common procedure.

[20] *Khilāfa*, 17/11.

[21] *Ibid.*

[22] *Ibid.*, 19/12.

[23] *Ibid.*, 19–20/12.

[24] *Ibid.*, 20/13. For a further assertion of the contractual nature of the *bay'a*, see also *ibid.*, 42/24–25.

Rashīd Riḍā has implied by the foregoing that the *bay'a* must be constituted by what amounts to an elective process, by prior consultation either before nomination by a single person or nomination by a group acting together; that in either case the choice must enjoy the concurrence of the Community through the judgment of the *ahl al-ḥall wa 'l-'aqd*; that the *ahl* must possess effective influence in the Community so that their decision will be assured of enforcement; and that the *ahl* are the final authority, speaking for the full body of believers. While recognizing the vagueness of traditional references to the *ahl al-ḥall wa 'l-'aqd*, however, he has not come a great deal closer to a clear definition. He has introduced the qualification of influence, which is a noteworthy contribution; yet when he comes to enumerate the formally required qualifications of the electors, he merely cites Māwardī's enumeration: moral probity (*'adāla*), knowledge (*'ilm*) of the required qualifications of the candidate, and judgment and wisdom (*ra'y wa ḥikma*) with which to apply knowledge.[25] He does not call attention to Māwardī's omission of influence or power as a qualification, although he does subsequently say: "It is understood from the foregoing that the title *ahl al-ḥall wa 'l-'aqd* is meant to apply to those who enjoy that title by power and by actuality. These are the leaders whom the Community follows in its general affairs, of which the most important is the establishment of the Imamate."[26]

After establishing that the *ahl al-ḥall wa 'l-'aqd* are the legitimate representatives of the Community, Riḍā goes on to establish an identity between them and the Community as a whole, whether the latter is termed *jamā'a* or *umma*. Although in some instances in the ḥadīth sources it is clear that *jamā'a* signifies the whole body of Muslims, in references to questions of authority the term means "those holding authority among the Muslims, the *ahl al-ḥall wa 'l-'aqd* and those whose consensus is accepted as binding" (i.e., the qualified initiators of *ijmā'*).[27] Among these are the "most important rulers and those whom the imam consults."[28]

The restriction of the meaning of *umma* and *jamā'a* to the leaders of the Community is in a sense a play upon words. Fakhr ad-Dīn ar-Rāzī states that public leadership is a right of the Community (*umma*), since it has the right to depose the caliph for what it considers just

[25] *Ibid.*, 25–27/16–17.
[26] *Ibid.*, 28/17.
[27] *Ibid.*, 23/14.
[28] *Ibid.*

cause. But, asks Rāzī's commentator Taftazānī, if leadership belongs to the *umma*, then who are those who are led? According to Taftazānī, by *umma* in this context must be understood "the *ahl al-ḥall wa 'l-'aqd* who represent the Community by virtue of their positions of rank and prominence, their leadership being then exercised over the other individual members of the Community." This, agrees Rashīd Riḍā, is the correct interpretation. He adds that in the Prophet's time these leaders were "not [those holding the formal titles of] jurists, princes, and governors, but those leaders of the Muslims who were consulted" (by the Prophet).[29]

But the proposition that the Community can only exercise authority over itself through its representatives is really self-evident. To deduce from this, furthermore, that authority therefore really belongs to the representatives and not to the Community as a whole, is unsatisfactory on two counts. First, until the representatives are more clearly identified than as those in positions of authority, we still have no more than a self-evident proposition, namely, that authority belongs to those in authority, or that authority belongs to those capable of exercising it, which is another way of saying that might makes right. Second, the affirmation that these persons are the representatives of the Community offers no indication of the quality of the relationship between the two parties. Does the Community enjoy the power of control over the representatives or of selecting them or of exercising discretion as to whether to follow them? Apparently not; the representatives seemingly enjoy their status by virtue of what is assumed to be an undeniable and absolute capacity. They are representatives but not delegates.[30] Their authority, then, appears to be in the nature of an oligarchy rather than a kind of publicly exercised sovereignty. But in this case, it is all the more essential to define them specifically, or to indicate the means by which they are to be identified.

It should be noted that the question is one of the application of constitutional principles and not of their origin or sanction. It is in this sense that "sovereignty" or "right of leadership" (*ḥaqq ar-ri'āsa*) can be spoken of as belonging to persons rather than to the law itself or to God as institutor of the law. In this respect Rashīd Riḍā renders the service of bringing the issues down to the existential level, where they

[29] *Ibid.*, 24–25/15.

[30] Although on page 156/93 of the *Khilāfa* he calls them "delegates."

can be understood as rules for behavior rather than theological justifications. But it is precisely on this level that the need for positive definitions and procedures becomes essential. His inconclusive references to the *ahl al-ḥall wa 'l-'aqd* belong in what was described in chapter ii as the category of "self-sufficient facts": situations of juridical relevance, whose effects are theoretically legally valid or invalid, but for which no means of verification are provided.[31] For the purposes of applying the law such propositions are meaningless, though they may be relevant for morality and conscience. In the present example, however, Riḍā's definition of the Community representatives is not even sufficiently precise for his proposition to have moral relevance.

If he has not told us who the representatives are, however, Rashīd Riḍā has still said a great deal. He has proposed an identity of the terms *ahl al-ḥall wa 'l-'aqd*, *ūlū-l-amr*,[32] *jamā'a*, *umma*, *ahl ash-shūrā*, and *ahl al-ijmā'*. In a single body of men (who remain undefined) are associated the powers of election and deposition of the ruler, general influence and prestige among the subjects at large, representation of the rights of the Community, participation in decisions of state, and authoritative determination of the law. Consultation, which is recommended in Qur'ān and ḥadīth but receives little attention in the classical juristic writings and was never definitively institutionalized in Muslim history, is adopted by Rashīd Riḍā as the hallmark of his political theory and confided to a single body in the fields of election, constitutional interpretation, administration, and legislation.

The bare fact that Rashīd Riḍā characterizes this body as the representatives of the Community is not sufficient, however, to justify conclusions that he "considers the principles of consultation and *ijmā'* as democratic principles of the participation of the people in power,"[33] and still less that he conceives the Community to be sovereign in the sense of Rousseau's "General Will."[34] The most that can be said is that whereas the traditional juristic theory saw the caliph as exercising God's authority and responsible to the Community only in a manner

[31] See above, pp. 31–32.

[32] *Khilāfa*, 25/15: "Rāzī verified that by 'those in authority' [*ūlū 'l-amr*] in Verse iv:58 of the Qur'ān is meant the *ahl al-ḥall wa 'l-'aqd*, who represent the power of the Community."

[33] Gardet, *La Cité musulmane*, p. 352.

[34] Hazem Zaki Nuseibeh, *The Ideas of Arab Nationalism* (Ithaca, 1956), p. 126. See also A. Sanhoury, *Le Califat: son évolution vers une Société des Nations orientale* (Paris, 1926), pp. 94–95, for an attempt to liken the contract of the *bay'a* to contract in the theory of John Locke. Sanhoury closely parallels Riḍā in his entire presentation.

incidental to his religious responsibility, Riḍā appears to magnify the role of the Community (or rather, that of its leading members) to the point where it is they who are the vice-gerents of God and the caliph's responsibility to them becomes of primary rather than secondary importance.[35] The *ahl al-ḥall wa 'l-'aqd* have replaced the caliph as the human agency whose function is determined directly by religious considerations, and the caliph has become their executive officer. Collectively they stand in relation to the Community as a whole in approximately the same position as the caliph did in classical theory, in the respect that their authority derives from their capacity for the function they perform, and not from a delegation.[36] While they are called the representatives of the Community, they, like the caliph as traditionally conceived, are trustees rather than agents. The power of coercion in society is theirs: "True obedience is due only to God, and worldly authority belongs to the body (*jamā'a*) of the Community. The chief (*ra'īs*) is only a representative of its unity."[37]

This partial substitution of the *ahl* for the caliph is not intended by Riḍā as an innovation but as an expression of the true Sunna of the Rāshidūn caliphs. There is no intimation of a deliberate contradiction or significant alteration in the classical theory, and if under the stimulus of his apologetic motives his ideas sometimes "appear less as a simple working out of Muslim assumptions than as the Muslim recasting of Western assumptions,"[38] this is not his conscious intention, and he does not mean to accept the more revolutionary implications of such a process. He can still, therefore, refer to the Caliphate in the traditional phrase, "successorship to the Prophecy."[39] Likewise he can criticize Kemal Atatürk for declaring that "sovereignty belongs to the Nation [*umma*] represented by the Grand National Assembly, that this sovereignty is unlimited, and that no one, whatever his title, be he caliph or sultan, can claim to exercise the least influence on this assembly."[40] In part his criticism appears to be directed against Ata-

---

[35] As we shall see, the caliph as the leading *mujtahid* of the Community is subject to the concurrence of the *ahl*, whose combined *ijtihād* has the force of *ijmā'*.

[36] The difference remains, of course, that the *ahl* are not tied to the population by a contract; but the classical idea of the contract was only of secondary importance.

[37] *Khilāfa*, 217/129.

[38] Gardet, *La Cité musulmane*, p. 352. See also Laoust, *Essai*, pp. 573–574.

[39] *Khilāfa*, 218/130.

[40] *Ibid.*, 200/118. Riḍā is referring to the tract published by the Grand National Assembly in 1922 entitled *Hilafet ve Hakimiyet-i-milliye*; Arabic translation by 'Abd al-Ghanī Sānī Bey, *Al-Khilāfa wa Sulṭat al-Umma* (Cairo, 1924); French translation (anonymous) in *Revue du Monde Musulman*, LIX (1925), 5–81.

türk's substitution of the Turkish *umma* for the Muslim *umma*. But it also illustrates the shifting connotations of sovereignty in Riḍā's usage: earlier he himself attributed it in the sense of political leadership (*ḥaqq ar-ri'āsa*) to the *umma*;[41] here he denies it in the sense of authority above the law.

It is the caliph's function to protect Islam from innovation and promote its laws and beliefs, with the aid of the Community given through the process of consultation (*shūrā*). Riḍā maintains that

> This duty consists in effect of conserving the religious principles that the early Muslims agreed upon, while leaving the Community at liberty in individual matters of devotional practice to follow their own *ijtihād*. In political and judicial matters pertaining to government, the caliph may give preference to certain conclusions of *ijtihād* over others, after consulting the 'ulamā' among the *ahl al-ḥall wa 'l-'aqd*, particularly if he is not himself a qualified *mujtahid*.[42]

The leading jurists, he continues, have in the past obeyed the caliph in matters pertaining to government even when this was opposed to their own *ijtihād*, so long as this did not contradict explicit texts of the Qur'ān or Sunna.[43]

This formula serves for Rashīd Riḍā as a principle of limitation of power. In an earlier article in the *Manār* he gave much the same argument, adding that there is no requirement that the ruler's directives should conform to the *ijtihād* of the jurists, since *ijtihād* is only a matter of speculative opinion and is not infallible. As long as the ruler's directives do not contravene explicit texts, they should normally be followed. But, he adds significantly, if the *ahl al-ḥall wa 'l-'aqd* should meet and pass other decisions opposed to the ruler's policy, these are binding on him, "because they are the deputies of the *umma* and it is they who have the right to select the caliph; the Muslims have no imam except through their *bay'a*. If he should oppose them, the Community must support them against him rather than vice versa."[44]

On technical points of legal interpretation, then, the caliph must consult the jurists. He is himself the chief *mujtahid* of the Community,[45] with his powers limited by the combined and declared opinion of the

[41] *Khilāfa*, 24/15.
[42] *Ibid.*, 50/29.
[43] *Ibid.*
[44] *Manār*, XIV, 740–741.
[45] See *Khilāfa*, 133/79.

others. On nontechnical questions the whole Community is potentially a consultative body.[46] But Rashīd Riḍā, like Muḥammad ʿAbduh and other modernists who have stressed the importance of consultation, does not draw a distinction between the obligation to seek advice and the obligation to *defer* to advice; either one, for him, is a limitation of power.[47] An absolute ruler, to his mind, is not one who has the final power to make all decisions, but one who relies entirely upon his own information and judgment in making decisions.

B. *Power, Authority, and Necessity*

Rashīd Riḍā is able to adduce more detailed enumerations from traditional literature of the qualities required of the caliph himself than of the electors. The aggregate list includes the requirements that the prospective caliph be male, Muslim, adult, free, capable of *ijtihād*, of moral character, judicious, courageous, physically sound, and Quraishite.[48] These qualities are given by different writers in different combinations; we may note that power and influence are not among them. Riḍā concentrates his attention on the requirement of Quraishite lineage and suggests that it serves to ensure that the caliph will be a person of influence. The requirement, he asserts, was based on the consideration that the Quraish, because of their great prestige as the leading clan and as relatives of the Prophet, would command the respect necessary for effective leadership. At the same time the membership in Quraish was sufficiently diverse not to represent a dynastic principle properly speaking, nor promotion of family or factional interests over those of rivals; the members of Quraish were themselves divided into factions, and the real source of corruption was partisan favoritism within these factions, such as Umayyads and Hāshimites.[49]

Quraish is to the Arabs what the Arabs are to the Muslims as a body, according to Riḍā: a vital core of leadership.[50] It is the require-

---

46 *Ibid.*, 55–56/32.

47 *Ibid.*, 51/30: "The imam is not an absolute ruler as many people suppose. He is limited by the prescriptions of the Qur'ān and the Sunna, by the example of the Rāshidūn caliphs, and by consultation."

48 *Khilāfa*, 29–30/18. The writers whose enumerations are cited by Rashīd Riḍā are Taftazānī, Qāsim b. Qultubugha, and Māwardī.

49 *Ibid.*, 31–40/19–23.

50 Cf. *ibid.*, 38/22: he carries his championship of Arab leadership to the point of declaring that had the Muslim army defeated at Tours in 732 been mostly Arab rather than Berber, it would have overrun and Islamized Europe; it failed because the Berbers lacked the sincere Islamic spirit of the Arabs.

ment of Quraishite lineage, then, that serves as a principle of effective power in the Caliphate.

It may seem somewhat strange that Rashīd Riḍā considers that this lineage is still sufficient in the twentieth century to ensure strong leadership. As far back as the fourteenth century, Ibn Khaldūn had declared, rather more strongly than Riḍā, that the requirement existed as a means of ensuring influence, but then went on to imply that since Quraishite prestige had by that time dwindled away (that being the period of the shadowy Abbasid caliphate of Egypt), the requirement no longer served its purpose and was perhaps therefore inoperative.[51] Riḍā's refusal to accept this reasoning perhaps stems from his distrust of Ibn Khaldūn's principle of *'aṣabiyya*, or clan partisanship, which he considers contrary to Islamic social loyalties.[52] Since Ibn Khaldūn associated Quraish leadership with *'aṣabiyya*, Riḍā, who did not do so, may have been reluctant to follow Ibn Khaldūn's conclusions, though their initial premises do not really seem very different. Riḍā, however, evidently clings to the Quraish requirement out of consideration for something somewhat different from *'aṣabiyya*, namely, the moral prestige that is attached to Quraish lineage by Arabs even today, rather than any powerful group spirit among members of the Quraishite clan itself. It would therefore be unjust to suppose that by insisting on Quraish lineage he nullifies his effort to secure a principle of effectiveness among the qualities of the caliph.

In any case, the problem of the ruler's qualities and that of the electors' qualities are different in an important respect. Once the proper electors are identified, their choice of a caliph is authoritative and recognizable; the electors serve as an agency competent to determine whether a given candidate is or is not qualified. Whether the elected caliph has the material as well as moral capacity to perform his functions depends above all on whether the electors themselves possess sufficient influence to make their decision effective. Hence it is the qualifications and the process of identification of the electors, rather than of the caliph, that is the fundamental problem. Until this is solved more adequately than it has been by Rashīd Riḍā, the question of the caliph's qualifications remains abstract. In the classical writings, the question of the electors' identification remained only vaguely answered for a good reason: the theory itself was essentially a rationalization of the accumulated Sunnī record and a refutation of Shī'ite

---

[51] *Al-Muqaddima*, chap. iii, sec. 22; Rosenthal translation, I, 398–399.

[52] *Khilāfa*, 226–231/134–137.

allegations of violations by the Umayyads and Abbasids of Islamic standards. Hence the theorists could not afford to restrict their requirements to such a level as would cast doubt on the legitimacy of any practices in the history of the institution. In this position they could only offer a formula that would fit any and all of the various groups and individuals who had at least nominally been responsible for the choice of caliphs, and such a formula was bound to be vague to the point of meaninglessness. Certainly it was bound not to include specific procedures for the authoritative determination or recognition of the capacity of the electors.

Riḍā, on the other hand, sets forth his account of the structure of the Caliphate with an entirely different purpose and set of assumptions in mind. He seeks to provide the basis on which the "true" Caliphate can be restored in the present day. He is not concerned with defending the historical record of the various Sunnī caliphates after the Rāshidūn, and in fact challenges the legitimacy of the Umayyads, Abbasids, and Ottomans. These considerations should reasonably have rendered him free to ignore the obscurities of the classical juristic writers and come squarely to grips with the problems they could not afford to face. He need not have given much attention at all to the classical theory, and instead could have built again from the bare foundations of the Sunna of the Rāshidūn, and applied this to contemporary needs. Nominally, this is what he claims to be doing, but in practice he has not drawn the conclusion that if Umayyad and Abbasid history is irrelevant, then Māwardī, Taftazānī and the rest are irrelevant also. Perhaps this is because these classical writers, while justifying post-Rāshidūn practices, outwardly based their formulas in large part on the Rāshidūn record.

One qualification limiting the authority of the Community's representatives over the caliph which Riḍā has inherited from the traditional presentation is the stipulation that the caliph may only be deposed for cause; indeed, he cannot even abdicate.[53] This is an important limitation. Although Riḍā does not explicitly say so, it signifies that the caliph's function is defined by a source beyond the discretion of the Community or the *ahl*. Therefore he cannot be simply the agent of their will. Conversely, we are told elsewhere that "the 'ulamā' are agreed on the *obligation* to revolt against the imam who shows himself to be an unbeliever."[54] A distinction is drawn, however, between un-

[53] *Ibid.*, 70/40.
[54] *Ibid.*, 43/25.

belief (*kufr*) and individual contraventions of the religious law (*ma-'ṣiya*): it is only the former that justifies deposition, while in the latter case it is enough for the caliph to be advised to mend his ways.[55]

On the other hand, it is recognized that in some cases calling for deposition such action is not a practical possibility or at least could only be realized with the accompaniment of bloodshed and civil strife. Here the doctrine of necessity becomes relevant.

Rashīd Riḍā distinguishes between the duly constituted Imamate, in which deposition can only be for cause, and the Imamate of necessity. This latter comprises two subcategories: first, when it is not feasible to meet all the requirements in regard either to the qualifications of the candidate or to the functions of his office and scope of his jurisdiction, so that an imperfect solution must be voluntarily accepted; and second, when the office or its functions are usurped by force. In the former case the usual rules of deposition only for cause apply; in the latter, no obedience at all is due, and it is a duty to overthrow the ruler at the first opportunity.[56]

The doctrine of necessity in relation to the Caliphate is familiar in the medieval treatises. Two passages quoted at length by Riḍā set forth the argument. The first, by Kamāl ad-Dīn b. al-Humām (d. 861 H.), is reminiscent both of al-Ghazālī[57] and, in the last sentence, of Ibn Jamā'a:[58]

> If it is impossible that learning and moral probity be present in whomever holds the Imamate—if, for example, the office is held by a man who is ignorant of the laws or commits grave sins—and if to overthrow him unbearable civil strife must be fomented, then we proclaim that such an Imamate is lawfully contracted. Thus we would not be in the position of one who destroys a city to build a palace. Furthermore, we have admitted that the decisions of unjust rulers must be executed in the lands over which they have gained mastery because of compelling necessity. How then could we deny the validity of such an Imamate in view of the general harm that would be necessitated by its absence? And if another usurper should overthrow the first and supplant him, the one overthrown must be considered deposed and his successor becomes Imām.[59]

---

[55] *Ibid.*, 71/41.

[56] *Ibid.*, 60/35, 62/36, 65/38.

[57] *Al-Iqtiṣād fī 'l-I'tiqād*, p. 107 (quoted above, pp. 47, 48).

[58] *Taḥrīr al-Aḥkām*, p. 357 (quoted above, p. 50).

[59] *Khilāfa*, 63/37. The passage is from Ibn al-Humām's *Al-Musāyara fī Uṣūl ad-Dīn*, edition of 1316 H. (no page reference given).

The second quote is in the same vein. It is taken from Taftazānī as follows:

> If there are no candidates among the Quraish worthy of the Imamate, or if the election of an imam is rendered impossible by the prevalence of error, tyranny, and bewilderment, we cannot leave in doubt the legitimacy of accepting the judicial functions, of executing judgments, of applying the criminal sanctions of the Sharī'a, and of filling all the functions of authority dependent on the Imamate. It is the same when the imam of Quraishite origin is a man who is impious, tyrannical, or ignorant, let alone being unfit for *ijtihād*. In sum the theory of the Imamate rests on what is possible as well as on free choice. In case of helplessness and constraint, when oppressive, faithless, debauched men seize power and when despots impose their evil rule, then temporal leadership becomes a matter of sheer force, and by necessity the religious laws dependent upon the imam must rest upon this principle. No account is then to be taken of the lack of learning and moral probity and other qualifications, for necessity makes permissible what is forbidden. To God we turn in distress and in Him we put our hopes that our misfortunes will cease.[60]

These are persuasive and yet dangerous arguments, since they engender the risk that evils tolerated as exceptions in the name of necessity will through long practice become established principles. Riḍā recognizes this:

> This means that rule by forceful conquest is like eating the flesh of dead animals or of swine in case of necessity. It is imposed by force of arms, but it is better than anarchy. What it requires, however, is a constant readiness to put an end to it as soon as possible. People should not accustom themselves to its perpetuation, nor should it become like a ball to be tossed back and forth by usurpers, as is the case with nations oppressed or content with oppression because of their ignorance of their own latent power or because of the strength of their overlords. Those, on the other hand, who are enlightened by political awareness rise up to overthrow their tyrannical governments and rulers. The most recent group to do this was the Turkish people; but they only overthrew one form of forceful rule by means of another, although this may prove better than the first. What they did followed the example of proud nations, for the mass of the 'ulamā' of Turkey,

[60] *Khilāfa*, 64–65/37, quoted from *Maqāṣid aṭ-Ṭālibīn* (Constantinople, 1305 H.), p. 277.

> India, Egypt, and elsewhere had preached the duty to obey the Ottoman sultan-caliphs as long as these did not show signs of infidelity or apostasy from Islam, regardless of the oppression, corruption, economic ruin, and terrorization of the population their obedience might entail. This view was advanced by jurists devoid of rational insight and *ijtihād*. It is the most important reason for the widespread belief among them that the authority of the *shar'ī* Caliphate can dispense with temporal power and a life of political independence.[61]

Nor is Riḍā satisfied with a theory of delegation by a nominal caliph of political authority to the actual possessors of *de facto* power. Such delegation is mere deceit, since the caliph in such a case lacks effective power of his own to delegate and, when he wishes, to recall.[62]

> If they obstinately persevere in such attitudes, the Muslims will never have either an Imamate or an iman. The time has come, then, for them to understand that in transforming the laws of necessity, as applied to the caliph of usurpation, into a firm and permanent principle, they have destroyed the structure of the Imamate and done away with the sovereignty of the Community known by the term *jamā'a*.[63]

The real issue is the relation between power and authority: which logically precedes the other? The classical theory, as we have seen, never solved this problem, and tended either to ignore the fact of power or, under the guise of necessity, to declare in so many words that might made right. Riḍā has sought to strike a balance between these extremes, but has done so haphazardly and ineffectively because of his failure to be specific enough in identifying precise procedures and requirements. At times this leads him into sophistry. In discussing the question whether those holding *de facto* power are obliged to defer formally to a caliph whose authority is only nominal, he solves the problem by declaring that if in fact they did defer to him, then he would indeed thereby hold real power and would not be only a nominal ruler.[64] But this assumes a certain benevolence or renunciation on the part of those who voluntarily defer, and does not come to grips with the real issue.

Riḍā's own program for restoring the Caliphate rests, curiously,

---

[61] *Khilāfa*, 65/38.
[62] *Ibid.*, 115/68.
[63] *Ibid.*
[64] *Ibid.*, 62–63/36.

squarely on the doctrine of necessity, albeit of the type in which the Community *voluntarily* restricts its effort to what is practical under the circumstances. He acknowledges that few persons wish to revive the Caliphate along the lines of the classical theory, either because of their lack of understanding or because they think it impossible. The most, then, that can be hoped for now (i.e., in 1923) is a partial restoration which might serve as an opening wedge.[65] But the institution he proposes is in substance no more than a spiritual directory of the type he denounces so scornfully as represented by the post-1922 Ottoman Caliphate. The only political function he assigns it is the apparently nominal investiture of already existing rulers.[66]

It is Riḍā's interpretation of the role of the Umayyads in Islamic history and of the concept of *'aṣabiyya* that epitomizes the weakness of his entire theoretical approach to the problem of power and nullifies what recognition he does give, in passages already cited, to the importance of power for authority. In viewing the contemporary political situation he shows a certain pride in the achievements of Muslim groups who have secured sufficient power for themselves to stay free of European control.[67] But in viewing specific events of Islamic history, and in particular the advent of the Umayyad dynasty, he sees power as the inevitable corrupter of Islamic principles of government rather than as their necessary support.

> The great fault of the Umayyads for which they could never be pardoned was their perversion of the basic principle of government in Islam, which was that government was elective in nature and rested on the consultation of the electors among the *ahl al-ḥall wa 'l-'aqd*. They abolished this principle and replaced it by a material one, according to which might makes right. It was they, then, who were the first to destroy Islamic government. Later, many others followed their example.[68]

Transposed into milder terms, what this passage says is that the

---

[65] *Ibid.*, 112/67.

[66] *Ibid.*, 132–134/78–80. See below for a fuller discussion of this in relation to the question of a "spiritual" Caliphate.

[67] He sees this virtue in the Kemalist revolution in Turkey (*ibid.*, 238/141); for the same reason he earlier gave support to the Ottomans, for all their faults, against European influence (*ibid.*, 193/114). He supported 'Abdal'azīz b. Sa'ūd against Indian Muslim attacks "because he is the greatest Islamic power on earth since the fall of the Ottoman state and the rise of a nonreligious government in Turkey" (*Manār*, XXVII, 638).

[68] *Khilāfa*, 79/45–46.

Umayyads, as the strongest party, assumed exclusively for themselves the function of the *ahl al-ḥall wa 'l-'aqd*, which hitherto had not depended on the qualification of power. He continues:

> In sum, we wish to show how disastrous it was to have caused the Caliphate to deviate from the path traced for it by the Prophet and be made the plaything of clans and of the spirit of domination. This misfortune is the source of all others that struck the Muslims in their spiritual and temporal interests.[69]

This would seem to suggest that Islam demands that natural human ambitions be not merely channeled but actually laid aside in the interests of an institution whose functions are temporal but whose foundations are purely moral. It is of course an assumption common to various religions that men are doomed to the vicissitudes imposed by their own nature until they allow this nature to be transcended by faith. But it seems peculiarly characteristic of Islam, as interpreted both by Riḍā in the above passage and by the classical juristic theorists, to make the temporal political structure of society dependent upon this millennial assumption.

That the Umayyad failure to adhere to the Rāshidūn practices was the failing of human nature, Rashīd Riḍā apparently acknowledges in a later chapter of the *Khilāfa*. Islam, he writes, came to put an end to man's subjection to the cyclical swing in history of tyranny succeeding tyranny, by introducing a doctrine of moderation and consultation, by making the ruler responsible to the leaders of the people, and by making all men equal before the law. It was the failure of the post-Rāshidūn caliphs to follow these principles that caused Islam's temporal decline. This was due to certain human weaknesses—among them, greed, ambition, jealously—stirred up for the most part by enemies plotting against Islam[70] or by non-Arabs converted to Islam for ulterior reasons.[71]

The principle of force, he continues, was allowed to enter into Islam

---

[69] *Ibid.*, 81/47.

[70] Laoust notes that this idea of a "plot against Islam" is familiar in Riḍā's writings as it had been in those of Ibn Taimiyya centuries before. All weakening influences on Islam—secularism, imperialism, etc.—are interpreted by this mentality, remarks Laoust, as being part of a deliberate scheme (*Essai*, p. 574). See also Riḍā's attack on 'Alī 'Abd ar-Rāziq in *Manār*, XXVI, 100, which begins with the words: "The enemies of Islam who covet its destruction, the elimination of its authority and law, and the enslavement of its peoples, continue to wage their unceasing struggle against it. . . ."

[71] *Khilāfa*, 217–219/129–130.

by Mu'āwiya's example. It was then employed by the Abbasids, backed by Persian resentment against the Arabs and Manichean resentment against Islam, to establish Chosroism; then the rise of Turkish military leaders signified the complete collapse of the Caliphate. As a result of the social evolution following the initial introduction of arbitrary government, with the general weakening of the religious spirit, it eventually became impossible to reestablish a state based on the Rāshidūn principles.[72]

This is the closest Riḍā comes in his study of the Caliphate to recognizing that the issue he presents is in effect one between politically and socially expressed religious devotion on the one hand and the irascible tendencies of human nature on the other. He spoils it somewhat by attributing the failure of the former to prevail to an insidious ages-long plot, and also by casting Islamic principles in the mold of modern liberalism.

In taking the position he does, he runs into direct conflict with Ibn Khaldūn on the question of *'aṣabiyya*. Ibn Khaldūn had developed this notion into one of the fundamental motivating forces of political and sociological organization in his theory of history, to the extent where even the divinely revealed religious message could not be propagated effectively without its support. His classification of types of political authority included religious nomocracy as a subdivision of the larger category of rule by law (*mulk siyāsī*) in which power in the community was organized, but was still nevertheless power.[73]

Ibn Khaldūn used his theory of the inescapable need for the support of *'aṣabiyya* in politics to justify the role of the Umayyad dynasty and in particular Mu'āwiya's effort to secure acceptance of his son Yazīd as his successor. This action, he argues, was justified by Mu'āwiya's need to placate his fellow Umayyads in order to avert civil war, and was in the best interests of the Community, which depended for its unity and strength upon Umayyad solidarity.[74]

The Prophet's criticism of *'aṣabiyya*, furthermore, was directed only against its unbalanced use, as an expression of love of conquest or overweening pride. When directed to God's service, it is quite commendable. If it were to disappear altogether, there would be no effective force behind the application of the Sharī'a. In the case of temporal

---

[72] *Ibid.*, 220–223/131–133.

[73] See above, pp. 29–30.

[74] *Muqaddima*, chap. iii, sec. 26 and sec. 28; Rosenthal, I, 422–423 and 431–434. See above, p. 45.

rule, then, the spirit of domination is only condemned when it is immoderate and directed toward oppressive ends.[75]

Riḍā entirely rejects this interpretation and asserts that Ibn Khaldūn is mistaken in considering *'aṣabiyya* relevant to prophetic missions and to the Caliphate, whose whole social purpose is to supplant *'aṣabiyya* by the rule of law. The right of the clan of Quraish to the Caliphate is based on their high social prestige, not on their possession of the force and violence that underlie *'aṣabiyya*.[76]

These objections indicate, however, that Riḍā, like Muḥammad 'Abduh, relies on a definition of *'aṣabiyya* different from that of Ibn Khaldūn. Riḍā's and 'Abduh's definition is restricted to what Ibn Khaldūn himself condemned: pure force, not including social prestige, immoderately used for entirely selfish ends. Riḍā acknowledges that it is the social influence of the Quraish that entitled them to leadership; in Ibn Khaldūn's terminology this is an aspect of *'aṣabiyya*. On this point, then, the two writers are not far apart. But beyond this, when Riḍā denies the virtue of military prowess as a support of early Islamic government and takes Ibn Khaldūn to task for seeking to justify the conduct of Mu'āwiya,[77] it is clear that their conceptions of politics in the Caliphate are very different.

In the light of Riḍā's overall doctrine of the Caliphate it is difficult to define the extent to which he came to grips in his own mind with the problem of power and authority. His remarks on the *ahl al-ḥall wa 'l-'aqd* clearly reflect an awareness of the importance of power, while leaving the normative and moral aspects of authority obscure. His criticism of the idea of a "spiritual" Caliphate, especially the post-1922 Ottoman one, seems to indicate the same awareness, which is obscured, however, by the wholly spiritual character of the institution he himself proposes.[78] Finally, his treatment of *'aṣabiyya* gives the impression that he regards the Caliphate in its complete and duly established form as the expression of an ideal, transfigured, millennial society in which the historic failings of human nature have, by divine grace, ceased to exist.[79]

[75] *Muqaddima*, chap. iii, sec. 26; Rosenthal, I, 414–417.

[76] *Khilāfa*, 226–227/134–135.

[77] *Ibid.*, 227/135.

[78] See below, pp. 183–186.

[79] This is reminiscent of similar tendencies infrequently appearing in Muḥammad 'Abduh's writings, described above (pp. 139–142) as the cataclysmic-enlightenment view of historical evolution. See *Risāla*, 100/144.

C. *Spiritual and Temporal Authority*

Whether the caliph's authority is conceived as spiritual or temporal is largely a question of levels of meaning. It can be considered spiritual in the sense that the theoretical justification for the existence of the office is found in the religious-law source of *ijmāʿ* and in the presumed need to enforce the Sharīʿa; application of the divine law is, in fact, the essential function of the caliph. On the other hand, if this function is looked at in terms of the actions it involves—that is, the use of centralized powers of constraint to enforce a particular legal code, regardless of the origin of the code or the moral desirability of its enforcement—then it is a temporal function. We can harmonize these two points of view by saying that the Caliphate, in theory, served to provide temporal enforcement of a law much of which dealt with temporal matters, but that both the law itself and its application were considered to be imbued with religious significance and to have a religious sanction.

The classical theory, from a modern vantage point, seems vague and inconclusive because it took little cognizance of this distinction. Much of it is only intelligible on the religious level, although at the same time it purported to deal with questions whose importance was on the positive or existential level. This explains its failure to deal adequately with the problem of power and authority. By relying on the classical theory as his raw material, Rashīd Riḍā falls prey to the same weakness, as we have attempted to show.

On the question of spiritual and temporal authority, he is again often incoherent. This is partly because of the ambiguity of meanings in the theory he inherited and partly, perhaps, because of the pressure of apologetics under which he wrote, which led him, in his zeal to prove the soundness of his own doctrines and errors of others (Turks, Westernizing Arabs, and Europeans), to a tendency to dash off in several directions at once. In principle he recognizes that in traditional theory the caliphal power is temporal while its ultimate significance is spiritual—that God possesses sovereignty but man exercises it—and seeks at times to stress the temporal aspects and to demolish the notion that there can be such a thing as a "spiritual" Caliphate. His own proposals for a restored Caliphate, however, do in fact suggest a spiritual institution. This is partially explained by his belief that a more temporal office could not at the time be realized; yet in some of his theoretical passages he implies that the nature of the authority of even the true Caliphate is spiritual rather than temporal.

First, as for his emphasis on temporal authority, we have seen that he wrote at length of the political sovereignty of the representatives of the Community, the *ahl al-ḥall wa 'l-'aqd,* and the function of the caliph, as their nominee, to direct the common affairs of the Community and serve as the chief interpreter of the law. This law, Riḍā indicates in his chapter on "Islamic Legislation and the Caliphate," is in some respects temporal in content but spiritual in significance, and in still other respects devoid of religious importance and hence open to the discretion of the ruler to modify and adapt as he will, according to the best interests of his subjects. This last category includes the whole realm of political, administrative, financial, judicial, and military organization. Man-made legislation in this field is called by Riḍā *ishtirā'*.[80]

Furthermore, in applying the Sharī'a even in its more spiritual aspects, the strict rule is that conduct must be judged only in its external form, without presumptions as to the spiritual worth of the inner motivations of the parties. "The caliph in Islam is only the chief of a [constitutionally] limited government."[81] His political powers, then, are not themselves spiritual.

In his apologetic work *Shubuhāt an-Naṣārā wa Ḥujaj al-Islām*[82] Riḍā elaborates on this theme. Defining the content of the revealed Law is the task of the jurists in consultation with one another; enforcement of the Law is assigned to the caliph.

> The function of this leader [the caliph] is to protect the Faith and its adherents and to enforce the ordinances of the Sharī'a. He is not empowered over the people in religious matters nor has he independent authority to determine the *shar'ī* ordinances for them. His task is only to maintain order and enforce the laws. Thus his power is civil and subject to consultation, not absolute or exclusive. But Islam has required him to act in accordance with the revealed Law and has forbidden him to legislate in his own right. It requires obedience to him so long as this entails right conduct, just as it requires the Community to remove him from power if he obliges them to do what is unlawful. In this sense it is true that the civil power in Islam is dependent on religion and that thus it is a religious power. But it is false to

[80] *Khilāfa,* 154/92. (See also below, p. 189.)

[81] *Ibid.,* 209/123.

[82] Cairo, 1322 H., reprinted from a series of articles appearing in Volumes IV and V of *Al-Manār.*

> liken this to religious power found in other religions than Islam or to suppose that the leader in Islam combines two powers, one over spirits and minds and the other over bodies and actions.[83]

Nothing is more absurd, he concludes, than for Christians to advise Muslims that the path to their worldly salvation lies in withdrawing their political authorities from the constraint of the revealed Law and substituting legislation based on their own desires.[84]

Two chapters quoted in the *Khilāfa* from Muḥammad 'Abduh's *Al-Islām wa 'n-Naṣrāniyya ma' al-'Ilm wa 'l-Madaniyya* (whose general arguments are reproduced in substance in the *Shubuhāt*) argue much the same point: that Islam's mission has been, in part, to abolish the religious powers of clerical authorities, so that "there is no such thing in Islam as what some call spiritual authority." Unlike the Pope, who enjoys special infallibility in interpreting revelation and is not responsible to the body of believers, "the caliph is from all points of view a temporal ruler." It is the papal heritage that has led Christians to suppose that Islam similarly granted absolute powers in spiritual as well as temporal affairs to the ruler.[85]

The then recently established Ottoman "spiritual" Caliphate was contemptuously rejected by Riḍā as having nothing to do with the true institution.[86] In any case, he added, few persons took this new Turkish office seriously, except perhaps as a move to ward off British designs to secure the title for one of their own protégés.[87] He also blamed non-Arab Muslims for having over-glorified the office of the Caliphate in Abbasid and Ottoman times, with the result that now, by continuing the mere title of caliph, the Turks were able to convince some persons that the institution still remained in spiritual form.[88]

Riḍā first directed such allegations, in fact, against the Ottoman Caliphate even before the Young Turk revolution of 1908–1909. A passage in his *Shubuhāt*, originally written about 1901, seeking to deny the existence of sacerdotal powers in Islam, declares that the title

---

83 *Shubuhāt*, p. 78.

84 *Ibid.*, p. 79.

85 *Khilāfa*, 210–215/124–127, reprinted from *Al-Islām wa 'n-Naṣrāniyya*, pp. 61–67. See the discussion of the same passage above, pp. 148–150.

86 *Khilāfa*, 94/55.

87 *Ibid.*, 113/67. This is a reference to the Sharīf Ḥusain of the Ḥijāz, whom Riḍā attacked bitterly (*ibid.*, 123–127/73–76). It was not until March, 1924, however, that Ḥusain was proclaimed *Amīr al-Mu'minīn* by a small body of followers.

88 *Ibid.*, 209/123.

"Shaikh al-Islam" (applied to the chief *muftī* in Constantinople) is " . . . an invention of kings and amirs who were themselves far removed from any appearance of religiosity and so sought to benefit from whomever had that appearance, out of consideration of the effect this would have on the spirits of the unquestioning masses."[89]

These arguments contribute to his position not only that spiritual power does not exist but also, conversely, that the political or temporal role of Islam is essential. In a letter he addressed in 1919 to Lloyd George, he wrote: "The Muslims consider that their religion truly exists only when a strong and independent Muslim state is established that can put the laws of Islam into application free from all foreign opposition and domination."[90]

His insistence on Islam's temporal and political message comes to a head in his attacks on ʿAlī ʿAbd ar-Rāziq, the Azhar graduate whose revolutionary treatise *Al-Islām wa Uṣūl al-Ḥukm*[91] denied on the one hand that Islam was intended by the Prophet to apply to politics, and on the other that the Rāshidūn caliphs were more than purely temporal rulers whose authority had no Islamic sanction. Rashīd Riḍā sums up what he considers objectionable in ʿAbd ar-Rāziq's assertions as follows:

> That Islam has no caliph nor imam nor government nor political or judicial legislation; that it is a purely spiritual religion like Christianity as understood by the Protestant sect; that all that the Muslims have believed from the time of Abū Bakr to the present day regarding the Imamate and Caliphate is void in word and misguided in deed and is corruption on the earth, in its attribution of religiously and divinely sanctioned power to the caliph; that a group of Muslims misled secular rulers into imposing their power on them, and that Abū Bakr was only a king of the Arabs who wanted to achieve their unity; that . . . all those who rebelled against him in refusing to pay the *zakāḥ* were not apostates from Islam, and that the war against them was not religious but political, in defense of the Arab state and its unity; that Islam itself does not oblige the Arabs or any other Muslims to have a state or unity; rather, every party of Muslims, Arabs or non-Arabs, may establish for themselves a

---

[89] *Shubuhāt*, 77.

[90] *Khilāfa*, 194/114.

[91] Cairo, 1925; French translation by Léon Bercher, "L'Islam et les bases du pouvoir," *Revue des Études Islamiques*, 1933, pp. 353–390, and 1934, pp. 163–222.

government to their liking, and the religion of Islam does not limit them in this in any way.[92]

These views were anathema to Riḍā because they presented the Caliphate as a wholly temporal, in fact secular, institution, and particularly because they seemed to impugn the special sanctity of the Rāshidūn caliphs, beginning with Abū Bakr himself. 'Abd ar-Rāziq's party claimed that his ideas were faithful to the teachings of Muḥammad 'Abduh and that the great reformer, had he lived, would have defended the book against the attacks of Riḍā and the Azhar shaikhs. Louis Massignon expresses what would seem to be fully justified skepticism in this regard, principally on the grounds that 'Abduh's denunciation of allegations of spiritual powers in Islam was limited to a denial of the existence of a theocratic clerical class, and that 'Abduh could scarcely have accepted 'Abd ar-Rāziq's assertion that the administration of justice is an entirely secular function.[93]

In reality Rashīd Riḍā and 'Alī 'Abd ar-Rāziq were in partial agreement on a number of points. In arguing that the political organization and activities of the caliph and his appointees were devoid of spiritual powers and were therefore "civil" or "temporal"; that in matters of political, military, judicial, and administrative organization the caliph was free to "legislate" according to his own judgment; that the Community held supreme political authority through its representatives—in these assertions, Riḍā seemingly championed a secular characterization of authority. But these views had only to do with the exercise of authority, whose ultimate origin and sanction in Riḍā's mind re-

[92] *Manār*, XXVI, 101–102. The condemnation of 'Alī 'Abd ar-Rāziq is continued in *Manār*, XXVI, 230–232, and XXVII, 715–717. The text of the judgment of the "Council of Leading 'Ulamā' of the Azhar" condemning the book and stripping 'Abd ar-Rāziq of his diploma appears in *Manār*, XXVI, 363–382; other documents relating to the affair, culminating in 'Abd ar-Rāziq's removal from his judicial post, are published in the same volume, pp. 212–217 and 383–393. A lengthy refutation of 'Abd ar-Rāziq's main ideas was published by Shaikh Muḥammad Bakhīt under the title *Ḥaqīqat al-Islām wa Uṣūl al-Ḥukm* (Cairo, 1926), and another by Shaikh Muḥammad al-Khiḍr Ḥusain, *Naqs Kitāb al-Islām wa Uṣūl al-Ḥukm* (Cairo, 1925). Both 'Abd ar-Rāziq's and Bakhīt's books are summarized in A. H. Hourani, *Arabic Thought*, pp. 183–190; see also Adams, *Islam and Modernism*, pp. 259–268; H. Lammens, "La Crise intérieure de l'Islam," *Les Études*, CLXXXVI (1926), 129–146; M. Fakhry, "The Theocratic Idea of the Islamic State in Recent Controversies," *International Affairs*, XXX (1954), 450–462.

[93] *Revue du Monde Musulman*, LIX, 313. The appeal by 'Abd ar-Rāziq's party to 'Abduh's name in support of their views appeared in the Cairo weekly *As-Siyāsa*, July 6, 1925.

mained in the Divine Law, so that with due consistency he could castigate the Turkish Grand National Assembly for proclaiming the doctrine of full "national sovereignty."[94] 'Abd ar-Rāziq meanwhile denied the religious origin as well as function of political authority.

Another publication that symbolized for Riḍā the secularist error into which an increasing number of Muslims were falling has already been mentioned. This is the tract "The Caliphate and National Sovereignty" (*Hilafet ve Hakimiyet-i-Milliye*) published in 1922 by the Turkish Grand National Assembly in justification of the replacement of the Ottoman Sultanate by a "spiritual" Caliphate.[95] Briefly summarized, this work offers the following argument:

> The Prophet's neglect of discussion of his political succession shows its secondary importance. The Caliphate is therefore a matter for the Muslims to organize for themselves. Only clear texts of Qur'ān and ḥadīth are properly speaking religious law; all else is only the "law of *ijtihād*," on which there is little consensus. In these the government is free to choose what is temporally most expeditious. The caliph's authority resembles that of the president of a republic, resting on a general delegation of authority.[96]
>
> Unless the caliph is instituted by the free choice of the nation, his office is entirely fictitious. Arbitrary rule has no place in Islam. But when the required qualifications are not present in any candidate, it is valid to choose a lesser personage by a process of free election.[97]
>
> The community alone can confer authority. The contract of the Caliphate is essentially one of agency, which consists, in the words of the *Mecelle*, of "one person empowering some other person to perform some act for him."[98] As the nation's mandatory, the caliph is always subject to recall for the abuse of power. A *walāya* cannot by law be exercised without the subject's consent, except in cases of minors; only in the latter case is it freely exercised by virtue of inherent capacity alone; otherwise it is by delegation from the subject.[99]

---

[94] *Khilāfa*, 233/138.

[95] The Arabic translation by 'Abd al-Ghanī Sānī Bey did not appear until 1924, after the publication of Riḍā's *Khilāfa*.

[96] *Revue du Monde Musulman*, LIX, 5–16.

[97] *Ibid.*, 17–26.

[98] See C. A. Hooper, *The Civil Law of Palestine and Trans-Jordan* (Jerusalem, 1933), I, 375 (*Mecelle*, Art. 1449).

[99] *Revue du Monde Musulman*, LIX, 28–42. It is this interpretation of the *walāya*

> The obligation to establish an Imamate is no more than the obligation to have a competent ruler. He need not have full powers if governmental functions are adequately performed by others. No one since the Rāshidūn has been ideally qualified; therefore, *a fortiori*, the imam's powers should be limited. These limitations are left to peoples of each historical age to work out for themselves.[100] One form is to require the caliph to delegate his authority to other bodies: this is what the new Ottoman caliph has done. Properly speaking, the question of the Caliphate is not a religious one but is only a matter of avoiding anarchy. The means for this should vary with the times.[101]

It is interesting to compare these principles with those of Rashīd Riḍā. What the Turkish argument supports, of course, is not a spiritual Caliphate in the sense of an office having the function of supervising or directing the religious beliefs and practices of the subjects. It maintains, on the contrary, that the Caliphate is a wholly temporal office, to an extent greater than that envisaged by Riḍā. On the other hand, by arguing that the temporal power of the caliph himself can legitimately be reduced to nought, it leaves the institution, if anything, an aura of tradition and ceremony which might represent to the minds of some Muslims a spiritual function—though assuredly not a spiritual power.

The fact is that Rashīd Riḍā himself argues the case for national sovereignty over the caliph in a strikingly similar manner. For him, as for the authors of the Turkish pamphlet, the caliph's *walāya* or title to authority rests on a contractual delegation from the representatives of the Community, and is thereby strictly limited; it is for this reason described in both works as temporal authority, and the caliph is compared by both to the chief of a limited or constitutional government. Both seek by this means to withdraw the theory of the Caliphate from the realm of theology and secure it on the plane of positive human relationships. By contrast, the earlier jurists, while they did not accept the popular term *khalīfat Allāh* in the sense of "successor to God," in substance viewed the caliph as the deputy or agent of God on Earth. The *walāya* for the earlier jurists, as the second chapter of this book

as applied to the caliph that represents the primary departure of this presentation—and that of Rashīd Riḍā—from the classical theory, in which the caliph's *walāya* had been more comparable to that over a minor resting on inherent, rather than contracted, capacity.

[100] *Ibid.*, 45–53.

[101] *Ibid.*, 59–70.

attempts to show, rested in the office of the Caliphate not by virtue of delegation from the Community but by virtue of the inherent incapacity of the Community to govern itself and the capacity of the ruler, by virtue of his particular qualifications, to do so. This is therefore to be compared to a *walāya* over a minor, as in the example—often used by the jurists—of a guardian's authority over a marriageable girl. The contract of the *bay'a* in these circumstances was a matter of recognition by both parties of their inherent relationship; both Rashīd Riḍā and the anonymous spokesman of the Grand National Assembly made it an instrument of delegation of authority.

Turning now to Riḍā's own proposals for a revived Caliphate, we find these concerned principally with no more than the elements of a spiritual and cultural directory, with political authority nominally delegated (in the manner so distasteful to him in other passages)[102] to its *de facto* holders.

Riḍā would first establish a seminary for the training of qualified jurists and potential caliphs, whose function as a body would be the exercise of *ijtihād* or interpretive endeavor, under the leadership of the caliph, whose most important quality would be that of chief *mujtahid*.[103] A system of election of the caliph by the *ahl al-ḥall wa 'l-'aqd* would then be established.[104] Finally, a bureaucracy of the following offices, each in the form of a consultative council, would be instituted:

a. General consultation;
b. *Fatwās* (legal opinions) and religious publications;
c. Investiture of deputies, heads of Muslim states, governors, *qāḍīs*, and *muftīs*;
d. General surveillance of the government;
e. Propaganda and missionary work;
f. Sermons, preaching, spiritual guidance, *ḥisba*;
g. Collection of the *zakāh*;
h. Supervision of the pilgrimage and service of the two Holy Cities;
i. Correspondence.[105]

There is no indication that the functions of (*c*) and (*d*) would be more than ceremonial, although apparently Riḍā hoped that this system would germinate into a full-fledged government and the politi-

[102] *Khilāfa*, 115/68.
[103] *Ibid.*, 132/78.
[104] *Ibid.*, 133/79. But there is still no means of deciding who the *ahl* are.
[105] *Ibid.*, 134/80.

cal realization of pan-Islam. For the time being, pan-Islam is admittedly only a spiritual and cultural ideal, and it is recognized that the opposition from the colonial powers will be especially stiff to the extent that the movement is frankly political. "Conversely, opposition will be much attenuated if these motives are purely religious and tend toward no other goal than to reestablish the Law of Islam as God promulgated it."[106] Riḍā maintains that

> If our program were instituted in even a small area, the whole Muslim world would not fail, out of religious discipline, to accept the legitimacy of this new caliph; none of the Muslim governments would find themselves authorized to criticize it and none of the Muslims subject to foreign rule would be able to renounce it. Every Islamic people would then seek attachment to it, so that those who were unable to follow the government of the true imam because of the constraint of a foreign power would strive at least to follow the main body of Muslims and their imam in fulfillment of God's command, in matters over which their own government exercised no control having to do with the organization of religious education and instruction and laws of personal status. Indeed, every government exercising control over Muslim subjects would find itself compelled to conciliate them to an extent commensurate with their unity and public opinion in permitting them to follow the religious guidance of their caliph, as the Catholics do with the Pope.[107]

This curious reference is the Papacy is one of several in the *Khilāfa* which suggest the attraction exerted by that institution on Riḍā. While denying that the spiritual powers of the Pope were duplicated in the office of caliph, evidently he is impressed by the success of the Roman Catholic Church in maintaining cohesion and organization among its worshippers and leadership over them, as well perhaps as providing a systematic means of progressive interpretation of dogma. "Have the Muslims never taken note of the action of the Papacy," he

---

[106] *Ibid.*, 200/118. Is Islamic law then purely spiritual? Laoust, in a note to his translation, notes the contradiction between Rashīd Riḍā's "political pan-Islamism and his confessional internationalism" (p. 271, note 56).

[107] *Khilāfa*, 174–175/103. It is interesting to note once again the assumption, common among medieval Muslim writers as well as with Riḍā, that moral truth where it exists will be assured of recognition and in turn will be observed. Just as sound moral qualities in the ruler were traditionally considered a guarantee of good government, so now we find that if the Caliphate is properly reestablished, Muslims everywhere can be counted on to adhere to it.

asks, "which succeeded in organizing its religious power socially and financially? We have copied the foreigner in his faults, but we have not imitated him when it would be to our advantage."[108]

Again, he argues that the failure of the Muslim 'ulamā' to present an effective exposition of Islam with which to stem the drift among Muslims toward Western secularism—let alone their failure to win new converts to Islam in the West—is due to the fact that the "Muslims do not have a leader and an organized body to undertake such a task with the necessary organization and funds in the manner that it is done by the leader of the Catholics, the Pope, and the patriarchs and bishops and missionary societies in Christian lands."[109]

These references to the Papacy carry no enthusiasm for the idea of infallible proclamation of dogma nor for powers of spiritual intercession. Still, they represent a desire on Riḍā's part to organize a form of spiritual leadership and authoritative—as distinguished from infallible—interpretation of questions of religious law if not of theology. He is proposing in effect to organize into a definitive institution what has never been organized in Sunnī Islam before, under the auspices of the Caliphate, which had never since the Mu'tazilite inquisition in the third century of Islam exerted direct influence over the body of 'ulamā'.

While the emphasis on religious supervision in Riḍā's program for the Caliphate is partially to be explained by considerations of necessity, it must be acknowledged that at the same time the functions he proposes have the character of positive spiritual authority in their own right. His proposal is for more than simply a ready framework for temporal powers which he hopes will accrue to the caliph in course of time: it is also for a spiritual directory which would exert its interpretive religious authority without waiting for the fulfillment of its political mission.[110]

---

108 *Ibid.*, 82/47.

109 *Ibid.*, 109/65. It is speculative but not implausible to imagine that Riḍā's plan for a training college for future *mujtahids* and caliphs was inspired in part by the example of Christian clerical education in the theological seminaries. Could he even have been the victim of a misunderstanding of the meaning of the College of Cardinals?

110 Nonetheless he is unwilling to confide such powers to a Muslim government that is not properly constituted or motivated, whatever its temporal power. In an article in 1913 he cited a maxim of Ghazālī: "Either be a Jew in practice or do not play with the Torah," drawing from this the moral that the Ottoman Empire must either "found an Islamic government free of imitations of the West and its laws . . . and give the Caliphate its rightful place in reviving the call to Islam, applying the legal sanctions

Thus, Riḍā's view of the relation of spiritual to temporal authority presents the same ambiguity as does his treatment of the relation between power and authority, with the difference that in developing his considerations of the spiritual significance of authority in Islam, he proceeds a step beyond the classical writers, who were content to leave the spiritual aspects of authority indeterminate, unorganized, and therefore less extensive. Spiritual authority to Rashīd Riḍā, despite his initial denial of its existence in Islam, is not only a matter of the origin and sanction of temporal authority; in the institution he proposes, it is a positive function as well.

---

and maintaining religious freedom," or turn over all supervision of religious affairs except those clearly of an official character to private religious societies, individuals, and religious endowments, extending them the necessary financial aid and protection (*Manār*, XVII, 77).

VI

MUḤAMMAD RASHĪD RIḌĀ: LEGAL DOCTRINES

Rashīd Riḍā's theories of jurisprudence generally follow logically from Muḥammad 'Abduh's concept of the identity of natural law with the Sharī'a. He adopted this concept as his own and built upon it a liberal method of legal reasoning, in which the guiding principle was *maṣlaḥa*.

But as in the case of his constitutional ideas, his legal ideas tended to remain on the theoretical level. He appeared to distrust efforts to apply them to particular situations when this led to results resembling those arrived at through secular means in the Western manner. This was particularly the case when he sensed, after World War I, that it was no longer the tradition-bound 'ulamā' but the rising class of Westernizing Muslim intelligentsia who represented the strongest challenge to his views. Consequently, while his legal theory was more or less progressive (albeit ambiguously so), when it came to drawing concrete conclusions he was sometimes recalcitrant. In this, as in his constitutional theory, he showed himself to be an ideologist bound by traditional idealism rather than a practical reformer.

A. *The Maṣlaḥa as a Legal Source*

Riḍā's chief purpose in his writings on legal questions was to show that the Sharī'a was intended and suited to be a comprehensive legal structure for Islamic society, rather than either a purely millennial set of ideals or a system whose operation is restricted to matters of personal status. Indeed, to him piecemeal application of the Sharī'a ordinances is even harmful in some cases: by neglecting one part of the Law it is impossible to apply the rest properly, since profound changes in social custom and attitude will result and consequently the whole structure of social institutions will be altered.[1]

He takes sharp exception, therefore, to those Muslims who argue that the principle of legislation by the Community or nation is of Western invention and suppose that the Sharī'a is limited to a few inadequate prescriptions from the Qur'ān and Sunna, the elaboration of which was cut short with the closing of the gate of *ijtihād*. These persons assert that this is the reason for Muslim backwardness and that the only remedy is to adopt Western secular codes. To this Riḍā replies:

> This is the opinion of those who are ignorant of the fundamental principles of the Islamic Sharī'a and the basis of legislation in it. They do not distinguish between the [traditional] juristic usage and the modern usage of the word "legislation" [*tashrī'*], so that the difference in usage hides the truth from them. That is because the terms *dīn* and *shar'* can be used as synonyms, although they are respectively general and particular terms. For they [i.e., the ignorant ones] often restrict *shar'* to mean judicial or practical rules to the exclusion of the fundamentals of doctrine, authority, and ethics, which are principles of religion and are related to the welfare of both this world and the next. Thus they divide jurisprudence into two parts, *'ibādāt* and *mu'āmalāt* [ritual devotions and social transactions], and the jurists themselves distinguish between religious faith and the execution of justice, saying, "This is permissible from the legal but not from the religious point of view." But practical rules are called "religion" in consideration of the fact that God is served by their observance and they are followed in submission to His commands and prohibitions. It is in this sense that the term "lawgiver" [*shāri'*] is applied to God; it is applied to the Prophet only in the sense that he is the transmitter and elucidator of the law. . . .
>
> The real truth is that all this [i.e., both religious faith and the execution of justice] is of particular religious significance, having been legislated to enable man to come close to God in the case of the *'ibādāt*, and to enable him to avoid evil and disapproved actions and observe the truth in the case of the *mu'āmalāt*, and both together being a means of purifying the soul and of preparing it for the life to come. Among the *mu'āmalāt* there are those acts which have a religious importance, such as respect for the

[1] *Al-Khilāfa au al-Imāma 'l-'Uẓmā* (Cairo, 1923), 168/100.

> person, honor, and property of others, giving them sincere advice, and abstention from sin, oppression, aggression, deceit, treachery, and predatory consumption of other persons' property.
>
> As regards other things than these, such as formulation of policy, the organization of judicial administration, conduct of government, tax-collecting, and the rules of warfare, all of which do not involve piety and closeness to God in their various applications beyond good intentions—in all of these the Prophet was a legislator [*mushtari'*] for his own time by his own *ijtihād*, being commanded by God to consult the Community in these matters, particularly those in authority who are the repositories of its confidence in its general interests and who represent its will, from among the 'ulamā', chiefs, and leaders. . . .[2]

The true distinction between religious and nonreligious law, then, is not between the *'ibādāt* and the *mu'āmalāt*, but between *'ibādāt* plus those parts of the *mu'āmalāt* having a moral significance on the one hand, and on the other hand those parts of the *mu'āmalāt* that are purely questions of administrative organization or practical convenience and therefore have no inherent moral importance. The function of the religious law in Islam, properly understood, is to regulate *all* human actions having any connection with religious morality.

But the distinction between *'ibādāt* and *mu'āmalāt* is nevertheless valid in another way, and it is here that we find the basis of the Community's power of legislation. This other distinction is explained in a series of articles that Rashīd Riḍā published in early numbers of *Al-Manār* entitled "Debates Between the Reformer and the Slavish Imitator" (*Muḥāwarāt al-Muṣliḥ wa 'l-Muqailid*). The young reformer (who, of course, speaks for Rashīd Riḍā) takes the view that the fixed *shar'ī* principles in the *mu'āmalāt* are of only a general character, allowing for considerable adaptation by successive generations of Muslims in the light of the demands of their worldly welfare, while it is only the *'ibābāt*, governing matters of ritual and worship, that do not admit of interpretive change.

> The principles of the Islamic religion are true belief, formation of good character, self-cultivation, and worship of God in the prescribed manner, as well as the general fundamentals of the *mu'āmalāt* such as protection of life, honor, and property. All these principles were laid down in the Prophet's lifetime.

[2] *Ibid.*, 153–154/91–92.

> . . . Creed and ritual were completed in detail so as to permit neither additions nor subtractions, and whoever adds to them or subtracts from them is changing Islam and bringing forth a new religion. As for the rules of the *mu'āmalāt*, beyond decreeing the elements of virtue such as the necessity for justice in laws and equality in rights and forbidding rebelliousness, aggression, deceit, and treachery, and establishing penalties for certain crimes, and beyond imposing the principle of consultation, the Lawgiver delegated the affair in its detailed applications to the leading 'ulamā' and rulers, who according to law must possess knowledge and moral probity, to decide by consulting one another what is most beneficial for the Community according to the circumstances of the times. The Companions understood this without need for a textual revelation from the Prophet, as is known from the ḥadīth concerning the mission of Mu'ādh b. Jabal to Yemen. . . . Indeed it is related that the Companions, if they saw benefit in anything, used to judge in favor or it, even if this opposed the usual custom followed, for they saw that the correct principle was to adopt whatever course was beneficial rather than to cling to the details and subsidiary rules of laws. . . .[3]

The Ḥanafī principle of *istiḥsān*, continues Rashīd Riḍā's "reformer," is essentially an application of this spirit. "*Istiḥsān* means that ruling in which a benefit to the Community is confirmed;" it is not really a "hidden *qiyās*," as is sometimes alleged; the latter explanation was only invented to escape the ḥadīth partisans' allegation that *istiḥsān* raised personal opinion to the status of an independent source of law.[4]

The dividing line between the area in which faithfulness to the specific content of revelation is enjoined, and the area in which consideration of circumstantial utility becomes the guiding rule, emerges less clearly in one of Riḍā's later writings. This is a little book entitled *Yusr al-Islām wa Uṣūl at-Tashrī' al-'Āmm* ("The Accommodating Spirit of Islam and the Sources of General Jurisprudence"),[5] containing a lengthy review of the principle of *qiyās* followed by a discussion of *maṣlaḥa.* In the preface Riḍā explains, in his usual fashion, that he favors a middle path between those rigid conservatives whose legal

---

[3] *Manār*, IV, 209–210.

[4] *Ibid.*, 211 and 860.

[5] Cairo, 1928. The book amplifies his commentary on Q. v:101 in 'Abduh and Riḍā, *Tafsīr al-Qur'ān al-Ḥakīm* (Cairo, 1346–1354 H.), Vol. V.

interpretations are all tied to one traditional sect or another, and those secularists who at most use Islamic "symbols" but are ready in practice to disregard Islam entirely and to borrow legal codes from Europe or evolve new ones on the basis of local convenience.

> The moderate advocates of Islamic reform are those who affirm that it is possible to resuscitate Islam and renew its true guidance by following the Qur'ān and the true Sunna and the guidance of the Virtuous Forefathers [*as-salaf aṣ-ṣāliḥ*], and by seeking the help of the learning of the Imams [i.e., the great scholars of the past], without cleaving to particular sectarian books and teachings around which the first group has solidified. They also affirm that it is possible to combine this with the noblest forms of civilization and organization which the second groups calls for. Indeed, they believe that religion and the most modern techniques of civilization and power, on both of which they advocate primary reliance, are two friends in agreement, not in conflict, and that each adds to the power and nobility of the other.

Most of the section of the book dealing with *qiyās* consists of extended quotations from the medieval Ḥanbalī scholars Ibn Ḥazm (d. 1064) and Ibn Qayyim al-Jauziyya. The central issue is the relation between *qiyās* and the revealed texts of Qur'ān and Sunna. Ibn Ḥazm, a sweeping opponent of *qiyās*, had argued that whatever actions were neither commanded nor prohibited by the revealed sources were thereby discretionary, and that to introduce new commands or prohibitions through *qiyās* would amount to changing the divinely prescribed character of discretionary acts.[6]

Ibn Qayyim al-Jauziyya, on the other hand, distinguishes between the valid and invalid uses of legal reasoning. Some, he says, are definitely sound, namely those that stem from the clear implications of revealed texts through identification of their *'ilal*. Others are definitely false, in that they contradict revealed texts or involve idle speculation on theological questions, or treat the Sacred Law as an object of riddles and fanciful questions. A third category consists of those judgments involving problematical comparisons (*ishtibāh*): they cannot be binding, but may be resorted to by individuals in case of need.

Qiyās, according to Ibn al-Qayyim, is therefore valid to the extent

[6] *Yusr al-Islām wa Uṣūl at-Tashrī' al-'Āmm* (Cairo, 1928), pp. 30–37, quoting Ibn Ḥazm's *Al-Muḥallā bi 'l-Āthār fī Sharḥ al-Mujallā bi 'l-Iqtiṣār* (Cairo, 1347–1352 H.).

that it conforms to revealed texts, and invalid insofar as it is contrived (*iṣṭilāḥī*).[7]

Ibn al-Qayyim criticizes both the extreme opponents of *qiyās* and its extreme partisans. Both parties, he states,

> . . . shut themselves off from one of the paths to truth and consequently were impelled to widen some other path beyond its capacity. Thus the opponents of *qiyās*, when they excluded the process of seeking similarities and causes and considering motives and interests behind the law [*ḥikam wa maṣāliḥ*]—which are a part of the justice and equity of God's revelation—had to broaden [their reliance on] literal meanings [*ẓāhir*] and on *istiṣḥāb* [continuing to apply a past ruling, on the basis of presumption, for lack of acceptable evidence of present inapplicability], resorting to them beyond the limits of need and stretching them farther than they would stretch. By their affirmation of textually indicated rulings without consideration for what lay behind them, [in effect] they rejected them and resorted to *istiṣḥāb*.[8]

This narrow approach led this group to ignore the clear implications that sometimes are present in the texts, and to abuse the method of *istiṣḥāb* by carrying it beyond the bounds of plausibility, with the result that they tended to assume the invalidity of certain actions until positive proof was furnished of their validity, which is the reverse of the correct presumption.[9]

On the other hand, the extreme partisans of *qiyās* are condemned by Ibn al-Qayyim for their disregard of revealed texts and for failing to recognize the comprehensive relevance of these sources for all human actions.

> They widened the paths of *ra'y* [personal opinion] and *qiyās*; they advocated the method of *qiyās ash-shabah* [purely external analogy], linking rulings to attributes to which it is unknown whether the Lawgiver linked them or not, and identified *'ilal* on whose account it is unknown whether the Lawgiver issued laws or not. . . . [They also erred] in their belief that many rules of the Sharī'a were at variance with justice and analogy. . . .[10]

---

[7] *Yusr*, pp. 39–44, quoting Ibn al-Qayyim's *I'lām al-Muwaqqi'īn 'an Rabb al-'Ālamīn* (Cairo, n.d.).

[8] *Ibid.*, p. 45.

[9] *Ibid.*, pp. 46–47.

[10] *Ibid.*, p. 48.

In truth, Ibn al-Qayyim assures us, nothing in the Sharī'a opposes sound *qiyās*, and if it seems to do so, either the particular analogy is unsound, or the revealed text in question has been misunderstood. His criterion of soundness is that of specific and logical derivation from a textual ruling, in the same manner as Qarāfī:

> The valid *qiyās* is one in which the *'illa* to which the original [textually revealed] ruling is tied is present in the derivative case, without any impediment in the matter to nullify it. A *qiyās* of this kind is in no way opposed by the Sharī'a. Similarly, the *qiyās* of 'elimination of what is contrary' [*qiyās ilghā' al-fāriq*], in which there is no discrepancy between the two cases that is relevant to the ruling, is also not opposed by anything in the Sharī'a. Inasmuch as the Sharī'a provides for the restrictive application [*ikhtiṣāṣ*] of certain rules by a judgment that diverges from parallel cases, that category must be restricted by an attribute compelling its restriction to the ruling and preventing its extension to other cases.[11]

After quoting all this with evident approval, Riḍā summons the further support of Muḥammad b. 'Alī ash-Shaukānī, who declares:

> The *qiyās* which is acceptable is the one based on an *'illa* which gave rise to the original textual ruling. . . . Furthermore, it is not hidden from those of sound mind and understanding that the general and particular contents of the Qur'ān and Sunna make provision for every event that occurs. . . . There is no disagreement over use of the *'illa* if it has been textually specified. Disagreement only arose over the question whether its use should be classified as *qiyās* or as acting in accordance with the revealed texts. Most [of the jurists] took the former view, while the opponents of *qiyās* took the latter view. Thus the difference over this is only verbal. For this reason the matter is of little importance, and what has been regarded as of great moment in the dispute over this question is really only small.[12]

While agreeing with Shaukānī on the textual basis of *qiyās*, Riḍā takes exception to his minimization of the dispute, for the problem, he says, is that some opponents of *qiyās* do not concede the general applicability of *'ilal* even if textually specified.[13] The implication is impor-

---

[11] *Ibid.*, pp. 56–57.

[12] *Ibid.*, pp. 68–69, quoting from Shawkānī's *Irshād al-Fuḥūl ilā Taḥqīq al-Ḥaqq min 'Ilm al-Uṣūl.*

[13] *Ibid.*, p. 69.

tant for Riḍā, for his central purpose is to establish the comprehensive relevance of the Qur'ān and Sunna to all human problems. If extension of their meaning by analogy is denied, not only will rigid conservatism be confirmed in its unwillingness to deal with the modern world, but secularists will likewise be confirmed in their assertion that Islam as such is incapable of doing so.

What is curious in his book is the seemingly unconscious and rather unclear shift in his assumptions when he turns his attention, in the concluding pages, from *qiyās* to *istiṣlāḥ*. We have seen that for Qarāfī, Ibn Taimiyya, and other medieval jurists *istiṣlāḥ* was but a logical extension of *qiyās*, whereby a consideration of utility neither explicitly enjoined nor excluded by the revealed texts would be assumed to be valid as a basis for judgment. Rashīd Riḍā at least nominally adopted this rationale, acknowledging in the process that the conclusions of *istiṣlāḥ* were accordingly not legally binding in the manner of a firmly grounded *qiyās*, for no individual is entitled to require or forbid others to perform an act without divine authorization. Indeed, this is equally the case with a *qiyās* whose textual foundation is not entirely precise in its meaning.[14]

On the other hand, in matters of public policy this apparently does not prevent the government from enacting whatever ordinances it sees fit, provided the government rests on the proper foundations of consultation (*shūrā*) among the *ūlū 'l-amr* and provided such ordinances do not actually conflict with specifically revealed rights and obligations, for "God commanded us to obey those in authority among us only in mundane matters and in matters pertaining to mundane interests, on condition that this shall not entail disobedience to Him."[15]

Riḍā goes so far as to imply that much of the structure of the Sharī'a traditionally built up through the meticulous process of *qiyās*, with all that it entailed not only of deductive reasoning but of semantic study of texts of the Qur'ān and ḥadīth, was merely a roundabout way of arriving at the same conclusions that could be reached by the equally valid (but much simpler) process of *istiṣlāḥ*. This suggestion is made in a discussion of the Spanish Muslim jurist ash-Shāṭibī (d. 790 H.), whom he characterizes as exceptionally outspoken in his resort to *maṣlaḥa*. After citing ten examples given by Shāṭibī of decisions based on

---

[14] *Ibid.*, pp. 78–79.
[15] *Ibid.*, p. 79.

maṣlaḥa, Rashīd Riḍā notes that many of these decisions can be drawn strictly by deduction from the Qur'ān or Sunna or from *qiyās*.[16]

The same holds true, he continues, for most questions of public interest falling under the jurisdiction of political rulers.

> It is quite clear that [these questions] . . . all fall under the principle set forth by the ḥadīth *lā ḍarar wa lā ḍirār* ["no injury and no counter-injury"].[17] . . . From this is taken the principle of averting evils and conserving interests, with due consideration for what is known from textual sources and for what is known of the Law's intent. . . . However, the main body of the jurists always declare that all ordinances are derived from the previously mentioned principle [i.e., deductive reasoning from the revealed texts]. . . .
>
> Most of the 'ulamā' of the Community avoided explicit reference to the principle [of *maṣlaḥa*] because of their fear—as Qarāfī says—that tyrannical leaders would take it as an excuse for following their own desires and imposing their absolute power on the property and persons of the population. The 'ulamā' therefore thought to guard against this by tracing all laws back to revealed sources, even when this necessitated recourse to [so-called] hidden analogies. They converted the notion of *maṣāliḥ mursala* into one of the most technical forms of the *'illa* in *qiyās*, so that it was not subject to the interpretation of princes and governors. This fear was justified at the time, but the Community did not thereby guard itself sufficiently against the desires of its rulers, for every tyrant could always find corrupt 'ulamā' to prepare the way for him to follow his own inclinations to some extent.[18]

The solution to the problem, he concludes, is to reform the political structure so that decisions of public law and policy rest in the hands of qualified persons—the *ahl al-ḥall wa 'l-'aqd*, or *ulū 'l-amr*—acting in consultation with one another, with the ruler responsible to them.[19] This is preferable to "denying the principle of *maṣāliḥ* or narrowly restricting the derivation of legal ordinances from it." If this is done, "then there will be no reason to fear that the *maṣāliḥ* will be consid-

---

[16] *Ibid.*, pp. 73–75.

[17] The ḥadīth on which Najm ad-Din Ṭaufī built his doctrine of *maṣlaḥa* (see above, pp. 97–102). Rashīd Riḍā summarizes Ṭaufī's position with evident approval in *Yusr*, pp. 72–73.

[18] *Yusr*, pp. 75–76.

[19] *Ibid.*, p. 76.

ered a means for corruption . . . and no need to restrict the means of deducing legal ordinances, as the great mass of the jurists have done."[20]

The problem, then, is a political one, and the highly technical methodology of jurisprudence can be immensely simplified once the 'ulamā' no longer need to consider themselves the sole guardians of the law against governmental corruptions.[21] The solution is to place political authority in the hands of jurists. We have seen, however, that when Riḍā tries to develop this solution, his definition of "those in authority" is inconsistent and obscure.

It is difficult to conclude from *Yusr al-Islām* precisely what respective roles Riḍā means to assign to *qiyās* and *istiṣlāḥ*. On the one hand, if the very extensive quotations from Ibn Qayyim al-Jauziyya and Shaukānī mean anything, it is that Riḍā wished to demonstrate the possibility of extending the revealed texts through analogical deduction to cover all fields of life, implying that no process less closely tied to God's revealed commands (such as secular legislation, or simple considerations of utility for that matter) can be binding on the Muslim Community. But at the same time he also seems to say that on some occasions, at least, considerations of utility can be substituted for the complex traditional methods of deduction, without the revealed content of the Sharī'a being jeopardized. Whether these occasions are confined to matters of public policy is not entirely clear. To an undefined extent, then, *maṣlaḥa* becomes a basic source of legal interpretation in its own right and is no longer dependent on the particular indications of textual sources. Logically, the traditionally elaborate methods of reasoning involved in *qiyās* seem open to drastic simplification or even total abandonment. The *'illa* need only be some attribute contributing to social utility, and need not be deductively determined

---

[20] *Ibid.*

[21] Historically the point seems well taken. Having failed to develop rapidly enough to keep pace with the expanding political power in early Islam and so to maintain a large measure of direct influence over the ruler's policies, the religious and juristic classes appear to have evolved, by a date early in the Abbasid period, into a separate institution. By conserving their authority to determine the specific rules of law, free from governmental dictation, they preserved the Sharī'a as a specifically Islamic social instrument. (See Gibb, "The Evolution of Government in Early Islam," *Studia Islamica*, IV [1955], 5–17; also Gibb, "An Interpretation of Islamic History," *Muslim World*, XLV [1955], 4–15, 121–133.) Certainly the complexity of legal methods served to protect the jurists' position, although the motive behind their doctrines can only be a moot question.

from some specific indication. And indeed, if *maṣlaḥa* is taken as a legal source in its own right, *qiyās* itself can often be dispensed with, and positive rules can be decided upon directly on utilitarian grounds without the use of analogy, for the "wisdom" (*ḥikma*) behind the revealed Law is no longer inscrutable. But these are only implications, and they are not spelled out by Riḍā himself. We shall see that when such conclusions were explicitly drawn by others from premises similar to his own, he was often moved to object strenuously.

B. *Maṣlaḥa, Ijmāʿ, and the Problem of Positivism*

One of the most important implications of Riḍā's appeal to the *maṣlaḥa* as a legal source is that, by introducing a broad and flexible process of reinterpretation into the law, it makes necessary the recognition of some agency entrusted with the task of implementing the process, while at the same time it presupposes subjecting the accumulated *ijmāʿ* of many centuries to critical review and replacing it by a new *ijmāʿ*. Rashīd Riḍā proposes in effect to combine these undertakings by considering the electors (*ahl al-ḥall wa 'l-ʿaqd*), the participants in the process of consultation (*shūrā*), the "persons of authority" (*ūlū 'l-amr*), and the *mujtahids* all members of a single body in which the sovereign powers of the Community lie and whose executive the caliph is. This body is at once legislative and judicial, for its agreement to institute particular ordinances has the force of *ijmāʿ*, in the sense that it is an authoritative pronouncement of law valid for its particular time and place.[22]

It is at once apparent that this incorporation of *ijmāʿ* into a formal institution would be a new departure unprecedented in Islamic history, and that the value of *ijmāʿ* as a source of dogma might have to be

[22] There does not seem to be available a comprehensive and systematic statement by Riḍā on the various types of *ijmāʿ* or on their respective values as legal sources. The institutionalized form envisaged in the *Khilāfa* is apparently not placed on a level with the consensus of the Companions of the Prophet, which he often cites as authoritative justification for his own views; organized contemporary *ijmāʿ* is collective *ijtihad*, valid as a political decision rather than as an infallible pronouncement of dogma. Laoust claims that Riḍā considered even the consensus of the Companions valid only for its own place and time, and their opinions no more than *ijtihad*, but cites no source for his claim (*Essai*, pp. 569–570). Jomier, on the other hand, finds that the *ijmāʿ* of the Companions in Riḍā's view is final and binding for all time, unlike the later *ijmāʿ* of the Schools or of the present day (J. Jomier, *Le Commentaire coranique du Manâr* [Paris, 1954], pp. 201–204).

reexamined in the new circumstances. Riḍā recognizes that *ijmā'* has not previously been formally expressed, and suggests even that for lack of such expression it is doubtful to what extent it can be said truly to have existed in relation to particular points. It was, however, for lack of practical means of communication that there was no institutionalization in earlier times, and this is what he proposes to remedy.[23]

In identifying the problem of *ijmā'* in relation to that of the *maṣlaḥa*, we must return to our discussion of the latter. The basis of the difference between those ordinances of the Sharī'a that are subject to human adaptation and those that are not, says Riḍā, is a matter of epistemology: what values can be discerned by human reason and which ones can not? This distinction is set forth in another "debate between the reformer and the slavish imitator," in which the reformer declares:

> God's ordinances are of two categories. The first category is the one in which reason is not sufficient by itself to know the sources or applications of the Law; this category is the purely spiritual. . . . Reason can grasp its worldly value and benefit on the whole but commits the matter of its benefit for the afterlife to God, as for example belief in the Unseen. This applies to questions dealing with the afterlife and the forms of ritual and worship. . . . This category is to be accepted from the Lawgiver without reason's presuming to add to it or subtract from it. . . .
>
> The second category is one in which reason can know the aspect of utility by reflection, speculation, examination, and analogy, but is liable to error and misguidance in some matters, sometimes because of its weakness and sometimes because of its inclination to caprice. Therefore the Law established general principles so that its derivative ordinances might be made known on their basis. This is the category of wordly transactions (*mu'āmalāt*) based on the principle of repelling injuries and securing benefits and of preferring the lesser of two evils in case one or the other is inevitable. . . . It is in this category that the general public must unquestioningly follow those in authority, who in turn must be well versed in the sciences of religion and in worldly matters. . . .[24]

This means that in political questions the decisions of the leading *mujtahids* having to do with matters of public interest are authorita-

---

[23] *Khilāfa*, 172/102: "A great scholar" said, "It is impossible to ascertain the consensus of the Community, if indeed it exists."

[24] *Manār*, IV, 858–859.

tive and binding, and their *ijmā'* is a "legal source" (*ḥujja shar'iyya*), although this is not true in purely religious matters. These *mujtahids* are obliged to take a broad view of all considerations affecting the public interest rather than to "take literally the example set by the Prophet in all its particulars even when this obliges them to ignore the public interest." This obligation is implicit in the Prophet's saying, "The witness sees what the absent person does not see":[25] that is, a particular question can only be adjudged properly in the light of its particular circumstances. Textual limits must of course be respected:

> But the independence of judgment which this ḥadīth sanctions does not negate the obligation in explicitly defined cases to consult the text of the Qur'ān, just as it does not negate the obligation to follow the other principles of legal methodology that govern deduction and interpretation; on the contrary, these are required, though by another proof.[26]

Still, the Qur'ānic texts are only intended to be used as general principles: "For God did not reveal Qur'ānic verses corresponding to the number of occurrences befalling men and say, 'Judge by these, they are justice,' but rather what He gave us is a measure by which we ascertain truth on the basis of probability."[27]

This reference to probability is of crucial importance. It suggests an acknowledgment by Riḍā that if the main body of the *mu'āmalāt* is to be determined by broad interpretation of current social needs and not by a purely philological study of the exact texts of Qur'ān and ḥadīth, then there is no avoiding a partial intrusion of human guesswork and error, which are inherent in any judgment of probability. Probability can only represent a mere external facade of the true meaning of the Divine Law as it is applied to a given case. A certain amount of this corruption-by-exteriorization is inevitable, to be sure, no matter what the means of interpreting a law that in its pure form is nothing less than eternal Truth. But there is a great deal of difference between an interpretation that is confined to semantic distinctions and formally logical deductions, and one that seeks to determine questions of social moral value with only the most general and often vague scriptural principles to give guidance. Although the statement is often reiterated that the texts supply general principles, we are never told with any

[25] *Ibid.*, 860.

[26] *Ibid.*

[27] *Ibid.*

precision what these principles are, beyond protection of life, honor, and property, and general benevolence toward others.

If, however, it is admitted that judgments made under this plan are reached only as a matter of probability, then at least the limitations of this utilitarianism are brought into the open and too much will not be expected of the method. We might expect the further admission that the agreement of the *mujtahids* and "those in authority" on questions of public welfare, while having the force of positive law, are in the first place not necessarily a true representation of the Divine Law, and therefore are valid only in their own time and place, that is, subject to review, and second, that disagreement is always to be expected and resoluble only by some rather arbitrary procedure, such as a majority vote, which will provide not dogmatic certainty but only a convenient and orderly method of decision.

The first of these corollaries seems in fact to be accepted by Rashīd Riḍā. As for the second, he prefers to lapse into the traditional argument that presupposes that the Qur'ān and Sunna provide clear answers to all problems, and ignores the practical need for a means of authoritative interpretation:

> We affirm that God permitted legislation [*ishtirā'*] in Islam, delegating it to the Community to be decided upon by those posssessing knowledge and judgment in consultation among themselves. In truth power belongs to the Community, so that if their interpretation can be sought on a matter and they should reach unanimous agreement, their decision is binding on all. Neither the caliph nor other officers have the right to contradict or oppose their *ijmā'*, nor to oppose their representatives and delegates who are the *ahl al-ḥall wa 'l-'aqd*. The agreement of these latter, if they are limited in number, is called *ijmā'* by the jurists, provided only that they be persons qualified for *ijtihād*.
>
> Should they disagree in their interpretation, the subject of their disagreement must be referred to the two basic sources, the Qur'ān and the Sunna. Action must then be taken on the basis of what is indicated by one or both of these two sources, in keeping with the Qur'ānic verse [iv:58] that, after commanding obedience to God, the Prophet, and those in authority, says: "And if ye dispute in anything, then refer the matter to God and the Prophet, if ye are believers in God and the Judgment Day; that is the best interpretation." This means that this is better and sounder than other procedures, such as acting on the opinion of a majority of the delegates of the nation in enact-

> ing the statutes of Europe and her imitators, for our Law is opposed to them in this matter. It is one of the advantages of our Law that a dispute within the Community ceases with the giving of judgment by the Qur'ān and the Sunna, and that all the delegates of the Community are satisfied with what appears to be the most likely indication in them, so that there is no room left for rancor and dispute.[28]

It should be noted that this passage was written over twenty years later than the preceding one in which reference was first made to probability. But Riḍā's initial premise has not changed, but in fact is reaffirmed repeatedly, in his later writings: that legislative interpretation is to be carried out on a broad scale on the basis of the concept of public benefit. It is therefore surprising to find this bland assertion that the Qur'ān and Sunna provide the criteria for resolving all disagreements, especially when one considers that it is precisely the question of how to interpret textual principles that must give rise to disagreement in the first place. How can disputes over the meaning of the Qur'ān be decided by referring to the Qur'ān? And if the Qur'ān and Sunna do provide clear answers to all questions, what has become of the bold process of interpretation that Riḍā elsewhere describes so tirelessly? What need can there then be for *ijtihād* or *ijmā'?*

But this circular argument of Riḍā's should not be taken at face value. Any implication that in this perplexing passage he has reverted to orthodox conservatism and thrown off his usual liberal view of *maṣlaḥa* is quickly belied in the passage immediately following, in which he declares that even in the absence of textual stipulations for a liberal interpretation of the Law, "necessity alone would suffice as a legal source to justify the process of deduction known today as *tashrī'*."[29]

This is a broad use indeed of the concept of necessity. Necessity, we are told in effect, not only suspends standing rules in special circumstances but actually creates new ones as dictated by human needs. In this sense it is virtually synonymous with *maṣlaḥa*. The entire superstructure of substantive law arising from the general textual foundations is dictated by human need, whether under the name of public interest or necessity. This equation of interest and necessity, put forth in such a manner as to make formal deductions from the revealed

---

[28] *Khilāfa*, 156/93.
[29] *Ibid.*, 158/94.

sources only a secondary confirmation of what the law should be, amounts to an affirmation of natural law.

Since Riḍā continues to hold this view, then, how are we to account for his assertion that all disputes can be resolved by reference to the Qur'ān and the Sunna? Why does he not follow his position through, admit the consequences of interpreting on the basis of probability, and recognize that disagreement among legislators—perhaps even political partisanship—is inevitable and cannot be resolved in any final and authoritative way?

An answer to this is suggested if we recall the problem of positivism versus idealism discussed in our first chapter. The classical writers on constitutional theory tended to shy away from fully developing their systems on the level of application of law and preferred to formulate general rules whose supposed divine origin was always within sight. The dogmatic justification for their formulas of the Caliphate was their chief concern, rather than the operation of law as a humanly applied institution for the resolution of human conflicts. As a systematization of Sunnī practice, or recording of Sunnī *ijmā'* by which the various constitutional procedures were given the stamp of doctrinal sanctity, their theory did not answer practical questions of how observance or nonobservance of the rules set forth was to be determined and verified within the society. Thus the classical theory never clearly attributed sovereignty to anyone but God, and never progressed in its treatment of sovereignty beyond the religious to the existential or positive level. Such practical questions were beyond its function. The question of procedures for legislative interpretation was therefore excluded: the Sharī'a was a universally acknowledged divine law to be enforced by the ruler as an exercise of his divinely instituted office; the content of the Sharī'a was taken for granted, that is, it was whatever the Qur'ān, Sunna, *qiyās*, and *ijmā'* indicated.

Constitutional theory, then, provided no blueprint for institutional procedures of legislative interpretation by which open questions could receive positive resolution. Nor was such a blueprint offered anywhere else in traditional theories of jurisprudence in Islam. The "science of the sources of law" (*'ilm uṣūl al-fiqh*) was confined to defining the so-called "hierarchy of proofs" (*tartīb al-adilla*) and examining each of the sources within itself in order to classify their subdivisions (strong and weak haḍīths, local and universal *ijmā'*, *ijmā'* of the scholars and *ijmā'* of the Community at large, etc.). The means for authoritative validation of particular interpretations was of course *ijmāʻ*. But the nearest thing to a formal institutionalization of this was the gradual crystallization of learned opinion in the great Sunnī *madhāhib* or "schools," and this process was not really formal at all; indeed, it could not have been, without the schools becoming political affiliates or wards of the government. A formalized *ijmāʻ*, and *a fortiori* a political *ijmāʻ*, in losing its indeterminate, semi-articulate character, would lose its traditional function as an expression of the cumulative, time-tested general conscience and become instead a declaration of the general will and a blueprint for policy. This transformation could only serve to separate the concept of *ijmāʻ* from the religious ideal of the Sharīʻa and reconstitute it as a convenient but imperfect tool for the application of law. Thus it would cease to be a legal source, on the same level as the Qur'ān and Sunna, and become a political agency, combining the always fallible powers of practical judgment offered by the *shūrā* (the ruler's consultants) with the temporal power of decision of the ruler himself. *Ijmāʻ* in this sense is a process of positive legislation, not a canonical proof. If it is to do its new work, there is clearly no room for a principle of unanimity.[30]

Riḍā's difficulty is that while he seeks to organize *ijmāʻ* into a formal institution, equates it with the *shūrā*, and perhaps even recognizes that this will produce legal rules of quite different value from those agreed upon by the Companions of the Prophet (whose consensus was infallible), at the same time he is the unwitting prisoner of the idealist theoretical tradition. Whereas the tradition was simply not concerned with the problems of positive verification and application of legal interpretations, Riḍā is often unaware of them. As a Muslim apologist he is more than ready to declare that the Sharīʻa permits progressive and humane evolution, justifying his claim by outlining the means of a liberal interpretation and application; but he cannot possibly afford to acknowledge that the results will be no more inspired than Western quantitative, partisan democracy. To avoid this conclusion he takes refuge in the ideal quality of the Islamic sources—the categorical validity of the revelations of Qur'ān and Sunna, on whose authority there can be no disagreement—and then slips back into the realm of positive application, declaring that in *interpreting* the sources there *will* be no disagreement. By the same unconscious process, he man-

---

[30] For a similar view see Gardet, *La Cité musulmane* (Paris, 1954), pp. 119–134.

ages to attribute to *ijmāʿ* as a positive application the same quality of unanimity—and hence infallibility—that it enjoyed as a canonical source on the ideal level. In short, he has taken a traditional concept of the religious source and justification of the Law and used it to characterize the Law's positive application. This is the same process he followed in his constitutional theory of the Caliphate, mistaking a doctrine of authority for a program of action and ending by attributing sovereignty to a circularly defined group of "those in authority."

The point is not that Rashīd Riḍā was given to contradictions and garbled reasoning, nor that he saw no distinction between the criterion on which a decision is based and the procedure by which the decision is reached. It would be more just to consider that he was painfully aware, as were his fellow modernists, that the prescribed criteria had long been ignored, partly for lack of a more adequate procedure, and in their disuse had become stultified and ill-understood. He sought to recast the criteria in a more favorable light and at the same time to describe procedures by which they could be implemented practically. But the traditional theories that constituted his intellectual heritage dealt with moral ideals and criteria, not with positive applications and procedures; his education was in the religious and legal sciences, not in methods of critical historical or political analysis. As heir to an idealist rather than positivist tradition, it is hardly surprising that he should be imperceptibly bound at times by the limitations in scope of the former, even when seeking to escape them, and that when in positivist territory he is misled by occasional wishful thinking.

Nevertheless, these understandable predilections could lead Riḍā into some very blind alleys indeed, and when they did, much of his potential appeal to progressive minds was destroyed. It is a curious paradox that his general doctrine of the criteria of legal interpretation, if it invited criticism on any grounds, did so by appealing so widely to human value judgments in the form of *maṣlaḥa* as virtually to negate the supposed ideal and imperative character of the law, while on the other hand his attempts to find positive means of effectively instituting such interpretation were crippled by a hangover of idealism. In these circumstances, for lack of a realistic attitude toward the law's implementation and practical meaning, Riḍā's progressive doctrine of interpretation, instead of contributing to a revived recognition of the Sharīʿa as a living foundation on which to build an entire modern legal structure, may have served if anything as an opening wedge toward a frank espousal by others of the principle of secular legislation.

C. *Reaction to Secularism*

By the early 1920's Rashīd Riḍā was embittered to discover that his most formidable opponents were not the tradition-bound 'ulamā' of the Azhar but the Western-educated secularists, who were ready to push his own utilitarian principles beyond the bounds to which his intellectual background restricted him. The vehemence of his attack on 'Alī 'Abd ar-Rāziq was very likely due in part to the fact that 'Abd ar-Rāziq, as an Azhar graduate of pious family who had early been exposed to the benevolent influence of Muḥammad 'Abduh, should—following only one year's stay in England—not only come forth with an outright call to secularism but base his historical interpretations on premises not always very different from those adopted by Riḍā himself.[31] For 'Abd ar-Rāziq to claim the late 'Abduh's backing for some of his positions was only to add insult to injury.[32] Likewise Aḥmad Ṣafwat, an Egyptian lawyer contemporary with Rashīd Riḍā, was subjected to violent denunciations for preaching a doctrine of interpretation of the *shar'ī* sources which, judging by Riḍā's own description of it, seems in keeping with the general spirit of the latter's writings. Here is Riḍā's account of Ṣafwat's position:

> In the name of Islam he allowed nonadherence to the texts of the Qur'ān in particular matters, and thought it enough to bear in mind the intention and purpose in what it forbade, and the intended wisdom in what it commanded; what it permitted, every ruler could forbid.
>
> In the case of the Sunna, all the rulings and decisions of the Prophet which it confirmed need not be followed by later generations. This contradicts God's words in the Qur'ān, "Follow him [Muḥammad], that ye may find success." In this view, the Muslims are obliged in every time and place to follow their rulers' prescriptions, permissions, and prohibitions, even if the latter are in clear opposition to an explicit Sunna of their Prophet . . . or to a text of the Qur'ān. For in his opinion, all that the Muslims are obliged to do is to bear in mind what they understand of the wisdom and intended meaning of the texts. If they are able to remember this wisdom and assimilate this meaning by means other than following the enunciated verses,

---

[31] Particularly that Muḥammad had laid down only general moral principles of conduct, allowing latitude for individual judgment.

[32] See for instance *Manār*, XXVII, 715–717: "Al-Monsieur 'Alī 'Abd ar-Rāziq yanzi' al-'imāma. . . .

there is nothing objectionable in that. As the writer himself put it: "There is no harm in arriving at an intended goal by the most beneficial and convenient means."

As an example, he would allow a marriage contract to be made official without participation of witnesses, and would consider most of the period of pregnancy sufficient, after divorce, before remarriage, rather than the length of time prescribed by the Qur'ānic text. Indeed, it would [presumably] be equally suitable, if we knew by an X-ray examination of the inside of the womb that the woman was not pregnant, to let her remarry on the very day of her divorce, or let her husband not pay alimony if she should not remarry.

By this principle there remains nothing forbidden that cannot be committed legally by whoever claims authorization by virtue of what he considers the intended meaning of the Qur'ānic prohibitions, such as drinking wine, marriage with one's daughter, and such like.[33]

It is apparently when a specific conclusion is drawn from the liberal methods of interpretation that Rashīd Riḍā senses a danger to the revealed basis of the law. Ṣafwat is too practical in thinking ahead to particular situations that might arise in the future (such as questions dealing with marriage); Riḍā, while he has much to say about the humanist values of the Sharī'a, says very little about concrete examples.

Some of the more extreme statements in this passage can be discounted as representing no more than Riḍā's own projections and exaggerations of the point of view he attacks. Evidently Ṣafwat does not dismiss the body of Qur'ānic and Sunna sources as of no account, but in Riḍā's mind this is what he does to all intents in saying that it is sufficient to implement their understood purposes. Likewise he is offended by Ṣafwat's statement, "Thus the obligation is dissolved to cling to the literal meanings of the legislative pronouncements appearing in the Qur'ān."[34] In general, he considers Ṣafwat guilty of "trying to destroy Islam through interpretation."[35]

---

[33] *Manār*, XXIII, 545–546. Ṣafwat is not mentioned by name, but a statement is cited in the passage identical with one specifically attributed to him in *Manār*, XXVI, 104: "Thus the obligation is dissolved to cling to the literal meanings of the legislative pronouncements appearing in the Qur'ān." For one of Ṣafwat's own statements of his position, see his "The Theory of Mohammedan Law," *Journal of Comparative Legislation and International Law*, II (1920), 310–316.

[34] *Manār*, XXIII, 546; XXVI, 104.

[35] *Ibid.*, XXIII, 546.

Riḍā himself, in passages quoted earlier in this chapter and elsewhere, had long since proclaimed a similar doctrine of liberation from the shackles of literal meanings and of judgment on the basis of utility. For example: "The Companions, if they saw benefit in anything, used to judge in favor of it, even if this opposed the usual custom followed, for they saw that the correct principle was to adopt whatever course was beneficial rather than to cling to the details and subsidiary rules of laws. . . . "[36] And again: "God did not reveal Qur'ānic verses corresponding to the number of occurrences befalling men and say, 'Judge by these, they are justice,' but rather what He gave us is a measure by which we ascertain truth on the basis of probability."[37]

He had, furthermore, in 1906 published in the *Manār* the text of Najm ad-Dīn Ṭaufī's radically utilitarian fourteenth-century treatise on *maṣlaḥa*. In a brief introduction Riḍā recalls that he has on earlier occasions reminded his readers that the protection of general interests is the first principle of jurisprudence in the *mu'āmalāt*, and that "this indicates that *maṣlaḥa* takes precedence over a textual source."[38] There is no question but that he endorses Ṭaufī, and he appears to have published the latter's treatise in support of his own position.[39] Had the work been written in Egypt in 1923 by an Aḥmad Ṣafwat, it seems hard to imagine that he would have welcomed it. The criticism to which both Ṭaufī's doctrine and Riḍā's more liberal appeals for utilitarian interpretation and for the institutionalization of *ijmā'* and *ijtihād* are most liable—namely, that they open the door for human value judgments wide enough to destroy the religious basis of law and secularize the criteria as well as the applications of civil legislation—this criticism could not be more effectively expressed than in the words by which Riḍā himself attacks his selected secularist enemies.

Perhaps the confusion that might be found in these reversals of attitude can be explained in terms of the great gulf in educational background and cultural exposure between persons like Rashīd Riḍā, whose intellectual formation was achieved in entirely orthodox and traditional surroundings, and the Western-educated classes, who had no real knowledge of their own Muslim cultural heritage. Riḍā had no effective exposure to the Western intellectual tradition. Yet in every

[36] *Ibid.*, IV, 210 (quoted above, p. 190).

[37] *Ibid.*, 860 (quoted above, p. 199).

[38] *Ibid.*, IX, 745–746.

[39] This appears to be confirmed in Riḍā's brief but favorable account of Ṭaufī in *Yusr*, pp. 72–73, and in his own recourse to Ṭawfī's ḥadīth *la ḍarar wa la ḍirār* in *ibid.*, p. 75.

departure he made from traditional Islamic views, he was inescapably subject to particular Western ideas. His intent was to repel the Western invasion of Muslim culture, yet he had no sufficient ideological basis on which to build new doctrines, other than a dimly understood Western one. Unconsciously, he was distrustful of the very ideas he put forward and hence found no difficulty in discarding them when a few years later it was the "secularists" who were presenting them.[40]

[40] For remarks on Riḍā's growing reaction to the introduction of Western ideas and institutions after 1918, see Laoust, *Essai*, p. 562. It was not until 1918 that he championed the Wahhābī movement, nor until 1925 that he began publication of the works of Ibn Taimiyya, Ibn Qudāma, and Ibn Qayyim al-Jauziyya (*ibid.*, pp. 561–562).

VII

CONCLUSION: SEQUELS AND IMPLICATIONS

In attributing a general spirit of permissiveness and adaptability to the Qur'ān and Sunna, modern Muslim writers have often been the victims of two alternative but concurrent tendencies. The first is to carry the argument to the point where Islam seems to stand for nothing in particular except permissiveness itself. The second is to overlook the substantial renunciation of independence in judgment that is implicit in depending on the Qur'ān and Sunna for authorizations of flexibility. Thus, for instance, to praise *qiyās* as a principle of adaptability is also, in the nature of the case, to acknowledge the comprehensive authority of the sacred texts on which *qiyās* is based, and therefore to submit to their restrictions. In broader terms, the problem is one of the Muslims' epistemological view of the Qur'ān. As long as it is regarded as no less than God's final Truth, verbally revealed, then every idea to which Muslims attach value must be harmonized with it.[1]

The dilemma is illustrated in a book by a contemporary of Rashīd Riḍā, the poet and political agitator 'Abdal'azīz Shāwīsh (1876–1929), entitled *Al-Islām Dīn al-Fiṭra wa 'l-Ḥurriyya* ("Islam, the Religion of Nature and Freedom").[2] Shāwīsh asserts, in the familiar modernist

[1] See N. Safran, *Egypt in Search of Political Community* (Cambridge, Mass., 1961), for a general exposition of this point with relation not only to the Islamic reformist movement but also to westernizing liberal intellectuals in Egypt, who, as he shows, failed to grasp the central importance of this issue and consequently "joined the Islamic Reformists, and even the orthodox, in subordinating reason to the faith, but with this difference: that whereas, to the orthodox, faith was really a way of perceiving the truth, and its content was a practical guide to life, to the 'repentant' Liberal Nationalists faith only remained as a limitation on the intellect, and the interpretation of its content a means of vain intellectual aggrandizement" (p. 250).

[2] Cairo, n.d. (reprint, *ca.* 1960).

fashion, that Islam is not a detailed and rigid code of rules in social matters but a set of fundamental principles of permanent validity, on the basis of which men can enact specific rules appropriate to the occasion. Of these principles Shāwīsh lists eleven examples, all of which turn out to be of an essentially procedural rather than moral nature and purport to establish permissiveness, though in several cases falling prey to the second of the two alternative tendencies mentioned above. The principles are: (1) the validity of *ijtihād*, which is defined as derivation of conclusions from a proper understanding of the Qur'ān and the true Sunna; (2) God does not require of man what is beyond his capacity; (3) men should abstain from injury and counter-injury (*lā ḍarar wa lā ḍirār*); (4) the legality of means is subject to the legality of their ends; (5) conversely, what leads to a prohibited or reprehensible end is itself to be considered prohibited or reprehensible; (6) reason takes priority over the apparent (*ẓāhir*) meaning of the Sacred Law in case of contradiction; (7) what the Prophet decreed as legislation is binding, but what he said of ordinary matters of life is not binding; (8) all individuals are equal before the law; (9) only those who participate in an action are responsible for its consequences; (10) the Qur'ān and Sunna decree specific penalties for only a small number of offenses, and in other cases the authorities may establish suitable penalties at their discretion up to the limit reached in the specified cases; (11) local customs and conditions are valid criteria in determining the extent of application of the rules of the Sharī'a in many cases.[3]

Thus the skeletal structure of the Sharī'a came to be defined primarily in terms of its empty spaces. The dividing line between Islamic modernists and westernizing liberals became an essentially emotional rather than intellectual one, particularly inasmuch as liberals found it expedient to accept an Islamic sanction for their positions. Rashīd Riḍā and others of his school found it difficult to accept certain modern practices because they bore a secular label, but it proved equally difficult to put anything else in their place. Thus what passed for an Islamic revival became, in practice, an uneasy process of ideological assimilation.

This has enabled Islamic modernism to become an established tradition as a medium of expression, despite its intellectual and political failure. Indeed, were we to judge the vitality of an intellectual movement by the flow of publications, we should be led to the conclusion

[3] *Ibid.*, pp. 40–49.

that today Riḍā's reformism was a potent force. In recent years many books have continued to appear declaring that Islam is a divine system that prescribes fundamental rules of political, legal, and social life. These books vary in tone from angry protest to contentment with the existing state of affairs, but many of them carry the duality of theme that we have already seen in the ideas of Muḥammad 'Abduh and Rashīd Riḍā: on the one hand, that Islam, unlike other religions, carries its own revealed message in public matters and that this message must be taken seriously; on the other hand, that Islam endorses, in effect, the modern liberal values familiar in the West and does not deprive men of independence and latitude of judgment and action. The authors of these books, like the modernists of the previous generation, are still engaged in establishing the comprehensive relevance of the Qur'ān and Sunna, yet forever seeking permission from the Qur'ān and Sunna (and, happily, obtaining it) not to be bound too restrictively by the Qur'ān and Sunna.

A clear example of this is the book *Daulat al-Qur'ān* ("The Qur'ānic State") by Ṭāhā 'Abdalbāqī Surūr.[4] The author complains at considerable length of the corrosion of the Islamic spirit attending the political and social revitalization of the Arab and other Muslim states. In many Muslim minds, he says, Islam has been reduced to empty rituals and forms or has been denied altogether as a social principle. "Our culture has banished faith from the reality of our lives, and kept it [only] as a heritage and a memory."[5] Properly understood, Surūr insists, Islam is not simply a system of private piety but a source of political, economic, and social principles, which Muslims can ignore only at the price of negating the value of their individual devotions. To obey Islamic principles selectively is hypocrisy, even apostasy; if we renounce the social teachings of Islam, let us be frank and abandon religion altogether.[6] As for the scientific and material achievements of the West, let us adopt these without the culture that accompanies it, for modern culture is the enemy of Islam, and Islam offers a complete substitute that combines the technical progress of Europe with the social benefits that Europe lacks.[7]

> We must believe first and foremost that Islam is not a civilization among others containing both useful and harmful elements,

---

[4] Second edition; Cairo, 1961 (first published 1955).

[5] *Ibid.*, p. 20.

[6] *Ibid.*, p. 64.

[7] *Ibid.*, pp. 47–51.

> and that it is not a fruit of human ideas and efforts containing both erroneous and correct elements. Rather it is a law [*sharī'a*] which God laid down the day He laid down belief in it, that His slaves should act in accordance with it for their good, their happiness, and their glory.[8]

What, then, are the principles of the Islamic polity? As Surūr describes them they seem hardly distinctive, though they can be traced back to the Qur'ān and Sunna. Islamic government, he declares, is not properly speaking a religious government, for its officers are not clerical officials but men of experience and professional skill. Thus for instance the first two caliphs, Abū Bakr and 'Umar, appointed 'Amr b. al-'Āṣ and Khālid b. al-Walīd as military commanders on grounds of competence although their piety as Muslims was doubtful.[9] Piety alone is no qualification for public office, and according to a ḥadīth it is even sinful not to choose the best technically qualified man.[10] Furthermore, Islam preaches popular sovereignty, embodied in the social contract of the *bay'a*, the duty of consultation (*shūrā*), the legislative principle of *ijtihād* and *ijmā'*, and the right to overthrow tyrannical rulers. To these notions of responsibility to public opinion Islam offers a further guarantee of good government in its appeal to the moral conscience of the ruler.[11]

Despite what is thought, Islam does not lay down detailed blueprints for the forms of institutions but provides for flexibility, enunciating only broad principles. Thus it insists on impartial justice but leaves open the pattern of judicial organization. It provides for popular election and consultation, again leaving the procedures open. It requires the ruler to enforce the law and promote the Faith, by whatever means are appropriate. The guiding consideration is that of public interest (*maṣlaḥa*), which is also the foundation of jurisprudence.[12] It is therefore false to suppose that Islam insists on reviving the Caliphate in its previous form. The Muslim Community after the death of the Prophet only created the Caliphate as a matter of public interest, not of dogma. A formally unified Islamic state is not required in the modern age if it is impractical; the supposed requirement that the ruler be a Quraishite is a myth; and it makes no difference whether the

[8] *Ibid.*, p. 65.
[9] *Ibid.*, p. 72.
[10] *Ibid.*, p. 75.
[11] *Ibid.*, pp. 80–85, 116–117.
[12] *Ibid.*, pp. 101–104, 148–163.

ruler is officially titled "Caliph" or "President of the Republic."[13]

Thus having begun in a manner that may seem to suggest a condemnation of the present Egyptian or certain other contemporary secular Near Eastern regimes, Surūr ends by providing the means by which they might be considered legitimately Islamic—for one might ask, is not the present Egyptian government responsive to public opinion, considerate of the public welfare, competently officered, and presided over by a man of virtue and conscience?[14]

Many other recent books are available to provide Islam with a fashionable image. Muḥammad ash-Sharqāwī, in his *Ad-Dīmuqrāṭiyya 'Ind al-'Arab* ("Democracy Among the Arabs")[15] equates the Arab heritage with Islam and finds, like Surūr, that according to Islam the *umma*—ambiguously, the (Islamic) Community or the (Arab) nation—is the source of authority, that the ruler is to be popularly elected, that women, slaves, and (*n.b.*) military officers are not barred from participation in public affairs, that freedom of thought and expression should prevail, that social justice should be promoted, and so forth.

A more specialized and scholarly sample of recent literature in this vein is 'Abdalkarīm al-Khaṭīb's *As-Siyāsa 'l-Māliyya fī 'l-Islām wa Ṣilatuhā bi 'l Mu'āmalāt al-Mu'āṣira* ("Financial Policy in Islam and Its Relation to Contemporary Transactions").[16] Parts of the book appear to reflect the prevailing current of official economic ideology in Cairo: for example, that private wealth and investment are permissible in principle provided they are not used for the exploitation of others, and that monopoly endangers the rights of society and that Islam permits price-fixing or forced sale as a remedy.[17] Of greater importance are passages in which the author considers certain distinctive financial provisions of the Sharī'a and seeks to justify them and demonstrate their practical implications in modern contexts. In regard to the Islamic rules of inheritance, for instance, Khaṭīb defends the Qur'ānic principle of allotting to male heirs twice the amount allotted to their female counterparts by explaining that men's natural capacities make

[13] *Ibid.*, pp. 109–113.

[14] Among the author's other works are *Jamāl 'Abd an-Nāṣir, Rajul Ghayyar Wajh at-Tārīkh* ("Jamāl 'Abd an-Nāṣir, a Man Who Changed the Face of History") and *Ṣalāḥ ad-Dīn al-Ayyūbī* ("Saladin").

[15] Cairo, 1961.

[16] Cairo, 1961.

[17] *Ibid.*, pp. 94, 125–133, 190–192.

them more responsible than women for the support of their families. If it be argued that the Qur'ān is unduly rigid in this and fails to allow for changing conditions, he continues, the fact remains that no one has ever demonstrated convincingly that in any modern society the sexes are in fact equally responsible, and where individual exceptions may exist, it is questionable whether such exceptions are healthy.[18] Thus the question of reinterpreting or disregarding the Qur'ānic provisions does not arise.

Likewise in the matter of lending money at interest (*ribā 'n-nasī'a*), Islam prohibits this as socially pernicious, and also prohibits other practices that rest implicitly on the same principle. In principle it is therefore illegitimate for banks to lend money to individual clients at interest, though they may lend it in exchange for a share in the profit or loss of the borrower's enterprise. But Muslims need not feel compelled to risk destroying the economic and financial structure of their society by abandoning the practice of lending at interest, if no satisfactory alternative can be arranged. As for banks, insurance companies, or other institutions paying interest on individual deposits, this is entirely acceptable, since the social injury at which the Qur'ānic ban was directed does not arise.[19] By the same token, the Sharī'a in principle prohibits the advance sale of presently nonexistent commodities (e.g., fish before they are caught, agricultural produce before the harvest), in order to preclude speculation or subsequent conflict and misunderstanding; but a well-regulated modern stock and commodity exchange system largely removes the cause of the ban and is therefore legitimate.[20]

Another writer explains that despite the prevailing assumption, Islam respects absolute freedom of religion, including paganism and even apostasy from Islam. Verses in the Qur'ān calling for war against unbelievers are either superseded by others, particularly ii:256, which disavows compulsion in religion (*lā ikrāh fī 'd-dīn*), or are to be interpreted as having a political rather than religious objective. Leniency toward apostates is affirmed by a ḥadīth from the jurist Mālik b. Anas concerning the policy of the Caliph 'Umar. "I praise God," writes the author in his introduction, "who has enabled me to establish the religious freedom of the apostate from Islam, by virtue of which re-

---

[18] *Ibid.*, pp. 102–106.

[19] *Ibid.*, pp. 134–148, 175–189. Cf. a similar discussion of *ribā* by Fatḥī 'Uthmān, *Al-Fikr al-Islāmī wa 't-Tatawwur* (Cairo, n.d. [*ca.* 1961]), pp. 31–76.

[20] Khaṭib, *As-Siyāsa*, pp. 149–174.

ligious freedom in Islam is absolute and unrestricted. Thus Islam takes precedence over the legislators of our age in regard to the freedom of belief which they have enacted in their modern constitutions."[21]

The "legislators of our age," for their part, have been adept at invoking the support of Islam for their enactments. In the area of family law they have had to pay a price for this, for here the provisions of the Sharī'a are too specific and have been too continually enforced to be explained away by vague references to *maṣlaḥa* or *ijtihād*. Progress has nonetheless been made, not by the kind of explicitly Islamic methods that have been advocated by Riḍā and his school, but by a series of administrative devices and selective interpretations. Unlike Turkey, which abandoned the Sharī'a altogether in the 1920's, and Tunisia, which recently adopted a civil law of marriage, in Egypt the family law of Islam continues to be formally recognized—although no longer in special religious courts[22]—and has made the process of reform complicated, but it has not really stood in the way of what needed to be done. In the field of civil law, meanwhile, the Sharī'a has posed no material problem at all, and mere lip service to it has sufficed.

Family law, including matters of marriage and divorce, guardianship, and inheritance, has long been, together with the law governing pious foundations (*awqāf*), the special preserve of the Sharī'a not subject in principle to legislative tampering by the ruling authorities. Islamic tradition has always recognized the ruler's right to delimit the jurisdiction of individual judges and *muftīs*, both in territory and in subject matter. But even the Ottoman government exercised this right with circumspection, not using it as a means of influencing the applied content of the law itself, so that it could not be said that the civil authority actually enjoyed the power of defining the sphere of validity to be assigned to the Sharī'a. The most that the Egyptian government did prior to 1920 in delimiting the family law of the Sharī'a was to accord an official status to the Ḥanafī School.

The codification of family law that was promulgated in the Ottoman-controlled territories in 1917 and the piecemeal family legislation

[21] 'Abdalmuta'āl aṣ-Ṣa'īdī, *Al-Ḥurriyya 'd-Dīniyya fī 'l-Islām* (Cairo, n.d.), p. 4.

[22] The Sharī'a courts, as well as the religious courts of non-Muslim minorities, were abolished at the beginning of 1956. Cases are now heard in civil courts, but still according to the religious law of the parties. See N. Safran, "The Abolition of the Shar'ī Courts in Egypt," *Muslim World*, XLVIII (1958), 20–28, 125–135; also G. N. Sfeir, "The Abolition of Confessional Jurisdiction in Egypt," *Middle East Journal*, X (1956) 248–256.

that began in Egypt in 1920 represented a new departure, first because they both introduced certain innovations, and second, because the very act of subjecting Ḥanafī law to statutory provisions signified the subordination of the Sharī'a to legislative power.[23]

In Egypt family law has not been reduced to a single comprehensive code comparable to the Ottoman law of 1917, but has been the subject of a series of piecemeal legislative provisions whose overall effect appears to be largely the same on the psychological level: making Ḥanafī law valid only on the sufferance of the legislature. Frequently the method adopted in modifying the effective substance of Ḥanafī law has been a circuitous process of devices involving an extended use of the right of the government to limit the jurisdiction of judges, carried to the extent of denying judicial relief to parties in certain cases. For example, according to a 1923 statute designed to limit child marriages, courts are forbidden to hear any claim (except paternity suits) arising out of a marriage in which the husband was under 18 years of age or the wife under 16 at the time of the marriage[24] or in which the marriage was not duly registered; and registration could not be granted to under-age couples. Thus the law did not actually prohibit under-age marriage but only denied enforcement of its legal consequences.[25]

In other cases the method employed has been to incorporate into statutes an eclectic selection of provisions from various of the four Sunnī Schools or even from the opinions of medieval jurists outside the Schools. This principle of eclectic selection is an extension of a traditionally recognized practice known as *talfīq*, according to which an individual might follow one School in marriage procedure, another in determining inheritance, and still another in establishing a *waqf* or in performing prayers. Usually *talfīq* was not recognized as legitimate within what is essentially a single process: for example, in the case of marriage it would not be acceptable to follow Ḥanafī rules governing consent and Shāfi'ī rules on the dowry. Yet in certain cases it appears that this method has now been followed, under the claim made by drafting commissions that they have chosen from among views of

---

[23] This fact is remarked on by Joseph Schacht, "L'Évolution moderne du droit musulman en Égypte," *Mélanges Maspéro*, III (1935) (Extrait des *Mémoires* de l'Institut Francais d'Archéologie Orientale, LXVIII), 324–325.

[24] Later amended to apply to the time of the suit rather than the time of the marriage.

[25] Discussed by J. N. D. Anderson, "Recent Developments in Sharī'a Law," *Muslim World*, XLI (1951), 48 (the second of a series of nine articles in *Muslim World*, XL, XLI, and XLII [1950–1952]).

reputable jurists on the basis of suitability. It is generally acknowledged that the selection of individual rules is not based on methodological considerations of *uṣūl al-fiqh* (other than *maṣlaḥa*). Nor do the drafters profess to have exercised full *ijtihād*. Despite denials in the explanatory memoranda of various commissions that *talfīq* has been resorted to within single matters, certain examples would seem to belie this.[26]

This extended version of *talfīq* might be considered a form of *istiḥsān*, inasmuch as a choice is made between equally reputable alternative interpretations. As such, it outwardly involves only a limited *ijtihād*, since it makes no pretense of reviewing the interpretations themselves, in a way that would make possible a new ruling different from any previous one; the limits of the sum total of existing interpretations are respected. But all this obscures the nature of the real *ijtihād* that has taken place, which is not bound by traditional methods at all. Given the complete liberty of choice among alternative Sharī'a rules regarding the details of a single question, it seems clear that the relative degree of adherence of these rules to the Qur'ān and Sunna was not a consideration. It would make no difference, for example, that the rules selected might stem from mutually contradictory interpretations of the textual sources.[27] This is why *talfīq* was not traditionally permitted to be carried to such an extent. The actual consideration motivating the legislative commissions has evidently been to draft laws that are equitable by "modern," that is, secular, standards. Thus when the 1946 law of wills was introduced in the Egyptian Senate, the reporter of the bill explained: "In the project on the law of wills the Government has not confined itself solely to the rite of the Imam Abū Ḥanīfa. It has searched for its source of inspiration in other rites with the goal of producing a law which will be adapted to circumstances and respond best to practical needs."[28]

Had the prime concern been to safeguard the Islamic character of the law, confirmation of the Ḥanafī rules would have sufficed. Alternatively, if *ijtihād* as advocated by Rashīd Riḍā had been employed, the legislators would not have been bound to choose between already

[26] Anderson in *Muslim World*, XL (1950), 253–255, and XLII (1952), 39. See also Anderson's *Islamic Law in the Modern World* (New York, 1959), *passim*.

[27] A point noted by Anderson in *Muslim World*, XL (1950), 255.

[28] Speech by Senator Aḥmad Ramzī Bey, March 25, 1946; quoted in H. Liebesny, "Religious Law and Westernization in the Moslem Near East," *American Journal of Comparative Law*, II (1953), 500.

existing rules of the four Schools, but would have been limited only by what they considered to be the intent of the Qur'ānic and ḥadīth sources themselves. This might have led to even greater changes in the substance of the law, but would have reflected a more wholly religious conception of the nature of law.

The secular conception is much more evident in the field of civil law. Much less of the substance of the Sharī'a, of course, has found its way into the 1949 Egyptian civil code and its Syrian and Iraqi counterparts than into family law. This is because of the historical record of adulteration of Islamic civil law by other elements, including the Western codes imported into the Ottoman Empire and Egypt in the last century. The present Egyptian civil code is the product of a group of jurists headed by 'Abdarrazzāq as-Sanhūrī, who since the mid-1930's had called for a code based on (1) appropriate features of European codes, particularly the French and German, (2) judicial precedent in Egypt since 1850, and (3) Islamic law. Outwardly he argued for the inclusion of Islamic law as a model on grounds reminiscent of Rashīd Riḍā: that the Sharī'a was innately evolutionary and adaptable through *ijmā'* and *ijtihād*, that a distinction should be made between its religious and temporal provisions, and that *ijmā'* should serve to "organize the practical functioning of deliberative agreement" (i.e., be institutionalized).[29]

As a practical lawyer Sanhūrī has no intention of attempting to reconstruct an entire legal system along the lines indicated by Rashīd Riḍā, based on an examination of the intent of revealed texts. He is content to give the Sharī'a third place among his sources, selecting certain useful general concepts from it[30] on a piecemeal basis in order to "perfect the fundamental bases of our legislation" and filling in gaps in existing legislation with provisions from the Sharī'a.[31] In the completed 1949 code, Sanhūrī told a Senate committee, three-fourths

---

[29] Sanhoury (Sanhūrī), "Le Droit musulman comme élément de réfonte du code civil égyptien," *Introduction à l'étude du droit comparé: recueil d'études en honneur d'Edouard Lambert*, II (Paris, 1938), 622–624. This article is a partial translation from Sanhūrī's fuller treatment of the entire question of the sources of a new civil code in his article "Wujūb Tanqīḥ al-Qānūn al-Madanī al-Miṣrī wa 'alā ayy Asās Yakūn Hādhā-l-Tanqīḥ," *Majallat al-Qānūn wa 'l-Iqtiṣād*, VI (1936), 3–144.

[30] Particularly the assumption that since law deals with externals, it should avoid excessive reliance on presumed intent, especially where intent is irrelevant, as in tort cases; on this question he finds Islamic law closer to German and Anglo-Saxon than to French law. Thus the Sharī'a influences Sanhūrī's choice between two European models.

[31] "Le Droit musulman comme élément de réfonte," *op. cit.*, p. 628.

to five-sixths of the provisions were "based on the decisions of Egyptian courts and on the existing legislation."[32] How much of this reflected genuinely Islamic jurisprudence would be very difficult to determine with any accuracy.

The other debt that the 1949 code owes to the Sharī'a lies in the provision that cases are to be decided according to the Sharī'a in default of any statutory rule *and* in default of any relevant custom.[33] This is a minor step forward for the Sharī'a, since previous to the new code only natural law and equity had been listed as a subsidiary basis for judgment.

Despite Sanhūrī's lip service to the ideal of an evolutionary Sharī'a, it is evident that the Egyptian civil code adopted the Sharī'a not as the basis of the entire system but as only one of a number of sources, from which rules could be drawn here and there and synthesized with rules from other sources into a unified system. The result is a law that is peculiarly Egyptian, not peculiarly Islamic. Provisions from the Sharī'a were included, as Sanhūrī had written in 1936, "because they are part of our heritage,"[34] which is after all the same reason that modern Egyptian judicial precedent was included. The Sharī'a thus occupies a place comparable to the place that had been occupied by custom in its own early historical development: it is merely suitable, not sacrosanct. It is not surprising that in drafting the various rules of the code, Sanhūrī avoided public discussion of the doctrinal issues involved. The synthesizing technique represents much ingenuity and, no doubt, wisdom, but the fact remains that it is a secular rather than religious conception of law that is implicit in the whole process.[35]

On the most explicit level, developments such as these have made a mockery of the aspirations of Riḍā and other modernists for the revival of Islamic jurisprudence. Riḍā's program, taken literally, would have required not only that a resort to *ijtihād* reflect a faithful and systematic dependence on the meaning of the revealed texts, but that all members of the Egyptian parliament qualify morally and intellectually as *mujtahids*. On another level, in terms not of Riḍā's intentions

---

[32] J. N. D. Anderson, "The Sharī'a and Civil Law," *Islamic Quarterly*, I (1954), 30.

[33] Liebesny, "Religious Law and Westernization," *op. cit.*, p. 499. The Syrian code of 1949 puts Islamic Law before custom.

[34] "Le Droit musulman comme élément de réfonte," *op. cit.*, p. 628.

[35] For a discussion on this point see M. Khadduri, "From Religious to National Law," *in* Ruth Nanda Anshen, ed., *Mid-East: World Center* (New York, 1956), pp. 220–234.

but of his ideological role, we may pay less attention to his espousal of pious ideals and more to the fact that he made a place for such modern secular notions as national parliamentary sovereignty and utilitarian legislation within the traditional Islamic political and legal formulas. The effort of Islamic modernists to justify the revitalization of the Sharī'a by appealing to such principles as *ijtihād*, *istiṣlāḥ*, and *ijmā'* has made it easier for many of their compatriots to accept the legitimacy of contemporary legislative developments without much concern for the niceties of the actual methods used. Since the legislation is progressive, and since assurance has been given that Islam encourages progressive legislation, the requirements of Islam have presumably been respected. Just as in the second century of Islam the fabrication of ḥadīths and the elaboration of a system of deductive legal reasoning had sanctified the assimilation of existing local customs and precedents into a unified Islamic system of law, so today the modernist principles may be said to have performed an assimilative function.

By the same token, it would be possible to discount the significance of Riḍā's desire to restore the Caliphate, which under the circumstances of the 1920's stood not the slightest chance of realization in any case. His revival of the classical theory of the Caliphate serves to remind us that the classical theory itself had not been a program for action but a hyperbolical, almost allegorical, rationalization. Correspondingly, Riḍā's own ideas may be considered the hyperbolical reflection of the mentality of those of his fellow Muslims who have shared a nostalgic consciousness of the great days of early Islamic history and a desire for political action within a national framework in the present age.

In this sense Riḍā's constitutional theory, despite his intentions, does not represent a serious program but a statement of ideals. It had no more prospects of adoption than that of Māwardī in the eleventh century. What Māwardī's treatise tells us is not how the state was actually organized in his time, but that government is a moral enterprise confided by God to the leaders of the Community, and that the moral quality of government must depend on their moral qualities and religious devotion. What Rashīd Riḍā tells us in the *Khilāfa* is that in 1922 the modern concept of popular and national sovereignty was strong enough to find room in his supposedly revivalist theory and that the parliamentary legislative institution is sanctioned by Islamic principles. The ambiguities and contradictions in his proposals largely serve to confirm that he conceives theory with the same allegorical imagination, though not the same purpose, as his classical forerunners.

Seen in this light, 'Alī 'Abd ar-Rāziq's great crime was to lend the sanction of a theory, and thus the sanction of an ideal, to something that he himself declared to be purely mundane. His theory did not attack an existing institutional structure, any more than Riḍā's theory upheld one. But by denying the very concept of an Islamic government, 'Abd ar-Rāziq was bound to offend even some persons who might be tacitly ready to accept the practical implication of his ideas, namely a secularly organized government.

Despite all that we have been saying about the assimilative function of Islamic modernism, common sense must remind us that to dwell on it is somewhat pointless, for its relevance to present-day ideological concerns is really only a minor one. It would be easy to go on to enumerate occasions, for instance, on which the present government in Egypt has invoked the support of Islam, sometimes in the form of *fatwās* from shaikhs of Al-Azhar, for its revolutionary policies; but the fact is that this is at best a secondary level of rationalization, the primary level being that of appeals to sentiments of nationalism and social justice. Rather than Islamic loyalties assimilating nationalism and secular institutions, it would be more to the point to say that the latter have assimilated Islam.

Furthermore, whereas the legal and constitutional doctrines of the Abbasid period served to preserve the legitimacy of the existing fabric of institutions in the face of anarchy, the need in the twentieth century has been for a principle of creation, innovation, and construction, by which revolution may be given a sense of moral direction. Muḥammad 'Abduh made it plausible to seek such a principle within the Islamic tradition; Riḍā embarked on the search, and emerged with unsatisfactory answers. Insofar as his answers inspired action, it was of the negative and destructive kind promoted by the Muslim Brotherhood, but more generally they inspired a passive, uneasy, ineffectual acceptance of European institutions and social practices, without providing these with any firm moral basis.

The nationalist sentiment of the present day provides no such moral guideline, or "regulative principle," as one writer has put it.[36] It is not

[36] Albert Hourani, *A Vision of History* (Beirut, 1961), pp. 145–160. Cf. his "Near Eastern Nationalism Yesterday and Today," *Foreign Affairs*, XLII (Fall, 1963), pp. 123–136.

in the nature of nationalism to do so, for nationalism is an assertion of identity and of solidarity, acknowledging nothing beyond itself and simply appropriating those social values that serve the cause of self-assertion. Nor can the concern for social justice, so explosively conspicuous in the Near East today, quite provide such a principle either, as long as it is primarily an instrument and an expression of nationalism.

It is nonetheless curious that today Arab nationalist intellectuals, including the Christians among them, tend to turn to Islam as a "national" heritage in which to find "Arab" principles of action distinctive from those offered by Western liberalism or by communism. And indeed Islam provides them with a number of important assets. It offers them a history, and therefore the sense of identity required for self-assurance. It provides an ethic of communal (i.e., national) solidarity in the struggle against enemies, and a sense of destiny in the world. It promotes concepts of brotherhood and equal dignity among citizens, of the importance of justice, and of the benefits of strong and virtuous leadership. If the Islamic modernists, and particularly Muḥammad 'Abduh, have one positive accomplishment to their credit, it is the revival of the optimistic, action-oriented spirit by which these aspects of Islam have been lifted out of the realm of chiliastic escapism and made relevant to the present world of endeavor. To this end two ideas in particular have been successfully advanced, whether on impressive intellectual grounds or not: that men are indeed the authors of their own actions, and that they are fully entitled to act on the basis of their own calculated interests. But as these ideas took hold, they broke loose from their theological and moral moorings. The capacity for action and for the pursuit of interests has tended to become the servant not of transcendent moral responsibility or devotion, but of the subjective willfulness either of the group or of the individual.

> The problem which was implicit in these national movements [writes Albert Hourani] was no longer how to preserve the law as standing above the community but how to create a common will. Political problems became problems of social engineering: how to generate the unity and dynamism which could create and maintain a state. . . . This explains why at one period those who wanted national independence also wanted parliamentary institutions; the example of Europe, they thought, showed that representative government was a means of gen-

> erating this active will. But it was only a means, and might be replaced by a better means. . . .[37]

The shift from traditional Islamic piety and acceptance of what was presumed to be a divinely ordained social order to the new ethos of "social engineering"—from the idea of divine voluntarism to that of human voluntarism—is symbolized, if not exactly explained, in the failure of the Islamic reformists of Muḥammad 'Abduh's and Rashīd Riḍā's generations to establish a middle ground. In Europe the corresponding theological tradition of divine voluntarism had gradually yielded either to the Thomist theology of natural justice or, later, to its secular derivative long before human voluntarist philosophies emerged. The latter have had their modern triumphs, some of them parading under superhuman banners and accordingly repulsive, but others tempered by traditions of civility. In the Islamic world the pace of change has been so fast—pressed, significantly, by manifestations of the West's will and power rather than its reasonableness—as to induce a transformation of attitude straight from the passivity of Ash'arism to the assertiveness that characterizes contemporary nationalism. In this process, the intellectual reformers who sought to provide answers to the most modern needs by fanciful appeals to the earliest period of Islamic history inevitably tended to fall between two stools, alternatively giving rise to impotent protests against the rootlessness of the modern social order or providing fuel for its militancy and self-esteem.

---

[37] *A Vision of History*, p. 156.

SELECT BIBLIOGRAPHY

SELECT BIBLIOGRAPHY

Works cited in the footnotes, aside from certain items to which only incidental reference is made, and a limited number of other items which have been found particularly useful and significant are included. More exhaustive bibliographies, covering a wider range of themes than does this book, may be found elsewhere. The reader is referred particularly to those in Albert Hourani, *Arabic Thought in the Liberal Age* (London, 1962), and H. A. R. Gibb and Harold Bowen, *Islamic Society and the West*, Vol. I, Part II (London, 1957).

The bibliography is given in two sections: I, Works in Arabic; II, Works in Other Languages.

I. WORKS IN ARABIC

'Abd ar-Rāziq, 'Alī. *Al-Islām wa Uṣūl al-Hukm.* Cairo: Miṣr Press, 1925. French translation by Léon Bercher, "L'Islam et les bases du pouvoir," *Revue des Études Islamiques*, 1933, pp. 353–390; 1934, pp. 163–222.

'Abduh, Muḥammad. *Al-Islām wa 'n-Naṣrāniyya ma' al-'Ilm wa 'l-Madaniyya.* Cairo: Manār Press, n.d.

———. *Risālat at-Tauḥīd.* Cairo, Manār Press, 1351 H. French translation and introduction by B. Michel and Moustapha Abdel Razik, *Rissalat al-Tawhid; exposé de la religion musulmane.* Paris: Paul Geuthner, 1925.

———. *Tafsīr al-Fātiḥa.* Cairo: Manār Press, 1901.

———. *Tafsīr Juz' 'Amma.* Cairo: Manār Press, 1341 H.

———. *Tafsīr Sūrat al-'Aṣr.* Cairo: Manār Press, 1321 H.

———, and Jamāl ad-Dīn al-Afghānī. *Al-'Urwa 'l-Wuthqā.* Cairo, 1927. Originally published as a periodical in Paris, 1884.

———, and Muḥammad Rashīd Riḍa. *Tafsīr al-Qur'ān al-Ḥakīm.* Cairo: Manār Press, 1346–1354 H. 12 vols.

Abū Ya'lā, Muḥammad b. al-Ḥusain. *Al-Aḥkām as-Sulṭāniyya.* Cairo, 1357 H.

Abū Yūsuf, Ya'qūb b. Ibrāhīm. *Kitāb al-Kharāj.* Cairo, 1937. French translation by E. Fagnan, *Le Livre de l'impot foncier.* Paris: Paul Geuthner, 1921.

Al-Afghānī, Jamāl ad-Dīn. *Ar-Radd 'alā 'd-Dahriyyīn.* Cairo, 1903. French translation by A. M. Goichon, *Réfutation des matérialistes.* Paris: Paul Geuthner, 1942.

Amīn, Aḥmad. *Zu'amā' al-Iṣlāḥ fī 'l-'Aṣr al-Ḥadīth.* Cairo: Maktabat an-Nahḍa 'l-Miṣriyya, 1948.

Arslān, Amīr Shakīb. *Li-mādhā Ta'akhkhara 'l-Muslimūn wa li-mādhā Taqaddama Ghairuhum.* Cairo, 1358 H. English translation by M. A. Shakoor, *Our Decline and Its Causes.* Lahore: Muhammad Ashraf, 1944.

———. *As-Sayyid Rashīd Riḍā au Ikhā' Arba'īn Sana.* Damascus: Ibn Zaidan Press, 1937.

Al-Ash'arī, Abū 'l-Ḥasan. *Al-Ibāna 'an Uṣūl ad-Diyāna.* Hyderabad, 1321 H. English translation by Walter C. Klein, *Al-Aš'arī's Al-Ibānah 'an Uṣūl al-Diyānah* (*The Elucidation of Islam's Foundation*). American Oriental Series, No. 19. New Haven: American Oriental Society, 1940.

Al-Azhar University. "Ḥukm Hai'at Kibār al-'Ulamā' fī Kitāb al-Islām wa Uṣūl al-Ḥukm," *Manār,* XXVI, 363–382.

Al-Baghdādī, 'Abdalqāhir. *Uṣūl ad-Dīn.* Istanbul, 1928.

Bakhīt, Muḥammad. *Ḥaqīqat al-Islām wa Uṣūl al-Ḥukm.* Cairo: Salafiyya Press, 1926.

Al-Bāqillānī, Abū Bakr Muḥammad. *At-Tamhīd fī 'r-Radd 'alā 'l-Mulḥida wa 'l-Mu'aṭṭila wa 'r-Rāfiḍa wa 'l-Khawārij wa 'l-Mu'tazila.* Cairo: Lajnat at-Ta'līf, 1947.

Al-Ghazālī, al-Imām Abū Ḥāmid. *Iḥyā' 'Ulūm ad-Dīn.* Cairo, 1289 H. 3 vols.

———. *Al-Iqtiṣād fī 'l-I'tiqād.* Cairo: Ḥijāzī Press, 1320 H.

———. *Al-Mustaṣfā min 'Ilm al-Uṣul.* Cairo: Muṣtafā Muḥammad Press, 1937.

Ibn Jamā'a, Badr ad-Dīn. *Taḥrīr al-Aḥkām fī Tadbīr Ahl al-Islām.* Edited by Hans Kofler in *Islamica,* VI (1934), 349–414, and VII (1935), 1–34. Partial German translation by Kofler, "Handbuch des Islamischen Staats- und Verwaltungsrechtes von Badr ad-Din Ibn Gama'ah," *Islamica,* VII, 34–65.

Ibn Khaldūn, 'Abd ar-Raḥmān. *Al-Muqaddima*. Edited by E. M. Quatremère. Paris, 1858. 3 vols. English translation by Franz Rosenthal, *Al-Muqaddimah: An Introduction to History*. New York: Bollingen Foundation, 1958. 3 vols.

Ibn Nujaim, Zain al-'Ābidīn. *Al-Ashbāh wa 'n-Naẓā'ir*. Istanbul, 1290 H.

Ibn Qayyim al-Jauziyya. *Aṭ-Ṭuruq al-Ḥukmiyya fī 's-Siyāsa 'sh-Shar'iyya*. Cairo: As-Sunna 'l-Muḥammadiyya Press, 1953.

Ibn Taimiyya, Taqī ad-Dīn Aḥmad. *Al-Ḥisba fī 'l-Islām*. Madina: Maktaba 'Ilmiyya, n.d.

———. *As-Siyāsa 'sh-Shar'iyya fī Iṣlāḥ ar-Rā'ī wa 'r-Ra'iyya*. Cairo: Maktaba Khairiyya, 1322 H. French translation by Henri Laoust, *Le Traité de droit public d'Ibn Taimiya*. Beirut: Institut Français de Damas, 1948.

———, and Ibn Qayyim al-Jauziyya. *Al-Qiyās fī 'sh-Shar' al-Islāmī*. Edited by Muḥibb ad-Dīn al-Khaṭīb. Cairo: Salafiyya Press, 1346 H. French translation of portion by Ibn Taimiyya by Henri Laoust, *Contribution à une étude de la méthodologie canonique de Taḳī-d-Dīn Aḥmad b. Taimiya*. Cairo: Institut Français d'Archéologie Orientale, 1939.

Al-Ījī, 'Aḍud ad-Dīn. *Kitāb al-Mawāqif*. Parts 5, 6, and Appendix edited by T. Sorensen. Leipzig, 1848.

Khallāf, 'Abdalwahhāb. *Maṣādir at-Tashrī' al-Islāmī fīmā lā Naṣṣ fīh*. Cairo: Arab League Institute of Higher Arab Studies, 1955.

Khaṭīb, 'Abdalkarīm. *As-Siyāsa 'l-Māliyya fī 'l-Islām wa Ṣilatuhā bi 'l-Mu'āmalāt al-Mu'āṣira*. Cairo: Dār al-Fikr al-'Arabī, 1961.

Khūrī, Ra'īf. *Al-Fikr al-'Arabī al-Ḥadīth*. Beirut: Dār al-Makshūf, 1943.

Maḥmaṣānī, Ṣubḥī. *Falsafat at-Tashrī' fī 'l-Islām*. Beirut, 1946. English translation by Farhat J. Ziadeh, *Falsafat al-Tashrī fī al-Islām: The Philosophy of Jurisprudence in Islam*. Leiden: Brill, 1961.

Al-Māwardī, Abū 'l-Ḥasan 'Alī. *Al-Aḥkām as-Sulṭāniyya*. Edited by Maximilian Enger. Bonn, 1853. French translation by Léon Ostrorog, *El-Ahkam es-Soulthaniya*, with introduction and commentary. Paris, 1901–1906. 2 vols.

Al-Qalqashandī, Abū 'l-'Abbās Aḥmad. *Ṣubḥ al-A'shā*. Cairo: Dār al-Kutub, 1916. Vol. 9.

Al-Qarāfī, Shihāb ad-Dīn. *Adh-Dhakhīra*. Cairo: Al-Azhar University, 1961. 2 vols.

———. *Sharḥ Tanqīḥ al-Fuṣūl fī 'l-Uṣūl*. Tunis, 1328 H.

Riḍā, As-Sayyid Muḥammad Rashīd. *Al-Khilāfa au al-Imāma 'l-'Uẓmā*.

Cairo: Manār Press, 1923. French translation by Henri Laoust, *Le Califat dans la doctrine de Raşid Rida*. Beirut: Institut Français de Damas, 1938.

———, editor. *Al-Manār*, vols. 1–35. Cairo, 1898–1935.

———. *Al-Manār wa 'l-Azhar*. Cairo: Manār Press, 1353 H./1934–1935.

———. *Shubuhāt an-Naṣāra wa Ḥujaj al-Islām*. Cairo: Manār Press, 1322 H.

———. *Tārīkh al-Ustādh al-Imām ash-Shaikh Muḥammad 'Abduh*. Cairo: Manār Press, 1931. 3 vols.

———. *Al-Waḥda 'l-Islāmiyya wa 'l-Ukhuwwa 'd-Dīniyya*. Cairo: Manār Press, 1367 H. (3d printing).

———. *Al-Waḥy al-Muḥammadī*. Cairo: Manār Press, 1352 H. (2d printing).

———. *Yusr al-Islām wa Uṣūl at-Tashrī' al-'Āmm*. Cairo: Manār Press, 1928.

Ṣa'īdī, 'Abdalmuta'āl. *Al-Ḥurriyya 'd-Dīniyya fī 'l-Islām*. Cairo: Dār al-Fikr al-'Arabī, n.d. (*ca*. 1961).

Sanhūrī, 'Abdarrazzāq. "Wujūb Tanqīḥ al-Qānūn al-Madanī al-Miṣrī wa 'alā Ayy Asās Yakūn Hādhā 't-Tanqīḥ," *Majallat al-Qānūn wa 'l-Iqtiṣād*, VI (1936), 3–144.

Ash-Shāfi'ī, al-Imām Muḥammad b. Idrīs. *Ar-Risāla*. Cairo: Būlāq Press, 1321 H. English translation with introduction by Majid Khadduri, *Islamic Jurisprudence: Shāfi'ī's Risāla*. Baltimore: Johns Hopkins University Press, 1961.

Ash-Sharqāwī, Muḥammad. *Ad-Dīmuqrāṭiyya 'Ind al-'Arab*. Cairo: Ad-Dār al-Qaumiyya li 'ṭ-Ṭabā'a wa 'n-Nashr, 1961.

Shāwīsh, 'Abdal'azīz. *Al-Islām Dīn al-Fiṭra wa 'l-Ḥurriyya*. Cairo, Dār al-Hilāl, n.d. (reprint, *ca*. 1960).

Surūr, Ṭāhā 'Abdalbāqī. *Daulat al-Qur'ān*. Cairo: al-Maktaba 'l-'Ilmiyya, 1955; 2d ed., 1961.

Aṭ-Ṭaufī, Najm ad-Dīn. "Sharḥ al-Ḥadīth ath-Thānī wa Thalāthīn min al-Arba'īn an-Nawawiyya," published in: *Majmū' ar-Rasā'il fī Uṣūl al-Fiqh* (Beirut, Ahliyya Press, 1324 H.); *Manār*, IX, 745–770; 'Abdalwahhāb Khallāf, *Maṣādir at-Tashrī' al-Islāmī fīmā lā Naṣṣ fīh* (*Cairo*, 1955), pp. 87–122; and Muṣṭafā Zaid, *Al-Maṣlaḥa fī 't-Tashrī' al-Islāmī wa Najm ad-Dīn aṭ-Ṭaufī* (Cairo, 1954), Appendix, pp. 14–48.

'Uthmān, Fatḥī. *Al-Fikr al-Islāmī wa 'ṭ-Ṭatawwur*. Cairo: Dār al-Qalam, n.d. (*ca*. 1961).

Zaid, Muṣṭafā. *Al-Maṣlaḥa fī 't-Tashrī' al-Islāmī wa Najm ad-Dīn aṭ-Ṭaufī*. Cairo, Dār al-Fikr al-'Arabī, 1954.
Zaidān, Jurjī. *Tarājim Mashāhīr ash-Sharq fī 'l-Qarn at-Tāsi' 'Ashar*. Cairo: Dār al-Hilāl, 1922. 2 vols.

II. WORKS IN OTHER LANGUAGES

Abdul Hakim, Khalifa. "The Natural Law in the Muslim Tradition," University of Notre Dame, Natural Law Institute, *Proceedings*, V (1951) 29–65.
Abu-Lughod, Ibrahim. *Muslim Rediscovery of Europe*. Princeton: Princeton University Press, 1963.
Adams, Charles C. *Islam and Modernism in Egypt*. London: Oxford University Press, 1933.
———. "Muḥammad 'Abduh and the Transvaal Fatwā," in *Macdonald Presentation Volume*. London: Oxford University Press, 1933. Pp. 13–29.
Ahmed, Jamal Mohammed. *The Intellectual Origins of Egyptian Nationalism*. London, Oxford University Press, 1960.
Aghnides, Nicholas P. *Mohammedan Theories of Finance with an Introduction to Mohammedan Law and a Bibliography*. New York: Columbia University Press, 1916.
Ameer Ali, Syed. *The Spirit of Islam*. London: Christopher's, 1922.
Amin, Osman. *Muhammad 'Abduh: Essai sur ses idées philosophiques et religieuses*. Cairo: Miṣr Press, 1944.
Anderson, J. N. D. *Islamic Law in the Modern World*. New York: New York University Press, 1959.
———. "Recent Developments in Sharī'a Law," *The Muslim World*, XL (1950), 244–256; XLI (1951), 34–48, 113–126, 186–198, 271–288; XLII (1952), 33–47, 124–140, 190–206, 261–276.
———. "The Sharī'a and Civil Law," *The Islamic Quarterly*, I (1954), 29–46.
Anshen, Ruth Nanda, editor. *Mid-East: World Center*. New York: Harper, 1956.
Arberry, A. J. *Revelation and Reason in Islam*. London: Allen & Unwin, 1957.
Arnold, T. W. *The Caliphate*. Oxford: Clarendon Press, 1924.
———, and Alfred Guillaume. *The Legacy of Islam*. Oxford: Clarendon Press, 1931.
El-Bahay, Muhammed. *Muhammed 'Abduh: eine Untersuchung seiner*

Erziehungsmethode zum Nationalbewusstsein und zur Nationalen Erhebung in Ägypten. Hamburg, 1936.

Berque, Jacques. *Les Arabes d'hier à demain.* Paris: Éditions du Seuil, 1960.

Binder, Leonard. "Al-Ghazali's Theory of Islamic Government," *The Muslim World*, XLV (1955), 229–241.

———. *The Ideological Revolution in the Middle East.* New York, London, Sydney: Wiley, 1964.

———. *Religion and Politics in Pakistan.* Berkeley and Los Angeles: University of California Press, 1961.

DeBoer, T. J. *The History of Philosophy in Islam.* Translated by Edward R. Jones. London: Luzac, 1903.

Carra de Vaux, Baron. *Les Penseurs de l'Islam.* Paris: Paul Geuthner, 1921–1926. 5 vols.

Caspar, Robert. "Le Renouveau du mo'tazilisme," Institut Dominicain d'Études Orientales du Caire, *Mélanges*, IV (1957), 141–201.

Colombe, Marcel. *L'Évolution de l'Égypte, 1924–1950.* Paris: Maisonneuve, 1954.

Coulson, N. J. "Doctrine and Practice in Islamic Law: One Aspect of the Problem," *Bulletin of the School of Oriental and African Studies* (London), XVIII (1956), 211–226.

———. "The State and the Individual in Islamic Law," *International and Comparative Law Quarterly*, VI (1957), 49–60.

Cragg, Kenneth. *The Call of the Minaret.* New York, Oxford University Press, 1956.

———. "The Tests of 'Islamicity'," *Middle East Forum*, Nov., 1957, pp. 15–17, 33.

Elder, E. E. *A Commentary on the Creed of Islam.* Translation of Taftazānī's commentary on the catechism of Abū Ḥafs 'Umar an-Nasafī. New York: Columbia University Press, 1950.

Faruki, Kemal A. *Ijma and the Gate of Ijtihad.* Karachi: Gateway Publications, 1954.

Fazlu-r-Rahman. "Internal Religious Developments in the Present Century Islam," *Journal of World History*, II (1954), 862–879.

———. "Modern Muslim Thought," *The Muslim World*, XLV (1955), 16–25.

Frye, Richard N., editor. *Islam and the West.* The Hague: Mouton, 1957.

Gardet, Louis. *La Cité musulmane: vie sociale et politique.* Paris: Vrin, 1954.

———. *La Mesure de notre liberté.* Tunis: Institut des Belles Lettres Arabes, 1946.
———, and M. M. Anawati. *Introduction à la théologie musulmane.* Paris: Vrin, 1948.
Gibb, H. A. R. *Modern Trends in Islam.* Chicago: University of Chicago Press, 1947.
———. *Studies on the Civilization of Islam.* Edited by S. J. Shaw and W. R. Polk. Boston: Beacon Press, 1962.
———, editor. *Whither Islam?* London: Gollancz, 1932.
———, and Harold Bowen. *Islamic Society and the West.* Vol. I, Parts I and II. London: Oxford University Press, 1950–1957.
Goldziher, Ignaz. "Du sens propre des expressions Ombre de Dieu, Khalife de Dieu pour désigner les chefs dans l'Islam," *Revue de l'Histoire des Religions*, XXXV (1897), 331–338.
———. *Muhammedanische Studien.* Halle, 1888–1890. 2 vols.
———. *Die Richtungen der Islamischen Koranauslegung.* Leiden: Brill, 1920.
———. *Vorlesungen über den Islam.* Translated by Félix Arin, *Le Dogme et la loi de l'Islam.* Paris: Paul Geuthner, 1920.
———. *Die Zahiriten, ihr Lehr-system und ihre Geschichte.* Leipzig: O. Schulze, 1884.
Guillaume, Alfred. *The Traditions of Islam. An Introduction to the Study of the Hadith Literature.* Oxford: Clarendon Press, 1924.
Haim, Sylvia G. *Arab Nationalism: An Anthology.* Berkeley and Los Angeles: University of California Press, 1962.
Hamidullah, Muhammad. *Muslim Conduct of State.* Lahore: Muhammad Ashraf, 1945.
Heyworth-Dunne, James. *Introduction to the History of Education in Modern Egypt.* London: Luzac, 1938.
———. *Religious and Political Trends in Modern Egypt.* Washington, 1950. (Privately printed.)
Horten, Max. "Muhammad Abduh, sein Leben und seine theologisch-philosophische Gedankenwelt," *Beiträge zur Kenntnis des Orients*, XIII (1916), 83–114; XIV (1917), 74–128.
Hourani, Albert H. *Arabic Thought in the Liberal Age.* London: Oxford University Press, 1962.
———. "The Decline of the West in the Middle East," *International Affairs*, XXIX (1953), 22–42, 156–183.
———. *A Vision of History. Near Eastern and Other Essays.* Beirut: Khayats, 1961.

Hourani, George F. "Averroes on Good and Evil," *Studia Islamica*, XVI (1962), 13–40.

———. "Two Theories of Value in Medieval Islam," *The Muslim World*, L (1960), 269–278.

Iqbal, Mohammad. *Six Lectures on the Reconstruction of Religious Thought in Islam*. London: Oxford University Press, 1934.

Jomier, Jacques. *Le Commentaire coranique du Manâr*. Paris: Maisonneuve, 1954.

Kabir, Humayun. *Science, Democracy, and Islam and Other Essays*. London: Allen & Unwin, 1955.

Khadduri, Majid. "Nature and Sources of the Shari'a," *George Washington Law Review*, XXII (1953), 3–23.

———. *War and Peace in the Law of Islam*. Baltimore: Johns Hopkins University Press, 1955.

———, and Herbert Liebesny, editors. *Law in the Middle East*. Washington, Middle East Institute, 1955.

Lambton, Ann K. S. "Quis Custodiet Custodes? Some Reflections on the Persian Theory of Government," *Studia Islamica*, V (1956), 125–148.

———. "The Theory of Kingship in the Naṣīḥat al-Mulūk of Ghazālī," *The Islamic Quarterly*, I (1954), 47–55.

Lammens, Henri. "La Crise intérieure de l'Islam, "*Etudes*, CLXXXVI (1926), 129–146.

Laoust, Henri. *Contribution à une étude de la méthodologie canonique de Taḳī-d-Dīn Aḥmad b. Taimiya*. Cairo: Institut Français d'Archéologie Orientale, 1939.

———. *Essai sur les doctrines sociales et politiques de Taḳī-d-Dīn Aḥmad b. Taimiya*. Cairo: Institut Français d'Archéologie Orientale, 1939.

———. "Le Réformisme orthodoxe des 'Salafiyya,' et les caractères généraux de son organisation actuelle," *Revue des Études Islamiques*, VI (1932), 175–224.

Levy, Reuben. *The Social Structure of Islam*. Cambridge: Cambridge University Press, 1957.

Lewis, Bernard. "The Concept of an Islamic Republic," *Die Welt des Islams*, n.s., IV (1955), 1–9.

———. *The Emergence of Modern Turkey*. London: Oxford University Press, 1961.

———. *The Middle East and the West*. London: Weidenfeld & Nicholson, 1963.

———, and P. M. Holt, editors. *Historians of the Middle East.* London: Oxford University Press, 1962.

Macdonald, Duncan Black. *Muslim Theology, Jurisprudence, and Constitutional Theory.* New York: Macmillan, 1903.

———. *The Religious Attitude and Life in Islam.* Chicago: University of Chicago Press, 1909.

Mahdi, Muhsin. *Ibn Khaldun's Philosophy of History.* London: Allen & Unwin, 1957.

———. "Die Kritik der islamischen politischen Philosophie bei Ibn Khaldun," *in* Dieter Oberndörfer, editor, *Wissenschaftliche Politik, eine Einführung in Grundfragen ihrer Tradition und Theorie* (Freiburg, 1963), pp. 117–151.

———, and Ralph Lerner, editors. *Medieval Political Philosophy.* Glencoe, Ill.: The Free Press, 1963.

Mahmassani, Sobhi. "Muslims: Decadence and Renaissance—Adaptation of Islamic Jurisprudence to Modern Social Needs," *The Muslim World,* XLIV (1954), 186–201.

Margoliouth, D. S. *The Early Development of Mohammedanism.* London: Williams and Norgate, 1914.

Massignon, Louis. "Études sur la notion islamique de la souveraineté," *Revue du Monde Musulman,* LIX (1st quarter, 1925): Turkey, Grand National Assembly: "Le Califat et la souveraineté nationale," trans. anonymous (pp. 5–81); Shaikh Muhammad Hilmi Tommara: "La Souveraineté islamique et le califat," trans. A. Sékally (pp. 83–112); Massignon, "L'Attitude actuelle des partis musulmans" (pp. 291–315).

———. "Introduction à l'étude des revendications islamiques," *Revue du Monde Musulman,* XXXIX (June, 1920), 1–26.

Nader, Albert. *Le Système philosophique des Mu'tazila.* Beirut: Institut de Lettres Orientales de Beyrouth, 1956.

Nuseibeh, Hazem Zaki. *The Ideas of Arab Nationalism.* Ithaca: Cornell University Press, 1956.

Ostrorog, Léon. *The Angora Reform.* London: University of London Press, 1927.

Pesle, Octave. *Les Fondements du droit musulman.* Casablanca, n.d.

Rosenthal, Erwin I. J. *Ibn Khalduns Gedanken über den Staat.* No. 25 of *Historische Zeitschrift.* Munich and Berlin, 1932.

———. *Political Thought in Medieval Islam.* Cambridge: Cambridge University Press, 1958.

Rosenthal, Franz. *A History of Muslim Historiography*. Leiden: Brill, 1952.

———. *The Technique and Approach of Muslim Scholarship*. No. 24 of *Analecta Orientalia*. Rome, 1947.

Safran, Nadav. "The Abolition of the Shar'ī Courts in Egypt," *The Muslim World*, XLVIII (1958), 20–28 and 125–135.

———. *Egypt in Search of Political Community*. Cambridge, Mass.: Harvard University Press, 1961.

Sakka, Ahmed. *De la souveraineté dans le droit public musulman sunnite*. Paris: Jouve, 1917.

Sanhoury, A. *Le Califat: son évolution vers une Société des Nations orientales*. Paris: Paul Geuthner, 1926.

———. "Le Droit musulman comme élément de réfonte du code civil égyptien," trans. René Sekkaly, in *Introduction à l'étude du droit comparé: recueil d'études en honneur d'Edouard Lambert* (Paris, 1938), II, 621–642.

Schacht, Joseph. "Classicisme, traditionalisme et ankylose dans la loi religieuse de l'Islam," in *Classicisme et déclin culturel dans l'histoire de l'Islam* (Bordeaux, 1957), pp. 141–166.

———. "L'Évolution moderne du droit musulman en Égypte," *Mélanges Maspero*, III—extract from *Mémoires de l'Institut Français d'Archéologie Orientale*, LXVIII (1935), 323–334.

———. "New Sources for the History of Muḥammadan Theology," *Studia Islamica*, I (1953), 23–42.

———. *The Origins of Muhammadan Jurisprudence*. Oxford: Clarendon Press, 1950.

———. "Problems of Modern Islamic Legislation," *Studia Islamica*, XII (1960), 99–130.

Sékaly, Achille. "Les Deux congrès généraux de 1926: le Congrès du Khalifat et le Congrès du Monde Musulman," *Revue du Monde Musulman*, LXIV (2d quarter, 1926), 3–219.

Shorter Encyclopedia of Islam. Edited by H. A. R. Gibb and J. H. Kramers. Leiden: Brill, 1953.

Smith, Wilfred Cantwell. *Islam in Modern History*. Princeton: Princeton University Press, 1957.

Tyan, Émile. *Histoire de l'organisation judiciaire en pays d'Islam*. Paris: Recueil Sirey, 1938; Beirut, 1943. 2 vols.

———. *Institutions du droit public musulman*. Vol. I: *Le Califat*. Paris: Recueil Sirey, 1954. Vol. II: *Sultanat et califat*. Paris: Recueil Sirey, 1957.

———. "Méthodologie et sources du droit en Islam," *Studia Islamica*, X (1959), 79–110.

———. "Notes sur la distinction du spirituel et du temporel dans le califat," *Annales de la Faculté de Droit*, Université de Saint-Joseph de Beyrouth, 1951, No. 1, pp. 5–17.

Vatikiotis, P. J. "Muhammad 'Abduh and the Quest for a Muslim Humanism," *Islamic Culture*, XXXI (1957), 109–126.

Von Grunebaum, Gustave E. *Islam: Essays in the Nature and Growth of a Cultural Tradition*. American Anthropologist, Memoir No. 81. Chicago, 1955.

———. *Medieval Islam. A Study in Cultural Orientation*. Chicago: University of Chicago Press, 1947.

———. *Modern Islam. The Search for Cultural Identity*. Berkeley and Los Angeles: University of California Press, 1962.

———, editor and contributor. *Studies in Islamic Cultural History*. American Anthropologist, Memoir No. 76. Chicago, 1954.

———, editor and contributor. *Unity and Variety in Muslim Civilization*. Chicago, 1955.

Von Kremer, Freiherr Alfred. *Culturgeschichte des Orients unter den Chalifen*. Vienna, 1875–1877. 2 vols. English translation by S. Khuda Bukhsh, *The Orient Under the Caliphs*. Calcutta, 1920.

Watt, W. Montgomery. *Free Will and Predestination in Early Islam*. London: Luzac, 1948.

———. *Islam and the Integration of Society*. London: Routledge and Kegan Paul, 1961.

INDEX

INDEX

Abbasids/Abbasid Empire, 14, 26, 27, 29, 36, 45, 46, 50, 51, 52, 64, 167, 168, 174, 178, 221
'Abd al-Ḥamīd (sultan), 147
'Abd al-Malik (caliph), 29
'Abd an-Nāṣir, Jamāl (Gamal Abdul Nasser), 15
'Abd ar-Rāziq, 'Alī, 158, 179–181, 205, 221
'Abduh, Muḥammad: general legacy, 12, 15, 16, 18, 211, 221–223; on reason and revelation, 84, 109–118; influence on Riḍā, 103–104, 153–155, 187; career, 104; chief concerns and approach, 105–109; on miracles, 119–121; and Mu'tazilism, 123; on esthetics, 123–125; on ethics, 125–129; on prophecy, 142–143; on ijmā', 143–145; Transvaal fatwā, 145–146; on politics and Caliphate, 146–152, 166, 175, 178; and 'Abd ar-Rāziq, 180, 205
'Abdurraḥmān b. 'Auf, 160
Abū Bakr (caliph), 44, 49, 98, 160, 179, 180, 212
Abū Ḥanīfa, al-Imām, 65, 76. *See also* Ḥanafī
al-Afghānī, Jamāl ad-Dīn, 104, 116, 136, 137, 139, 141, 143
Ahl al-bay'a, 34, 35. *See also* Ahl al-ḥall wa 'l-'aqd; Bay'a
Ahl al-ḥall wa 'l-'aqd ("people of loosing and binding"): electors of caliph, 33; parties to contract, 34–36; obedience to caliph, 41; identification of 43, 159–163, 175; and sovereignty according to Riḍā, 161–165, 172–173, 177, 183, 195, 197, 200. *See also* Bay'a; Caliph; Caliphate
Ahl ar-ra'y, 77. *See also* Ra'y
'Alī ar-Riḍā, 45
Amin, Osman, 123
Al-amr bi 'l-ma'rūf wa 'n-nahy 'an al-munkar ("commanding the good and forbidding the evil"), 128
'Amr b. al-'Āṣ, 212
Analogy. *See* Qiyās
Arab/Arabs, 173, 174, 176, 178, 179, 211, 213
Arab nationalism, 222. *See also* Nationalism
'Arābī Pasha, Aḥmad, 104
Aristotle, 78, 128
'Aṣabiyya (social solidarity): according to Ibn Khaldūn, 45, 46; according to 'Abduh, 137, 139, 151; according to Riḍā, 167, 172, 174–175
al-Ash'arī, Abū 'l-Ḥasan, 44, 59, 64, 111, 117. *See also* Ash'arite
Ash'arite/Ash'arism: and Mu'tazilites, 58–60; and modernism, 108; on free will, 111; on natural causality, 119–120; mentioned, 106, 117, 223. *See also* al-Ash'arī
al-Azhar (mosque-university), 104, 179, 180, 205, 221
Awqāf. *See* Waqf

al-Baghdādī, 'Abdalqāhir, 25, 44
al-Bannā', Ḥasan, 15
al-Bāqillānī, Abū Bakr Muḥammad, 25, 43–44, 52
al-Barā'a 'l-aṣliyya (presumptive exemption from judgment), 85, 97
Bay'a (oath of loyalty to caliph): as social contract, 23, 160, 161, 165, 212; only declaratory significance, 25, 35, 37,

44.10 a

KBP 1468 .K47 1966
Kerr, Malcolm H.
Islamic reform